Public Administration and Public Management

Government in any society delivers a large number of services and goods to its population. To get the job done, government needs public management in order to steer its resources – employees, money and laws – into policy outputs and outcomes. In a well-ordered society the teams who work for the state deliver under a rule of law framework – public administration.

Public Administration and Public Management provides a new perspective on the public sector by offering a concise and comprehensive analysis of what it is and how it operates. This book includes such issues as:

- the principal–agent framework and the public sector
- public principals and their agents
- the economic reasons of government
- public organisation, incentives and rationality in government
- the essence of public administration: legality and the rule of law
- public policy criteria: the Cambridge and Chicago positions
- public teams and private teams
- public firms
- public insurance
- public management policy

This book provides essential reading for those with professional and research interests in public administration and public management.

Jan-Erik Lane is professor of political science at the University of Geneva and has taught courses on government in several countries.

Public Administration and Public Management

The principal–agent perspective

Jan-Erik Lane

Routledge
Taylor & Francis Group

LONDON AND NEW YORK

First published 2005 by Routledge
2 Park Square, Milton Park, Abingdon, Oxon OX14 4RN

Simultaneously published in the USA and Canada
by Routledge
270 Madison Avenue, New York, NY 10016

Routledge is an imprint of the Taylor & Francis Group

© 2005 Jan-Erik Lane

Typeset in Baskerville by Keyword Group Ltd
Printed and bound in Great Britain by MPG Books Ltd, Bodmin

British Library Cataloguing in Publication Data
A catalogue record for this book is available from the British Library

Library of Congress Cataloging in Publication Data
A catalog record for this book has been requested

ISBN10: 0-415-37015-9 hbk
ISBN10: 0-415-37016-7 pbk

ISBN13: 9-78-0-415-37015-8 (hbk)
ISBN13: 9-78-0-415-37016-5 (pbk)

Contents

List of Figures

List of Tables

Preface

The purpose of this book is to suggest an entirely new perspective on the public sector, i.e. what it is and how it operates. In the existing literature there is a wide range of approaches to the analysis of government and non-market institutions and organisations, including public administration, public policy and policy implementation, political economy, public choice, organisational theory, neo-institutional theory, etc. No attempt is made here to cover all these different perspectives on the public sector, as such an ambition would go far beyond the format of this volume. This compact introduction to government and the public sector employs the principal–agent approach, applying it to the two classical perspectives on government, namely public administration (the rule of law) and public management (efficiency). What is new in this volume is the effort to base the understanding of government, its bureaux and agencies, as well as the state enterprises, upon game theory and the new economics of information, comprising *inter alia* the principal–agent approach.

Approaching the public sector in terms of the principal–agent framework leads one to see how transaction costs direct people to support government and its management of a public sector. The legitimacy problem of the modern state calls for constitutional government, or the rule of law. Understanding the modern state requires that one takes two fundamental considerations concerning government into account: efficiency and legitimacy. Both these objectives lead to the public principal contracts with a variety of agents in order to get the job done. Government may thus be analysed as a nexus of contracts. However, public sector contracting is not merely a replication of private sector contracting or market interaction. Public sector contracting has its specific features, which I will attempt to analyse below, especially the politics/administration separation, which can only be fully understood by means of the principal–agent framework.

I have divided the book into ten main chapters corresponding to the major themes in relation to government when analysed in terms of the economics of agency. All chapters were written for this volume, except that I have drawn on one published article ('Transformation and Future of Public Enterprises in Continental Western Europe,' in *Public Finance and Management*, 2002, Vol. 2: 47–66) plus a few review articles in *Public Management Review*. I have also drawn on an article written together with Florent Dieterlen ('The Mathematics of Management and Public Organisation: The Principal–Agent Framework,' in *Festschrift to Hannu Nurmi*, 2004, pp. 223–241).

This enquiry is the result of my teaching at Hong Kong University (in 2000 and 2002), at the National University of Singapore and at the Chinese University of Hong Kong (2003), where H. C. Kuan (Chinese University) provided a most stimulating environment for rethinking the art of government. I benefited especially from conversations with Ian Thynne (Charles Darwin University), whose knowledge of government was very helpful. Erik Verkooyen, André-Bruno Fischer and Daniel Martel (Dept of Political Science) contributed to the completion of the manuscript, and Sylvia Dumons (University of Geneva) assisted greatly in making the final version, correcting revision after revision without complaint.

Jan-Erik Lane
Geneva, November 2004

Introduction: the public and the private sectors

Every advanced society has three sectors: the public sector, the private sector and the third sector of voluntary non-profit organisations. The public sector comprises the general government sector plus all bureaux and agencies, including the central bank. The public enterprises are sometimes placed in the public sector and sometimes in the private sector, if organised as joint-stock firms. Principal–agent interaction arises in the public sector as one party, the principal, hires someone or a team of people, the agents, to get something done in exchange for remuneration.

The public sector consists of the services and the transfer payments of governments at various levels in the political system, as well as of the goods and services produced by the public organisations, by outsourcing or by the public enterprises. It comes with a price tag that must be covered by government taxation and user fees plus borrowing. Eventually, the costs of borrowing must also be covered by means of taxation.

The government sector consists of the following resident institutional units: all units of central, state or local government; all social security funds at each level of government; and all non-market, non-profit institutions that are controlled and financed by government units. This sector does not include public corporations, even when all the equity of such corporations is owned by government units. It also does not include quasi-corporations that are owned and controlled by government units. The economic aspect of the public sector is called 'public finance' and its size is measured for the 30 OECD (Organisation for Economic Cooperation and Development) countries by means of a system of statistics called 'National Accounts'. The Paris-based OECD publishes comparable public finance information every year. I shall employ this source to state an important distinction.

The general government sector consists of the totality of organisations which, in addition to fulfilling their political responsibilities and their role of economic regulation, produce principally non-market services or goods for individual or collective consumption, and redistribute income and wealth. The government sector includes central government or federal government, which tends to be the biggest subsector, at least financially.

The central government subsector consists of the institutional units making up the central government plus the bureaux and agencies that are controlled and mainly financed by central government. As the political authority of central government extends over the entire economy, it has the authority to impose taxes on all residents and non-resident units engaged in economic activities within the country.

The monetary authorities sector includes the central bank or the currency board and certain operations usually attributed to the central bank but, in some cases, carried out by other government institutions (or, in some instances, by commercial banks). Here we find the issue of currency, maintenance and management of international reserves – including those resulting from transactions with the International Monetary Fund (IMF) – and the operation of exchange stabilisation funds.

In the world of public finance there are two sets of countries which operate two different models for the public and the private sector. On the one hand, there are the welfare states with a mixed economy. On the other hand, there are the welfare societies, relying predominantly on the market economy. The delimitation of these two sets is somewhat arbitrary, as all countries have a public sector of some size. I shall draw the line at about 40 per cent total public expenditures of gross domestic product (GDP) for year 2001. Then the available data allows me to classify the following countries into these two sets (see Appendix):

- *Welfare states:* Austria, Belgium, Canada, Czech Republic, Denmark, Finland, France, Germany, Greece, Hungary, Iceland, Luxembourg, the Netherlands, Norway, Poland, Portugal, Slovak Republic, Sweden and Switzerland.
- *Welfare societies:* Australia, Ireland, Japan, Korea, New Zealand and the USA.

In both welfare societies and welfare states, difficult questions arise about public administration and management. Welfare states urgently need to address these questions, given their heavy reliance on the public sector. However, welfare societies should also address these questions in their search for public sector reform.

Corresponding to the separation of the public sector into three subsectors,

- government sector: allocation and redistribution
- public enterprises
- monetary authority

one must, in a traditional public sector, set up enquiries into four kinds of principal–agent relationships:

- governance of the bureaux
- governance of social security
- governance of the public enterprises
- making of monetary policy.

I will deal with the first three principal–agent relationships. That is not to say that there are not interesting principal–agent aspects of the making and implementation of monetary policy, which is one example of the general problem of public regulation. On the contrary, one may restate the two basic models of a monetary authority – Keynesianism and monetarism – as alternative models for the interaction between government as the principal and the Central Bank as the agent. However, the pros and cons of an independent monetary authority have been well researched recently. What opens a new perspective on the classical discipline of public administration, as well as giving the emerging discipline of public management theoretic coherence, is the application of the principal–agent approach to the government sector, its bureaux, agencies and enterprises or firms.

Thus, in any society one may make a demarcation between the public and the private sectors. This separation may not be crystal clear or neatly institutionalised, but it still exists. It is done in different ways in various societies. It is of profound significance however it is made. The public sector is the sphere of government, whether central, regional or local. The private sector is the family as well as the market and its firm organisations. The public–private distinction is a highly political one, as political parties go to elections on programmes to change the established division between the public and the private. No society can be either public or private, as all have a mixture. The public sector may be designated the 'state', but it gives the impression of a monolithic actor, which is quite wrong given the multiplicity of governments and authorities in the public sector.

The public sector consists of all the various activities of governments and their agencies. One may classify these into three categories: services – the provision of public goods and services (public resource allocation); transfer payments – income maintenance programmes (social security); and public regulation. The operation of these activities – allocation, redistribution and regulation – requires staff, meaning that governments must hire people and set up organisations. Thus, government faces two key problems that it must solve in public administration or public management: (1) how many employees to hire, and (2) how to organise these employees. I shall pinpoint the major changes in public administration and management that have occurred in the last 20 years, making it an interesting discipline in the social sciences. What I am referring to is the rise of New Public Management (NPM). I will discuss here the general model of NPM and in a later chapter return to country-specific applications when analysing public management policy.

Need for public administration or public management

In a well-ordered society the public sector has an impressive size, as there will be a fairly large set of public services, a decent set of social security programmes and a fair amount of public regulation of the private sector. The discipline of political economy deals with the politically highly sensitive question of *how much*, meaning the size of public resource allocation, the size of income redistribution and the amount of public regulation. The discipline of public management examines how the public employees are to be organised so that the job gets done. Various quantitative indicators have been developed in order to identify the demarcation line between the public and the private as well as to estimate the size of the public sector. One may employ different measures such as: the cost of the public programmes in terms of GDP; the number of public employees in terms of all occupationally active, and the number of laws and regulations for business.

These standard indicators give very different results and they must be used with caution. What they indicate is that the public sector in a well-ordered society ranges between 25 per cent and 60 per cent of GDP, in terms of expenditures as well as between 10 per cent and 40 per cent of those employed. Very few countries practice the extreme solutions of either a Manchester liberal society with a minimalist state or a Communist society with a maximalist state (Barr, 1993; Rosen, 1988).

We will not go into to the key problem in political economy of discussing the pros and cons of the welfare society and the welfare state, since both require a public sector and consequently public management. The core interest in this volume concerns how government organises its employees into *teams* for service provision, transfer payments and regulatory tasks. The main approach I suggest is the principal–agent framework looking upon public management as a *nexus of contracts* between principals and agents at various levels of government.

Public management or public administration deals with how governments set up organisations of people, motivating them in the performance of programmes as well as monitoring and evaluating their performance and results. Governments may choose *in-house* or *out-of-house* provision, meaning that it may also contract with private provider organisations or private individuals. Public administration management includes planning, budgeting, steering, monitoring and evaluation. Theories of public management attempt to explain how public organisations work, their accountability, efficiency and fairness. It is both an empirical and a normative enterprise, as theories of public management try to explain alternative institutional arrangements in various countries but also state recommendations about management reforms, and their feasibility and desirability.

The political nature of public management cannot be denied, referring to the distinction between politics and administration. All public administration and management is conducted within a political setting where the goals and means of activities are politically relevant. Public management is not neutral administrative action but consists of the execution of public policies. The principal–agent framework underlines this feature, as the basic principal of public sector organisations is the population, or *demos*. Political leaders rely on organisations or teams of people to get the job done in the public sector. The key question in public management is which organisational model to employ for the public teams and the conduct of their operations given the omnipresence of strategy.

New Public Management: the general framework

It is difficult to find one concise definition of NPM in the literature. The term NPM appeared in the early 1990s, and designated the ongoing public sector reforms in Anglo-Saxon countries. Since many countries have engaged in public sector reform one would like to identify the specifics of NPM in order to separate its key ideas from public sector reform in general. One must not assume that all public sector reforms during the last 20 years have been inspired by NPM. To identify what is distinctive about NPM I will first look at its rhetoric and then proceed to state two definitions, one *broad* and one *narrow* (Pollitt and Bouckaert, 1999; McLaughlin *et al.*, 2001; Hood, 2000; Thynne and Wettenhall, 2004).

Rhetoric of NPM

The language of NPM is different from that of traditional public administration, as well as that of public policy. The key words may be listed thus:

- *Service to customers:* Public organisations have only one rationale, namely the efficient provision of services to citizens. All the effort in setting up and funding public organisations must be directed towards the accomplishment of concrete objectives, i.e. services.
- *Leadership or entrepreneurship:* Public employees who are responsible for service provision need to be empowered, meaning provided with discretion to find the best means of achieving objectives. The complexity of service provision requires innovation and flexibility. Public employees cannot be restricted by red tape.
- *Contracting:* The leaders of public organisations must have great latitude to contract with their employees or buy goods and services from outsiders. Running a public organisation is about negotiating, writing and monitoring contracts with insiders or outsiders.

- *Governance:* A public organisation lives in a complex setting with other public and private organisations placed in a vibrant civil society. To accomplish goals, public organisations must recognise reciprocity and engage in networks of governance with other public and private organisations.
- *Re-engineering government:* Public organisations cannot be based on the traditional hierarchical and formal model of organisation, recommended in public administration. Front-line managers must be empowered. Policy advice should be separated from policy execution.

The key concepts in NPM were launched by practical people with an experience of business administration, but they have sources in academic reflection about the conduct of government bureaux and public enterprises (Hennessy, 2001). NPM comes in two versions. In a broad definition, NPM stands for public sector reforms that have been conducted in advanced countries lately, aiming at decentralisation and efficiency. However, in a narrow definition, NPM refers to a specific *governance model* that is entirely different from traditional public administration (Hood, 2000; Kettl, 2002).

Broad definition of NPM

Public sector reforms have been conducted in all OECD countries since 1980. One may characterise them by enumerating the key ideas in many of them as follows:

- *Emphasis on outputs and outcomes:* In traditional public administration the rule-of-law emphasis leads to a focus on inputs. Thus, administrative law as well as finance laws and budgetary regulations deal with the resources of the bureaux and regulate the conduct of behaviour on the part of individual bureaucrats and professionals. NPM looks upon the public sector organisations from the output or outcome perspective. It underlines the performance of the bureau as a whole, as well as that of individual team members. By emphasising outputs and outcomes in the public sector, NPM moves away from the cost concern typical of traditional public administration. Instead of rules the concentration is on *value*, meaning the benefits that the implementation of public policies result in for society.
- *Productivity and effectiveness:* Although value is far from easy to measure in the public sector, it still exists for public services just as for private ones sold in the marketplace. When public services are not allocated through the market, it is difficult to identify and measure their value. However, they do have a value to citizens, meaning that one can ask questions about efficiency, either as productivity (internal efficiency) or as effectiveness (external efficiency).

- *Customer service:* Value derives from the appreciation of citizens or consumers with public programmes. Bureaux have no right to exist but must prove their existence through the value they create in society. Far from being immortal, public organisations have no intrinsic rationale but act under a rationality assumption deriving from the value they create for society.

- *Downsizing or economy:* Governments in the OECD countries have in general tried to reduce commitments. It is not only a matter of increasing efficiency but also the cutting back of oversized programmes. Thus, all three parts of the public sector – allocation, redistribution and regulation – have come in for cut-back strategies.

- *Deregulation or reregulation:* Traditional public regulation in the form of entry regulation has been undone in major regulatory reform, increasing entry and thus competition. However, the move towards deregulation has often been followed by reregulation, setting up a new agency to check product quality, i.e. product regulations. Anti-trust regulation is often stressed in public sector reform, speaking about the relevance of the 'two Cs' to the public sector: choice and competition.

- *Decentralisation:* Offloading government has often meant moving tasks from central government to regional or local governments. Devolution is considered an essential strategy in public sector reform, whether in federal or unitary states. One may wish to distinguish between decentralisation (from state to local government) and deconcentration (from central level to provincial level in the state).

- *Privatisation or public–private partnerships:* Hiving off public policies to the private sector is one strategy that governments have started to consider more and more. There is actually a full range of options available from complete privatisation to only public ownership and government activity. In the network model there are all kinds of public–private mixtures, including third sector organisations.

- *Contracting out:* There is hardly any limit to what can be contracted out in the public sector. Sometimes even the contracting out of services is done out-of-house, though much outsourcing may hollow out government and lead to the concentration of asset-specific knowledge in the private sector.

- *Leaner or flatter organisation:* The typical transformation of the structure of private firms has been accepted also in public sector reform. Thus, middle-level managers have been removed and lower-level managers have been empowered. The giant hierarchy is no longer the optimal organisational structure, neither for private firms nor for public organisations.

One does not find all these ideas in each and every country doing public sector reform. As will be shown in Chapter 10, there have been great differences between the countries in their reform profiles. Yet sometimes NPM refers to a more specific and coherent set of reform strategies which call for a radically different way of doing the business of government.

Narrow definition of NPM

NPM as an entirely new philosophy of public sector governance harbours a few very precise ideas about how to get the job of government done. It relies on major ideas in economics, especially institutional economics and the economics of information, theorising the role of rules and incentives in organisations. Thus, NPM would employ the following market-inspired mechanisms:

- *Policy–provision split and purchaser–provider split:* Governments do many things, which is why it is essential to isolate the allocative part of governmental programmes. When governments produce goods and services, one may often ask whether the market could do it better. Allocative programmes must be broken out from regulatory tasks, and the provision of services can be done through outsourcing.
- *Contestability:* The separation of allocation from regulation and income maintenance opens up the possibility of market testing the production of goods and services. Since contestability is forthcoming when entry is open, governments should apply competitive tendering or bidding for all the services it wants to provide.
- *Contracting:* Using competitive tendering in allocation implies that government will employ its public procurement arm massively. Government becomes a contractor with alternative service providers, *contracting in* as well as *contracting out*. It may set up a purchaser–provider mechanism to handle an entire sector or a certain level of government such as a local government.
- *Incorporation:* Commercial matters in government are best handled through the employment of private law tools, e.g. the joint-stock company. Public enterprises are best run as incorporated businesses where the equity may be partially held by private partners. Any unit that engages in allocation and has an income or revenue stream can be incorporated, e.g. a hospital.

Agency theory and the economics of information predict that the use of the new market mechanisms in public management will enhance efficiency, as they mix rules and incentives in a more correct manner than traditional public administration. It remains to be discussed how the basic goal of rule of law in the public sector is to be satisfied by NPM in this narrow sense.

Theories behind NPM

Although it is true that NPM was put in practice by practical politicians and business gurus, it remains the case that the ground had been well prepared by new academic ideas. Let us mention the main origins of NPM within academia without pretending that they constitute a coherent source of inspiration. There were actually several sources of NPM unrelated to each other (Ashburner *et al.*, 1996; Pollitt, 2003; Kettl, 2000).

- *Public Choice:* This school broke most markedly with traditional public administration by underlining in an extreme manner the role of self-interests in the public sector with alternative groups of actors. If the public sector is populated by revenue-maximising politicians and budget-maximising bureaucrats, then is it perhaps better to offload most of the activity to the private sector? At least one would favour contracting out as the chief tool of government in order to reduce the possibility of Niskanen budget strategies from bureaux (Brennan and Buchanan, 2000, 2001; Niskanen, 2004).
- *Chicago School economics:* The theory about market efficiency was launched at the same time as scholars started to speak about government overload. Thus, the Chicago message could be applied all over the public sector, calling for cut-backs in order to restore markets. If markets are at any time efficient when left alone by governments, then it would be foolish not to rely upon them. When complete privatisation and deregulation was not feasible, governments could employ market-inspired mechanisms such as vouchers, the negative income tax, third-party access and workfare arrangements (Leube and Moore, 1986; Becker *et al.*, 1995; Coase, 1990; Solow, 1998).
- *The agency approach and the economics of information:* In the public sector the interaction between the key players tends to be a game between two parties that lasts longer than the quick buying and selling behaviour in the market. In traditional public administration the interaction between government and its bureaux was modelled by means of the rules about tenure, vocation and expertise through virtual monopoly. Principal–agent theory offers a better model of this dual interaction, while also recognising that agents tend to have the upper hand in this interaction, at least under the institutions of bureaucracy (Macho-Stadler and Perez-Castrillo, 1997).
- *Managerialism:* Private sector management tools have been recommended for the public sector ever since management was established as a subdiscipline of business administration. As a matter of fact, private management borrowed early quite extensively from Weber's theory of bureaucracy and Fayol's emphasis on formal hierarchical organisation. Thus, Taylor's scientific management in the firm was not much different from Wilson's approach to public organisation. However, private management has developed in an entirely different direction, away from hierarchy, formal organisation and in-house production. According to economic organisation theory, the firm is a nexus of contracts where the mix of long-term and short-term contracts is decided by considerations

of the opportunity costs of alternative contractual arrangements of insourcing and outsourcing. Public organisation is a need for a public management policy which outlines what is to be done in-house and out-of-house, as well as how much discretion managers may use given the requirements of rule of law (Pugh, 1997; Pugh and Hickson, 1997).

- *Network society:* The opportunity costs of alternative ways of organising teams depend on the evolution of society and technological change. Hierarchies are not the most efficient forms of organisation in a post-modern society where information is easily accessible and storable. The implication for public sector organisation is to find a governance model which fits the theory of the networking society (Kooiman, 2003; Shy, 2001).

Jan Kooiman's *Governing as Governance* (2003, a continuation of his edited volume *Modern Governance*, 1993) contains a clear and systematic exposition of the nature of public administration and management in the post-modern society, taking the governance approach to its logical completion. I shall first outline the basic points in his perspective in this highly theoretical book and then state one major reservation of mine.

- Governing today is governance as interaction in various arenas between public and private actors. Governance takes place equally in political and social arenas. Hierarchical governance is of limited use in the post-modern society. This is basically the Dutch network model made all-encompassing over the entire public sector.
- Interactive behaviour is orientated by means of subjective elements such as images. Public administration and management is more concerned with interpretation than behaviour. Problem solving results from how actors perceive the situation and position themselves in relation to others.
- Co-interaction plays the major role in bringing about outcomes meaning that cooperation among actors and stakeholders is crucial. Co-operation is the basic medium of exchange between all kinds of actors involved in policy implementation; it is dependent on how the actors perceive the situation and identify opportunities of joint action.
- Interaction occurs in arenas of different degrees of complexity, from simple problem solving to institutional decision-making. In addition there is meta-governance, where one reflects on the norms that all forms of governing must obey. Governance includes the process of arriving at agreements about the norms to guide the governing process.
- Societies have to respond to a number of governance challenges arising from social complexity. Governability depends basically on co-governance, but governability shows varying degrees of diversity, dynamics and complexity depending on the combination of the open and closed nature of interactions at the intentional and structural level.

Two kinds of objection may be raised when the governance model is taken to its logical completion. First, one may ask how applicable the model is empirically: how much of governing in the post-modern society is authority and how much is collaboration? I am not convinced that all governing is reciprocity. Second, one may debate whether this model includes the most relevant elements in any form of governing: what is the role of incentives in governance? One does not have to have an economistic mind to emphasise the role of incentives, which Kooiman almost entirely bypasses. Public administration and management is, in my view, first and foremost *strategy*, and incentives are crucial for determining the strategies of the players involved, whether the interaction is authority or reciprocity.

All the above theories paved the way for the arrival of NPM, underlining the relevance of market mechanisms and the irrelevance of central control over an increasingly complex society. Time was no doubt ripe for the propagation of these theories as the post-industrial society called for new governance structures. Yet these sources of academic inspiration of NPM are somewhat different: some have a special economistic tone, whereas others are more sociological in nature. In the so-called 'NPM countries', public choice theory and Chicago School economics were of profound importance. In other countries, e.g. the Netherlands, the network model was more important than economic theory. NPM was conditioned not only by new ideas in academia but also by fundamental social changes, the coming of the post-modern society, the theory of post-modernity and the risk society (Beck, 2001).

Conditions for NPM

Among the background conditions for the receptivity of the NPM philosophy I would like to underline the following:

- *Maturing of the public sector:* The twentieth century saw not only the rise of the tax state but also the coming of the regulatory state as well as the insurance state (Tanzi and Schuknecht, 2000). Government is present in society: allocative, redistributive and regulatory forms. Whether the public sector is measured by money, laws or employees, it is true that government is large in all OECD countries, especially so in the welfare states. It has become increasingly difficult for governments to pay for all their public policies. Since governments are more and more hesitant about running up deficits, they have to develop strategies that lead to more output with fewer resources. The question then becomes: Which public management policy is conducive to *value for money*?
- *Information revolution:* Large government operations such as education, health care and social security will be as much affected by technological change as private organisation. The potential use of computers is enormous in government where information is crucial, both in terms of

quality and quantity. Public organisations can be managed with the full employment of the potentialities of the information revolution – the coming of *e-governance*. Organisational structure will be affected by the computerization of work processes, as tasks are redefined and new skills identified (Oliver and Sanders, 2004).

- *Globalisation:* Although the globalisation wave derives its force first and foremost from the global market economy and the information revolution, it has clear implications for government operations. Public policy and policy implementation are affected by policy diffusion such as deregulation, global public procurement and migration from one state to another. The governance of the global society through international organisations conditions national policy-making, favouring competition. For instance, one major issue in international governance is whether regional coordination bodies such as the European Union (EU) and the North American Free Trade Agreement (NAFTA) or international bodies such as the World Trade Organisation (WTO) can require complete and open competition for contracts in the provision of public services (Hoekman *et al.*, 2002).
- *Civil society growth:* It is true that the twentieth century was the period of the growth of government. The literature on the expansion of the public sector shows that government grew on an average faster than the private sector, especially during war times. Yet the market sector has also expanded in a phenomenal way, as measured in the sustained positive and often high growth rates in the economy. Thus, the private sector has increased its capacity to provide services, meaning that offloading public sector tasks to the private sector is often a serious policy alternative (Deakin, 2001).

There was a widespread belief in the 1980s and 1990s that public sector growth had to be halted. Some political parties receiving considerable electoral support took the stance that government should be reduced – *downsizing*. Running a government with the revolution in information technology opened up a challenge that seemed highly relevant as globalisation pushed ahead in the 1990s. The old image of a huge bureaucracy seemed outdated, as the idea of a small flat organisation producing services in a customer-oriented fashion replaced the large formal organisation. Partnerships between the public and the private were suggested as more innovative and flexible structures for government in a strong civil society. And public management policy was devised, reforming the public sector organisations in accordance with the notions of NPM: market testing, competition, customer service, leaner and flatter structure, as well as managerial entrepreneurship. Yet there is more to public management than only management. One must add the rule of law and its implications for the conduct of government operations. How can justice be safeguarded in government?

Public management: merit and accountability

Public administration as a practical discipline for the governance of the state was founded on an antithesis that runs through all forms of public management, namely the tension between technical competence and political accountability (Ingraham, 1995; Natemeyer, 1978; Shafritz, 1997). Governments cannot implement their own policies for simple transaction cost reasons. Thus, they need various kinds of experts or agents with competence to put in practice government policies. At the same time, these agents must be accountable to the government, as they implement the objectives of government. If the proposed solution to this dilemma within public administration (neutral competence against political sensitiveness) in the form of a sharp separation between knowledge and values (administration versus politics) is not tenable, then how can public management combine these two entities: merit, on the one hand, and accountability, on the other?

One may outline the possibilities of combining competence and accountability by means of a simple 2 × 2 table (Table I.1) using the well-known concepts of Max Weber (Weber, 1978).

The move to set up major bureaucracies in the modern state, such as with the Northcote–Trevelyan Act in the UK and the Pendleton Act in the US, may be seen as attempts to arrive at the ideal solution of both high competence and high political accountability (Hennessy, 2001). The idea of Whitehall is that the civil servants are recruited only on the basis of merit but they serve their ministers completely, according to the doctrine of ministerial accountability (Johnson and Libecap, 1994). Civil servants will not be replaced when political power shifts from one party to another, because whichever party is in power needs competent people to implement policy. However, the civil servants will be loyal to the actual minister in power. Despite the effort to eliminate patronage from the Washington bureaucracy the number of political appointees remains much higher than in other OECD countries, reflecting the legacy of the *spoils* institution.

When bureaucratic cohesiveness is high, then the bureaucracy may start running the country. Weber predicted that the complex modern society could not be run without the bureaucracy, but he was well aware of the dangers of bureaucratisation. Two forms of low political accountability were identified by him, either *Beamtenherrschaft* (centripetal bureaucratic

Table I.1 Merit and accountability

Merit	Accountability	
	Low	*High*
High	*Beamtenherrschaft*	Weber's ideal solution
Low	*Satrapenherrschaft*	Patronage

power) or *Satrapenherrschaft* (centrifugal bureaucratic power). The history of political authority is full of examples of both forms, e.g. bureau autonomy (Dunleavy, 1991) and bureau capture (Becker *et al.*, 1995; Becker and Becker, 1997). The introduction of NPM affects the balance between merit and accountability.

NPM suggests the use of market mechanisms in public organisations. The purpose is to increase both political accountability and technical competence, but the outcomes need not be the intended ones. Several studies report on unintended results, such as increasing patronage in the distribution of contracts with suppliers, and elimination of public sector competence in favour of private sector competence (hollowing out), as well as increasing power and prestige for managers (Massey, 1997; Greene, 2003; Sanger, 2003; Shichor and Gilbert, 2000; Lavery, 1999; Flynn and Williams, 1997; Seidenstat, 1999; Raphaelson, 1998; James and Rhodes, 2003; Rothery and Robertson, 1995; Graham, 1998; Milgate, 2001; O'Looney, 1998). Moreover, the rule-of-law framework of public management cannot be undone in a constitutional democracy. It may be regarded as a goal in itself or as a means to competence and accountability in the public sector. I will look on the requirements of the rule of law as restrictions on efficiency in the public sector. Thus, the aim of public management is to deliver public services, but the organisations that are responsible for doing so must operate in accordance with the rule of law.

Public administration and public policy: a contracting perspective

Public organisations, authorities, bureaux, agencies, boards and enterprises increasingly face the demand for both transparency and efficiency. These are *macro demands* raised by the public at large and by the politicians. Often they surface in the deliberations of the governing bodies of public organisations, as well as in parliament. How, then, can the managers of public organisations meet these two challenges: transparency deriving from the rule of law (the public administration view); efficiency in the implementation of policies through outputs and outcomes (the policy perspective)? I suggest that this is to a large extent a matter for *micro contracting*, i.e. how the chief executive officers (CEOs) of these public organisations negotiate, write and enforce contracts with their employees that solicit a high work effort resulting in high quality and quantity outcomes.

The macro objectives of a public organisation laid down in policy documents and stated in public law can only be accomplished if there is micro management orientated towards efficiency within the organisation. The public policy approach underlines the relevance of the political process, resulting in the overall framework for the activity of a public organisation, or a set of public organisations when tasks are interdependent between several public organisations. Thus, it deals with legislation, budgeting and ministerial decision-making. The public administration framework targets the rule-of-law consequences of the operations of public organisations, including transparency, publicness and the possibility of complaint and redress. However, getting the job done in a public organisation is first and foremost a problem of contracting with people, motivating them to work to the accomplishment of the goals.

Contracting, from a micro view of the organisation, involves two things: (1) selecting the CEOs and (2) hiring the employees within insourcing or contracting out with other organisations. The achievement of the above macro goals of the organisation depends critically on how a whole set of micro contracts are made, starting with the CEO and his/her chief group of managers and ending with the contracts with each and every one of the employees. The quality of administration and the extent of policy accomplishments depend critically on how the entire set of contracts is handled, from negotiation up to evaluation. However, as I will show, there are some systematic difficulties in contracting that beset public management. They are best analysed within the principal–agent framework. Figures I.1 and I.2 may be consulted in order to clarify the bargaining problem where the principal has convex preferences and the agent concave preferences over effort and wage.

Figure I.1 targets the key importance of the effort of the agent, whether he or she works within an old regime of public administration or a New Public Management regime. 'Effort' (e) denotes all the factors which determine how employees or subcontractors deliver outputs (O) with a specific value – benefits – to the community in exchange for remuneration, or cost including a wage (W). Speaking generally, the principal would be interested in eliciting an effort that creates a positive benefit, meaning that benefits are higher than costs – the *gain* section in Figure I.1. And the principal would hardly be happy about a situation where costs are higher than benefits – the *loss* section in Figure I.1.

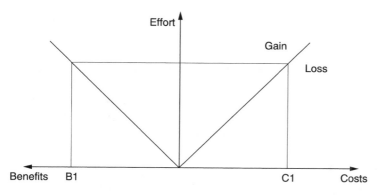

Figure I.1 Costs, effort and benefits.

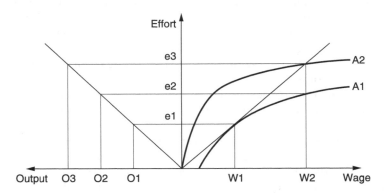

Figure I.2 Wage, effort and output (principal's convex preferences deleted).

This brings me to Figure I.2, where the two main solutions to the problem of creating value and minimising costs are outlined. Under old public administration, the principal would contract with one agent or team of agents for a wage *W2* against a promise of effort that would lead to an output of size *O3*. However, given the institutions of public administration, the agent would be tempted to shirk, delivering only *O2*. If the principal cannot correct this through monitoring, then he/she would be better off choosing *W1*, *O1*. The agent promises one behaviour *A2* but delivers another behaviour *A1* – moral hazard.

Under New Public Management, the principal would steer away from moral hazard by creating a bidding process involving two different types of agents, *A1* and *A2*, with low and high effort, respectively. Thus, the principal would offer two different contracts, depending on the nature of the agent, *A2* receiving *W2* and *A1* getting *W1*. However, if there is *asymmetric* information, then the principal cannot separate the agents. Adverse selection entails that the principal would be extremely hesitant to offer *W2* to *A2*, because he/she really does not know whether he/she deals with agent *A1* or *A2* – the agent pretending. The principal may decide to offer all agents *W1*, because the expected value of the game does not warrant offering the salary *W2* – adverse selection.

In a well-ordered society (Rawls, 1995) the public sector results from the resolution of two principal–agent games: first the population as principal and the politicians as agents, second the politicians as principals and the service teams as agents. To strengthen the population as principal, so-called citizen's charters have been enacted in public sector reform.

Citizen's charters

Charter programmes vary in content and purpose, serving the purposes both of New Right 'managerialist' concerns with rolling back of the state and achieving greater 'effectiveness, efficiency and economy', as well as communitarian aims of reinforcing local self-government and enhancing citizens' sense of community as a counterweight to the remote central bureaucracies. Charters come in different guises. Even when there is central guidance involved in the launching of national charter programmes, there cannot be a rigid format even within single countries. Recognition of the citizen as a customer is something more or less taken for granted in many service sectors in many countries, but this recognition is by no means universal, and even where the position is well-established, it did not happen overnight. Charters challenge the traditional image that the consumer-citizen should accept what he or she is given.

Several countries launched charter initiatives to encourage those responsible for the delivery of such services to improve their standards of performance, to operate in a more transparent way, to be more responsive to the needs and expectations of their 'customers' and to improve their complaints procedures. The basic objective has been to promote the empowerment of citizens by raising their critical awareness of the quality of services and (in theory at any rate) letting those who are dissatisfied seek out other providers. An important consideration, reinforcing this consumerist consensus, has been the desire to get better value for taxpayers' money in the provision of public services. The charters form part of public sector reform that has dominated the bureaucratic reform agenda in the OECD group of countries from the late 1970s (Hood, 1991, 1995, 1997).

The OECD Public Management Service (PUMA) lists Western European charter examples from the UK, Belgium, France, Italy, Portugal and the Netherlands (http://www.oecd.org.puma): indeed, it is now true to say that the phenomenon is a common one in almost all member states of the European Union. In January 2001, the Swedish Government announced a 'Servicedialog' pilot project, including an effort to develop citizen's charters in government agencies (http://www.servicedialog.nu/English/). Charter initiatives are to be found in every continent. In a memorandum submitted to the UK House of Commons Public Service Committee in October 1996, the Cabinet Office's Charter Unit claimed that some 15 countries have implemented or are implementing programmes similar to that in the UK, including Argentina, Australia, Canada, the United States, Belgium and Singapore. Hong Kong has its Performance Pledges, Malaysia has its Client Charters programme (1993). In 1997, the South African Government published 'People First' and The Caribbean may be mentioned (e.g. Jamaica, 1994) as Namibia, Costa Rica and, quite recently, Samoa – with its Service Charter, first published in July 2002, according to Drewry (2005).

Some charters are predominantly law-based. The French 'Charte des Services Publics' from 1992 announced the intention of adding to the traditional French public service principles of equality, neutrality and continuity, new principles of 'transparency, participation and simplification'.

The goals of the French charter comprised taking account of service users' needs and explaining and helping them with procedures; encouraging participation by citizens, while cutting delays and simplifying procedures, as well as increased accountability by means of quality indicators, as well as more recourse to conciliation and arbitration with regard to disputes (Flynn, 2002).

The NHS version of the UK Charter has recently been reinvented in the light of experience with charters. The numerous local patients' charters, adapted to particular medical practices and hospital trusts, that can also be found on the web, indicate clearly the progressive trickle-down effect of the original, centrally driven, charter programme. In UK public law the ombudsman system has expanded. There has been a significant increase in judicial review of administrative action, following a major overhaul of the relevant procedures in the late 1970s with an Administrative Court. European Union law and the European Court of Justice have impacted on the legal culture. The incorporation of the European Convention on Human Rights into domestic law by enactment of the Human Rights Act 1998 has already had a considerable impact on law and administration. References to the Citizen's Charter, John Major's 'big idea' of 1991, are infrequent, as the charter initiative has undergone an incremental metamorphosis, explaining its apparent disappearance. In June 1998, the Blair Government revamped and renamed its predecessors' charter 'Service First'. Drewry states: "The heavy top-down pressure from the Cabinet Office in the early days, reflecting strong prime ministerial involvement, has become less necessary as the charter principles have become absorbed into the bloodstream of public services – and are taken largely for granted by both the producers and the users of those services" (Drewry, 2005:25). The development in NPM contexts of more contractual and quasi-contractual modes of service delivery has had implications, some with legal significance.

Citizen's charters have today often a local or sectoral orientation, as not much remains of the central government conception of Mayor. But the politics of charterism in the UK covers both the New Right emphasis upon consumers and the New Left underlining of community. And citizen's charters may be interpreted as instruments for structuring the basic principal–agent interaction in the public sector, government referring to the interests of the ultimate principle of public service, i.e. citizens.

Osborne's trilogy: a critique of the management philosophy of David Osborne

Given the public attention rendered to Osborne's writings on public management, it is both timely and necessary to provide a critique of his key books with various co-authors. His message is a simplistic version of NPM without any foundation in organisational theory or rational choice.

His recommendations go against the wisdom of public administration and they are not strategy-proof from the point of view of asymmetric game theory.

Together with co-authors, David Osborne has produced a set of three books that has created much attention and most probably sold very well:

- *Reinventing Government* (1992) (with T. Gaebler)
- *Banishing Bureaucracy* (1997) (with P. Plastrik)
- *The Price of Government* (2004) (with P. Hutchinson).

His trilogy has no doubt had an impact upon public sector reform, at least in the United States, where he has created a group of 'reinventors' who regularly report on the outcomes of his management philosophy for the public sector. He has even published a huge handbook for helping people in transforming government: *The Reinventor's Field Book: Tools for Transforming Your Government* (Osborne and Plastrik, 2000).

Osborne's message in his three books is normative, as he wants to find the 'perpetuum mobile' of government, or the self-inventive agency, which steers itself towards economy and efficiency. Osborne launches a most impressive list of public sector reform ideas and he often provides evidence from how these ideas have been tried in various levels of government in the United States. Concentrating so almost exclusively upon the *ought*, one wonders whether Osborne has not bypassed a large literature in public administration and public management that underlines the recalcitrance of government towards lofty reform projects and promises of quick fixes.

In this section I wish to confront Osborne's key reform ideas with the lessons from extensive empirical research upon public organisations, as well as with basic theoretical results in asymmetric games, especially the principal–agent interaction. Osborne bypasses the lessons from organisational theory, as well as entirely the occurrence of gaming or strategy in public sector reform. He assumes that there is all the time a huge slack that can be squeezed without hurting the proper functioning of public programmes – a dangerous message with dire political consequences, if taken seriously in the consulting business. When it is argued that government, or public organisation, is inferior to private organisation – markets and entrepreneurialism, then one may place the problem either with the supply side – costs, or with the demand side – value. Osborne began by focusing upon costs that were too high (slack), but he now deals with the lack of priorities behind a goal structure of public programmes.

It would make things easy if one regarded Osborne's trilogy as merely another exercise in NPM. But I believe that Osborne's trilogy contains much more than the theory of NPM. And what it contains in addition to NPM is at odds with the established theories about government and public organisations. I shall pin down the difference between Osborne and NPM.

It is true that Osborne starts from the kind of reforms that constitute NPM and which he also endorses fully (Osborne and Plastrik, 1997: 8):

- decentralisation;
- re-examination of tasks and goals;
- downsizing and privatisation;
- cost-efficiency through contracting out and user charges;
- customer orientation and user fees;
- benchmarking and performance measurement;
- regulatory reform: deregulation.

However, Osborne not only wants to advocate these reforms, as he searches for something much bigger in terms academic achievement. One can search for evidence concerning these reforms, meaning whether they 'work' or not. In an evaluation of public sector reform in the last 20 years, finding the outcomes of these reforms is a most important research endeavour. Osborne presents numerous cases that are relevant in relation to the question: To what extent do findings about outcomes confirm the NPM philosophy that the above reforms increase efficiency? However, Osborne casts his nets much wider. He wants not only to correct government by taking away its *slack* but to change government entirely. It cannot be done, I will argue.

Government has, like all organisations or activities, two sides: value and costs. We value government because it brings us services we need, especially so in a democracy. However, we do not want to pay for the extra cost that government tends to generate, its X-inefficiency or waste. In a basic principal–agent approach to government with the population as the principal, the goal of the principal must be stated thus: maximise the value of government and minimise the slack of government. A number of mechanisms may be designed to accomplish this objective function, from fiscal constitutions to restrain revenue maximisation politicians (public choice theory) to tendering/bidding schemes in policy implementation (NPM). However, the purpose is to reduce slack and not undo government itself.

Osborne's almost 15-year-long crusade against government does not make this crucial distinction between eliminating waste, either with politicians or with bureaucrats, on the one hand and reducing basic government operations, on the other. Today government is on its knees in the American context: the US Government is broke. The 2004 federal deficit is the highest in US history. The US has suffered three years of record shortfalls. Cities, counties and school districts lay off policemen and teachers, closing schools and cutting services. Yet, *The Price of Government* (Osborne and Hutchinson, 2004) advocates competition, customer choice and a relentless focus on results to save millions while improving public services. Osborne believes that there is still 10 per cent more to save on each programme, of which

5 per cent can be handed over as bonuses to employees who find and make the saving. But a simple calculation tells us that 10 per cent savings year in and year out will lead to programme abolition sooner rather than later. This is nonsense, especially in the US context.

One cannot run government and receive its value without incurring costs. Value and costs are essential parts of any organisation delivering service. Once the fat is gone, any reduction in cost must lead to a reduction in output, meaning that value is also diminished. The X-inefficiency of government was revealed first by organisation theory and later public choice theory. We need no more of that now. There is basically no limit to slack in government, as it could run from 5 to 40 per cent of the costs. However, when the slack has been reduced, then further cost reductions must hurt valuable operations.

The US Government is about half the size of government in well-ordered democracies in Western Europe. Surely the fat must be gone? When government is pushed back so far that it cannot fund its essential operations, then it is not the time for a relentless search to save a few more dollars. It is time to state the value of government and attempt to measure it. What would society be like if law and order does not work, if children do not get proper education and if people cannot get basic healthcare?

Government is a difficult organisation to manage, not merely because it harbours complicated principal–agent relationships (Fukuyama, 2004; Lane, 2000), but even more so because the estimation of its value is not naturally forthcoming. Osborne started out with the cost side in *Reinventing Government* (Osborne and Gaebler, 1992), and in *The Price of Government* (Osborne and Hutchinson, 2004) he realises that the value side is as important. But he could not imagine that the only strategy that can buttress the value of government is to raise more revenues.

Improving government in the US context can only mean one thing, namely raising taxes. The difference between the US and the European scene could not be more telling. What is at stake in the unfolding management crises in the US Government is the value question: Do citizens want a decent and functioning government? In continental Europe it is still the cost side that dominates, as taxes cannot be raised further and user fees are at an all-time high.

Value in government is not forthcoming naturally because it is shared, entailing the $N-1$ and $1/N$ problems in collective action. A citizen would, all other things equal, wish to have government but pay less him/herself. And whatever a citizen pays for government will be shared with all others. Thus, taxes are a poor measure of value in government. And yet taxes constitute the main income source, because there is a limit to the rational use of user fees.

The value of government would need to be documented better in management research. Such research would inform society about how many people benefit from government and in what ways. This is difficult research, as it requires the development of new kinds of indicators tapping consumer satisfaction, coverage and appreciation of value. Osborne has nothing to say about how to promote this research on government.

According to Osborne, there is something fundamentally wrong in the design of the mechanism behind government. This echoes the Public Choice School. Osborne singles out the bureau as the 'wrong' institution in government. Bureaucracy destroys government because it has no mechanism of error correction. The market economy provides certain correcting mechanisms against error. These mechanisms work themselves out through the peculiar mix of incentives and institutions which characterise well-ordered or well-functioning markets. Could one find something similar for the public sector?

When government puts into effect the above-mentioned reforms of NPM, then the impact may be a great success in the short run. But what guarantees that the effects aimed at will be long-term ones? Osborne reports upon many short-term savings or increases in output, but clearly they can hardly be reproduced from one year to another in a long-run perspective. What can be done after NPM? If NPM shakes up a public organisation from its traditional protection against outside demands and breaks its established mechanisms of inertia, then would it not return to sleeping ugliness when the NPM reforms have been introduced through outside pressure? Osborne wants to maintain the momentum of NPM by finding what has eluded all theoreticians of public organisation, namely the self-inventing mechanism.

Osborne states that he wants to change the 'DNA of Government'. I shall quote from *Banishing Bureaucracy*:

> By "reinvention" we mean the fundamental transformation of public systems and organisations to create dramatic increases in their effectiveness, efficiency, adaptability, and capacity to innovate. This transformation is accomplished by changing their purpose, incentives, accountability, power structure, and culture (Osborne and Plastrik, 1997: 13–14).

This Copernican revolution in government will do away with bureaucracy and introduce a self-innovative organisation that accomplishes economy and effectiveness by itself as if these two goals had been built into the organisation. The prevailing wisdom in political science used to be that government bureaux are immortal, and that they have a momentum from within that is extremely difficult to change, as well as that governmental organisations display resistance to change. How, then, could Osborne accomplish this Copernican revolution in government?

This answer is as obvious as it is naïvely simple: Take the inherited wisdom from a course on private organisation and pin it down to five principles. Then apply them to government. Thus, we arrive at Osborne's five Cs:

- *Core strategy:* Clarify goals in a consistent hierarchy of priorities.
- *Consequence strategy:* Introduce private incentives everywhere.
- *Customer strategy:* Emphasise consumer choice.
- *Control strategy:* Allow for discretion and underline empowerment of employees.
- *Culture strategy:* Create entrepreneurialism and reduce resistance to change.

But precepts are one thing and reality another, as students of moral philosophy never fail to point out. What would be the relevance of these rational precepts, if the world of government obeyed the laws of complex organisation theory? Suppose we accept the lessons from 100 years of enquiry in organisation, public or private, and confront them with Osborne's five Cs (March, 1989; March and Simon, 1993). Then we would have the following contradictions:

- Organisational goals are complex and ambiguous.
- Government involves social values and vocation.
- Public goods or semi-public goods must be allocated to all or no one.
- Discretion entails a risk for arbitrariness.
- All organisations manifest resistance to innovations if they threaten vested interests.

In this hiatus between *Ought* (Osborne's five Cs) and *Is* (organisational theory) it is, of course, Osborne who must bend. If something is desirable (Osborne's five Cs), it is not necessarily feasible: Ought does not imply Can. In the world of genetics it is real DNA which determines the animal. If one wants to identify the chain of DNA in government, then perhaps empirical research is a better strategy than a mere normative selection of reasonable precepts?

Government has some characteristics which make it less suitable for the kind of reinvention strategy that Osborne recommends (and perhaps sells) to government. Government is after all *not* some kind of private organisation. I shall try to identify a few of these features of public organisations which do not rule out NPM but which restrict the applicability of private organisation precepts.

The logic of private organisation – markets, profit maximisation, incentives (private vices–public virtues), flexibility and adaptation – has a high esteem with Osborne. He sees no limit to the possibility of substituting private organisation for public organisation. Public organisation often displays features that are at odds with the philosophy of creative destruction and entrepreneurialism including: inertia, bounded rationality, stability, procedural accountability, social norms and vocation. Perhaps a well-ordered society needs both private and public organisation, and we should not attempt to replace one with the other. Government can benefit from private organisation, especially in its procurement activities. However, there is a limit to the substitution of private organisation for public organisation – a fact which Osborne never admits or takes into account.

Government cannot operate according to the logic of private organisation. Government does not come and go; only governments have short life spans. Long-run stability counts for much with government, meaning that the benefits that government produces are taken for granted and are often seen as intangible or non-fungible. Government, whether at the local, provincial or central level does not 'camp on the seesaw', as it must continue to operate under all conditions. Government flexibility is not the same firm adaptation in a market setting.

It is easy to be impressed by the logic of private organisation, especially when the state offers a legal system where private contracts and property rights can be enforced. However, government cannot operate according to private organisation. The market selects the winners and the losers from among the private enterprises as the business cycle unfolds, some companies expanding and others diminishing to the point of extinction. Government does not function according to this logic of growing and diminishing. It attempts to maintain its operations whatever the situation may be. Thus, public organisation underlines long-run stability through its institutions of competencies, tenure and non-profit activities.

Government, which is always founded upon public organisation in a well-ordered society, may employ private organisation and its mechanisms to a certain extent. Thus, it may use tendering/bidding extensively, as well as joint-stock companies. Outsourcing may be a sound strategy when government has expanded quickly or when government faces difficult demands from public sector trade unions. Public enterprises may be incorporated and put under a general competitive regime, levelling the playing field. But the core of government cannot abide the logic of private organisation. This is what Osborne never recognises, as he fails to see the limits of reinventing strategies.

Government is the exercise of public powers. The Leviathan can only be constrained by means of a rule-of-law regime. This is the basic lesson from public administration. Public organisation satisfies the basic Kantian requirements upon the state in order to have rule of law (Kant, 1996):

- legality and separation of powers
- openness and publicness
- complaint and redress.

Government must in its core procedures be organised so that it satisfies these requirements. Only public organisation can meet them. Osborne does not have a word to say about procedural justice.

Osborne's management philosophy targets a number of public vices that he wants to undo by the massive employment of the mechanisms of private organisation. Among these vices we find the basic facts about public organisation that scholars within organisational sociology have taken great pains to establish. Can they really be undone by introducing a self-correcting and self-innovative organisation? What are these public vices, more specifically? Let us reverse Mandeville's famous slogan and search for public vices as against private virtues (Mandeville, 1990).

Osborne attacks public organisation both from the supply side and the demand side. On the cost side, Osborne is of the belief that public programmes in general have huge slacks that can be undone without hurting the services delivered. Steering but not rowing, is what Osborne recommends on the cost side of government, meaning the use of tendering/bidding wherever it is possible.

On the demand side, Osborne argues that goals are not set in a clear and consistent manner. Priorities are not set for public programmes, meaning that there is a large set of low-priority programmes that somehow muddle through. If it is true that slack is typical on the cost side of public programmes and similarly that public programmes do not enter into a consistent objective function separating high-priority from low-priority programmes, then there would possibly be millions or billions to be saved.

Private organisation would undo these public vices, eliminating slack by means of tendering/bidding in combination with private remuneration for savings and reallocating resources towards high-priority programmes by clarifying priorities. However, all the lessons from organisation theory and public administration indicate that such reforms are more easily stated as desirable than implemented as feasible. Whatever organisation is chosen, public or private, there will be efforts to generate a slack. And in a democracy with organised interests seeking to favour their programmes, there can be no coherent list of priorities set for public programmes, as policy-makers differ in terms of the value they put on different programmes.

Osborne's theory of budgeting expresses his ideas about the vices of public organisation (Osborne and Hutchinson, 2004). His steps for rational budgeting for outcomes include:

- Set the price of government: How much are citizens willing to spend?
- Determine the priorities of government: the outcomes that matter most to citizens, along with indicators that measure progress.
- Decide the price for each priority outcome.
- Set outcome goals and indicators for each of the strategies and programmes, and make sure that results are measured.

- Decide how best to deliver each priority outcome at a set price: create steering organisations to act as purchasing agents and have them develop 'cause and effect' strategy maps and purchasing strategies.
- Solicit offers, and then choose which programmes and activities to purchase.
- Negotiate performance agreements with those providers, spelling out the key outputs and the outcomes to be produced, the indicators to be used to measure progress, the consequences for performance, and any flexibility granted to help an organisation maximise performance.
- Develop full cost accounting, which attributes all direct and indirect costs to a programme or strategy.
- Create a process to review performance against the targets, in both the executive-branch steering organisations and legislative committees organised to focus on the same outcomes.

The reader who has studied budgeting and public administration recognises this message as merely a version of the idea of programme budgeting combined with total quality management (TQM). One does not need to use incrementalism (Wildavsky and Swedlow, 2000) in order to argue that Osborne's budget theory is impractical. It is enough to employ the principal–agent model.

In order to state in a succinct manner that private organisation may also display vices and that no organisation, whether public or private, can be foolproof, one may state a simple principal–agent model, which covers both public and private organisation. Suppose that government as the principal hires a set of agents to implement policy. The agents would be the experts – thus there is asymmetric information. What institutional arrangement would be most suitable from the point of view of the principal in order to motivate the agents to deliver high effort against a reasonable remuneration (Rasmussen, 2001)?

There are two institutional arrangements that structure this principal–agent interaction in service delivery, where Osborne favours private organisation, meaning tendering/bidding, whereas mainstream public administration and organisational theory would recommend bureaucracy. The Osborne argument against bureaucracy is only a summary of the public choice criticism of long-term contracts in public organisation, resulting in either excessive supply or X-inefficiency (Mueller, 2003). If the principal instead chooses a short-term contracting regime involving market testing and bonuses to the agent, then the principal can avoid moral hazard, but he/she runs into the equally difficult question of adverse selection: How can one identify the bidding agents and select the best one? It is strange that Osborne does not bring up this fundamental problem in private organisation, which is well-known from, for instance the experiences with NPM in New Zealand.

I find the management philosophy of Osborne to be a crude and simplistic version of NPM. It bypasses all the empirical findings within public administration and organisational theory. And it is blind towards the theoretical insights in asymmetric information game theory. We should be more critical of this kind of consulting literature, which may have dismal political consequences for the safe and predictable delivery of public services. Implicit in all his books there is an unwarranted assumption that slack in public organisation is without limit.

Conclusion

In a well-ordered society, governments set up public organisations to run allocative, redistributional and regulation programmes. Whatever the institutional structure may be for these organisations, they involve collecting a team of people, motivating them and monitoring their performance against objectives. Running these organisations, or teams of people, is a task for management. Thus, there arises the need for a public management policy on the part of government (Kernaghan *et al.*, 2000).

The approach that I have chosen for the analysis of the main problems of public management is the principal–agent framework, originating in the economics of information and game theory. It leads us to emphasise that public administration and management is different from private management, because the principal of the entire fabric of organisation is government, representing the population. Public organisations may be seen as a nexus of principal–agent relationships, starting with the electoral contract between the population and the politicians or political parties and ending with the hiring of employees in agencies.

Public organisations operate under two logics, efficiency and accountability. This double objective function makes them fundamentally different from private organisations. What matters in relation to public organisations is both what they accomplish – their performance – and how they achieve their goals – accountability – in terms of a rule-of-law state (*Rechtsstaat*). I will approach the logics of public organisation with the principal–agent framework. What, then, does this new framework of analysis amount to?

Appendix

Table I.2 General government total outlays as percentage of nominal GDP 1986–2005

	1986	1990	1995	2000	2005
Australia	37.6	36.3	39.7	36.3	35.2
Austria	55.8	53.1	57.3	52.4	50.6
Belgium	58.9	53.4	52.8	49.4	49.3
Canada	47.5	48.8	48.5	41.0	39.9

(Continued)

	1986	*1990*	*1995*	*2000*	*2005*
Czech Republic	—	—	43.9	43.4	45.4
Denmark	53.3	57.0	60.3	54.7	55.8
Finland	47.9	48.6	59.6	49.0	50.4
France	52.7	50.7	55.0	52.5	53.6
Germany	45.4	44.4	49.4	45.7	47.6
Greece	45.2	50.2	50.0	49.7	46.2
Hungary	—	—	56.9	48.0	46.9
Iceland	40.6	42.4	43.7	42.8	42.9
Ireland	53.9	43.2	41.5	32.0	34.9
Italy	51.4	54.4	53.4	46.8	48.5
Japan	31.2	32.1	36.1	38.6	38.1
Korea	18.8	19.5	20.6	24.4	28.9
Luxembourg	—	43.2	45.5	38.5	46.4
Netherlands	56.9	54.8	51.4	45.3	47.8
New Zealand	—	53.3	41.9	40.2	39.9
Norway	48.3	52.8	51.6	43.4	49.4
Poland	—	—	47.2	45.3	47.2
Portugal	41.3	42.1	45.0	45.2	45.1
Slovak Republic	—	—	54.8	65.4	44.0
Spain	42.6	43.4	45.0	39.8	38.9
Sweden	62.0	59.4	67.6	57.4	57.5
United Kingdom	45.6	42.2	44.6	37.0	43.4
United States	37.0	36.5	36.4	33.6	35.7
Euro area	49.2	48.7	51.4	47.0	47.9
European Union	49.2	48.3	50.9	45.9	47.7
Total OECD	40.6	40.3	42.1	39.3	40.8

Source: OECD: National Accounts (www.oecd.org/home)

1 The principal–agent framework and the public sector

Introduction

The principal–agent framework (PAF) emerged in private sector analyses of human interaction that are more complex than the simple games studied in classical game theory (Gintis, 2000). The problem studied in the PAF is the following: If people interact longer than a one-shot game and if one party hires another as an expert of some kind, then how do they behave? This question is relevant to many private sector relationships that go beyond the simple adaptation in oceanic markets, including insurance, lawyers, agriculture (sharecropping), managing directors and health care (Rasmusen, 1994). How about public sector interaction? The application of the PAF to the public sector has not resulted in the same impressive list of new findings as with the private sector analysis using the PAF. The PAF comes up against the following perennial difficulties in approaching the public sector, such as:

- Who is the principal? The population at large or the elected politicians?
- What is maximised? The welfare of society or the private utility of the actors?
- Who is the agent? An entire organisation or single individuals?

It would perhaps be an exaggeration to demand that the PAF should clarify these eternal questions about the state, but one would like to see that the PAF moves the analysis one or two steps ahead when compared with other approaches to the public sector, such as public administration, public policy, public choice or management. The aim in this chapter is to suggest some clues as to how the employment of the PAF advances our understanding of the nature of the public sector, especially the logic of its organisations.

It is often stated that the PAF is merely another right-wing inspired theory advocating downsizing of the public sector. One should, however, distinguish between agency theory and the Public Choice School, as agency theory is neutral in relation to the preference between the public and the private. It argues basically that whether one employs public or private organisation, fundamental agency problems are bound to emerge in contracting. Government as the principal may face different agents: a service-providing bureau in the soft sector, a public enterprise in the business sector and the regulatory agency. How are the contracting games with these bodies to be modelled?

Why is the principal–agent framework popular?

It would be too simplistic to merely refer to the advances in the application of the PAF to private sector interactions. Although economics is the master science and the directions it goes into spill over into the other social sciences, there must be an isomorphism between private organisation and public organisation for the PAF to work in the study of government. Perhaps it is the growing relevance of the democratic regime which creates this isomorphism? The democratic state may be modelled as a principal–agent interaction in two separate phases. First, there is the principal–agent relationship between the population and its government, channelled through the electoral arena. Second, there is the principal–agent interaction between government and its agencies or public organisations. Thus, government is both agent and principal in this simple model of democratic policy-making, modelled as responsive to its principal, the demos, as well as giving direction to its agents.

Democracy according to the PAF would be a regime under which the population as the fundamental principal of the state instructs government and pays taxes to the politicians as their agents who set up a public sector with a carpet of organisation, staffed by people working as agents of the government. Thus, democracy is simply a double set of principal–agent relationships. Any student of public sector complexity would reject such a model of government as unrealistic at worse or simplistic at best (March and Olsen, 1996; Lindblom and Woathouse, 1994). One does not have to go far into the literature penetrating all the corners and muddy waters of modern government in the advanced democracies to realise that the PAF comes high on parsimony but low on descriptive realism. Yes, its normative appeal is obvious from the point of view of democratic theory.

After the re-engineering of government in the 1990s one needs a conceptual framework for analysing what some scholars call 'plural government' and other scholars describe as 'networking government'. To cut through so much organised complexity one would wish to employ a simple analytical approach which identifies the key players in an interaction and classifies them as either principal or agent. One does not have to agree with all of

Milton Friedman's ideas about government in order to endorse his recommendation to look for model simplicity as long as the predictive power of the model is satisfactory (Quine, 1992).

The popularity of the PAF derives to a considerable extent from the renewed surge in interest for game theory in all the social sciences. The key concept is strategy. It has certainly not been lacking from the writings of the great masters of public administration such as Max Weber and Aaron Wildavsky. However, the attention given to the concept of strategy and its immense elaboration with the Nash solution concept as well as with the idea of subgame perfect Nash equilibria is a new phenomenon in academia (Myerson, 1997; Fudenberg and Tirole, 1991; Ordeshook, 1986). It opens up a new systematic perspective on human interaction in general, the implications of which for government and its organisations in particular remain to be stated.

Suppose we regard government as a nexus of principal–agent interactions, then what new insights may we gain into bureaucracies, public enterprises and social security? It has been suggested that from the election emerges a principal–agent relationship between the voters and the politicians. This contract is, however, far more elusive than the contracts analysed in the PAF. Yet I shall look at the government provision of services in a broad sense as constituting a huge set of principal–agent interactions, stretching from the population to the agents over government as the main principal. I will confine the analysis to well-ordered societies, i.e. countries with democracy and the market economy (Rawls, 1995, 2001).

The agency framework is not an extension of the public choice approach to politics and administration, as the principal–agent model emerged from classical game theory and the economics of information (Laffont and Martimort, 2001). It can take into account the complexities of a public sector under plural government, as well as networking government, and it does not reduce behaviour to merely egoism, brutal or sophisticated. The PAF may be employed to illuminate the key ideas in public sector reform, such as the movement from public administration towards New Public Management (NPM). Why is there such an emphasis on entrepreneurial government and reregulation at the same time? May the PAF be employed to explain the main theories about the reorganisation of government in the early twenty-first century?

Principals and agents: contracting as the essence of interaction

According to the PAF, providing public services to the population is basically a contractual matter concerning the writing and enforcement of agreements between first, the leaders of government and an organisation responsible for service delivery, and second, the leaders of the organisation and single individuals. It makes little sense under the PAF to call the first contract 'politics' and the second contract 'administration'. From an institutional point of view, these contracts may look very different from one country to another. Different forms of law are employed when setting up these organisations and funding them – compare, for example, unitary and federal systems of government. And the organisations responsible for service delivery may employ alternative forms of contracting with individuals – compare bureaucracy with a competitive/tendering regime. Although the importance of public law is great in shaping these contractual relationships between government and public organisations, it remains true that the interaction between them adheres to the logic of contracting. I do not deny that alternative institutional arrangements matter greatly for how government and public organisations interact; this is why it is important to research the consequences of alternative institutions. Public sector reform in the OECD countries has resulted in such a wide variety of public organisations that one has started to use the word 'plural government' in order to emphasise that there is no longer any simple structure prevailing in the public sector (Ferlie *et al.*, 1996; McLaughlin *et al.*, 2001).

Whatever form or structure the public organisation has from a legal point of view, it is the case that government cannot get anything done unless there is an agreement between it and the public organisation about service delivery, i.e. a contract. Thus, underneath the paraphernalia of laws and instructions, budgetary appropriations and regulations, there is an agreement between the principal and the agent about what to deliver and how to be paid – a contract. One may perhaps not wish to use such a private law term as 'contract', but that is what the interaction between government and its organisations comes to.

The contract is more visible in the second principal–agent interaction, namely, that between the organisation and its employees. Whether the public organisation insources or outsources, it will, in any case, handle lots of contracts with individuals of varying length of time and with different contents. There may certainly be framework legislation that structures these individual contracts, but contracts they still are. Thus, one may look on the public sector as consisting of numerous teams of people working for government under varying institutional arrangements. Instructing and monitoring these teams is what the PAF concentrates its analysis on. To put the matter bluntly: the civil service is a *set of teams*, namely the professionals who work in schools, universities and hospitals as well as public enterprises and regulatory agencies.

After establishing the fundamental importance of the contract between government and the public organisations in the midst of all institutional details, which may change rapidly when public sector reform is frequent, the PAF concentrates on predicting the basic problems in the contracts that will be forthcoming between the principal and the agent. Alternative contractual arrangements will have different real-life outcomes. The PAF covers simple contracts between government and one agency as in many regulatory programmes, but the PAF may also cover complex contractual arrangements typical of networking where government contracts with several agents. Whether there is insourcing or outsourcing, the basis is the contract between government as the principal and the organisation as the team of agents.

Incentives: how is egoism and social value recognised?

The PAF underlines the role that incentives play in social interaction in general and in principal–agent games in particular (Laffont, 2003). However, it is not restricted to modelling only narrow self-interests as with the Public Choice School. As a matter of fact, one may employ the PAF to pin down a key difficulty in public administration or public management, namely the objectives of the principal. Herein rests the great and still unresolved mystery of incentives in the public sector (Breton, 1996): What is the objective function of the government – public, private, social, selfish? The incentives of the agent are basically mundane, and modelled by two principles:

- *The reservation price:* The principal must at least pay the agent what he/she can get in other employment.
- *Incentive compatibility:* The principal must compensate the agent for trying hard.

The agent will be offered a menu of contracts which all satisfy his/her reservation price and some of them will pay a higher wage to the agent if he/she promises a high effort or commitment. The agent is always risk-averse, meaning that he/she prefers employment to being an entrepreneur. The agent maximises his/her utility by combining salary, which is a positive, and effort, which is a negative. What, then, is the principal maximising?

The principal will want to supply a range of public services or public programmes. He/she may do this for a variety of reasons, egoistic or altruistic. Be that as it may, the basic idea in the PAF is that the principal contracts with the agent to get things done. The principal is dependent on the agent to get the job of government done, while the agent is dependent on the principal to get paid for his/her services. Thus, the objective function of the principal definitely comprises public services or public policies. Little is gained by speculation about whether egoistic or altruistic reasons matter most to the principal. Without supplying public services or accomplishing public policies he/she cannot reach egoistic goals such as power, prestige and money.

The supply of public services or public policies is the *quid pro quo* between the politicians and the population, the citizens accepting to pay taxes or charges in exchange for a menu of public programmes. The principal will use this income to pay the agent for his/her services and to pay him/herself a decent compensation. The capacity of the principal to raise income is related to the quality of services provided, meaning that the value of the public programmes implemented is crucial to the entire equation, starting with the population and ending with the agent. And here is the difficulty: How does one estimate the value of the services in the public sector? This is the crux of the matter in any theory about the output and outcome side of government.

In traditional public administration the principal simply picks up the bill from the agent and tries to cover it through taxation and user fees, if not by borrowing money. In NPM the idea is that the principal should focus on value for money and attempt to maximise the difference between the value of the services to the population and the costs of the operations of the agent. Thus, NPM recommends a whole set of strategies to reveal and estimate the value of public services:

- benchmarking, total quality management;
- results-based budgeting, accrual budgeting;
- user charging;
- privatisation;
- outsourcing.

The value of public services or public programmes is that entity which drives the entire set of principal–agent interactions, from the population over government to its organisations. Yet, it is elusive because it is difficult to measure (Moore, 2003). Principal–agent theory predicts that there will be conflict over the distribution of the social value of the public services. Thus, the agents will want to pocket a large part of the social value, especially if they are instrumental in producing it. And politicians would want their share of the cake, either at the expense of the population or through a reduction in the costs for the agents. This conflict over the social value of the public sector typifies principal–agent games. How recurrent are they in the public sector? Only empirical research can tell. I shall discuss the main games in order to see what they can illuminate about the public sector.

Principal–agent games

In the PAF the key distinction is that between post-contractual opportunism and pre-contractual opportunism, the relevance of which needs to be spelled out in relation to the public sector. I will distinguish between three main games that surface in the public sector of advanced countries like the OECD nations, combining democracy with the market economy.

The bureaucracy game

No governmental institution has been more analysed than the bureaucracy. One may classify the major scholars of government in relation to how they perceived this institution, starting with Wilson's and Weber's notion of bureau efficiency and ending with March and Olsen's garbage-can conception (Lane, 2000). The empirical study of bureaucracy resulted in several major findings feeding organisation theory such as Merton's insight into dysfunctional aspects of bureaucracy and Crozier's revelation about bureau rigidity. Can the PAF be employed to predict these various findings and explain why under some conditions bureaucracy works well, whereas under other circumstances it performs less well?

The bureau is typically to be found in the so-called 'soft part' of the public sector which is wholly or partially financed through taxes. It provides the population with a service such as education or health care. Its value tends not to be revealed through a demand revelation mechanism like the market. What, then, should the government as principal pay its agents for the service?

The bureau will supply its services with a cost tag, requesting that government picks it up. If government sleeps, then the bureau will set the price tag higher than the value of the service through various agent strategies. The bureau will engage in one of two strategies: excessive supply and/or excessive unit costs.

Government may of course collude with the bureaucracy as it did in historical periods, passing on the high price tag to the population in the form of an unbearable tax burden. However, in a democracy this is not the likely outcome of the principal–agent interaction. The loyalty of the politicians with their bureaucracy will have to be balanced by the dependency of the politicians upon popular legitimacy. Politicians will not usually want to pay the excessive cost or supply.

The outcomes of the bureaucracy game are clear: only if the principal puts active monitoring in place can he/she push the bureaucracy out of a suboptimal solution. Yet, it comes with a cost and a risk. If the principal does not want to engage in monitoring or cannot afford to do so, then he/she will offer a low salary. NPM teaches government to be vigilant in its dealings with its bureaucracies. Perhaps it goes too far when it suggests an entirely different set of mechanisms for contracting between government and its organisations, namely:

- tendering/bidding
- market testing
- short-term contracting or
- contracting in?

The public organisations tend to put up resistance when subjected to these private law mechanisms on a major scale. The strategy of cutting up the civil service, leaving a rich carpet of executive agencies, may lead to one dysfunction in bureaucracy, namely the lack of coordination.

Monitoring is, I suggest, a *sine qua non* as a government strategy. The monitors may come from special monitoring agencies such as an independent audit bureau or an efficiency task force with the Ministry of Finance. Government may employ two monitoring bureaux that are separate from each other. The problem with monitoring is again a principal–agent one: How can government trust the monitoring agent to try hard? The monitoring agency may collude with the monitored agency, or it may put in little effort for the same reason that the monitored organisation shirks. If this occurs, then government has run out of options. The only strategy left is major reorganisation to break up such coalitions or introduce better monitors (Laffont, 2001). The bureau model has two major implications. First, the bureaucracy in a Third World country will perform poorly. As long as the principal cannot offer decent remuneration, the bureaucracy will not try hard. Second, the bureaucracy in the First World will have to be shaken up from time to time in efforts at reorganisation in order to make monitoring effective.

The public enterprise game

The traditional public enterprise would be examined by the PAF in the same manner as the bureaucracy. It would, one may predict, be performing poorly, harbouring lots of employees sheltered by its monopoly position (World Bank, 1995). The interesting question is what games will be forthcoming when the public enterprise is given a new institutional setting, involving not only a new organisational form but also an entirely private law organisation, the incorporated firm (Dine, 1997).

The main source of inspiration for the re-engineering of the public enterprise was not public choice theory but Chicago School economics (Stigler, 1988, 2003). The public enterprise used to be part of the Ministry of Finance, run as a trading department in agreement with a regulatory scheme that allowed for only one provider. It happened that the public enterprise was both the sole provider and the regulator of the industry. Government handed over the licence to the public enterprise, which established its monopoly as part of a contract where government received a promise of a certain quantity of service at a certain quality. If the principal regulated both price and quantity, then surely it would be in the driving seat? No, predicted the PAF, as the outcomes would depend less upon legislative intention than upon the strategies employed and the information available. Government may end up as the real loser, with public regulation not being successful and losses running high. Here we have an example of the agent taking the entire social value of the public organisation and possibly even more.

Thus, government may find the Chicago public enterprise policy attractive as a more coherent solution to a principal–agent game. It comes as a rocket with three stages:

- deregulation
- incorporation
- privatisation.

All governments in the OECD set have pursued this kind of public sector reform all over infrastructure, as there are hardly any traditional public enterprises left. Where governments differed was in the extent of privatisation, some preferring to maintain partial or even full public ownership in a deregulated regime.

The Chicago model worked in one area with great success: telecommunications (Eliassen and Sjovaag, 1999). Here, deregulation meant true free entry with new operators coming in on a major scale in one country after another. The traditional public enterprise in telecom – in, for instance, the UK, France, Germany and Hong Kong – was transformed into a joint-stock firm in a competitive environment where entry was facilitated through technological innovations. But apart from telecommunications and perhaps also the airline industry, the Chicago model did not work out as envisaged. In the areas of electricity, water supply and taxis, deregulation has been either less successful, or less complete, and it has often been replaced by reregulation.

The policy of deregulation, incorporation and partial privatisation of the public enterprise brought about tremendous change in both the firm itself and in the market segment it was operating in. However, it was not without perils for the principal, the government. I wish to mention here the many examples of public firms engaging in strategies to increase market power in a deregulated setting. The agents of the new public firms have proven as difficult to control as the agents in the old public enterprise. The new regime has made it easier for agents – the CEOs – to increase their salaries, often quite dramatically, but what is even worse for the principal is that they have left some of these reorganised firms in a shambles. The CEOs of the new public firms have been inclined to take risks that the principal would not like to face when things turn out badly. The strategies of the CEOs of the reorganised public firms took on a regional if not global scale, often resulting in too quick an expansion, with great losses attending. The interesting thing here is that governments tend to become responsible even when they are not the main owners of the re-engineered firm. Thus, a partially privatised public enterprise, like French Telecom, which finds itself in difficulties will call upon government to help. The game involved here is called 'adverse selection' within the PAF. Government often fails to identify and stay away from agents who are too risk-prone, promising great results.

The reregulation game

Managerialism stands strong in present public sector reforms. There is even talk of creating 'entrepreneurial government' where government entrusts senior managers with the full responsibility for service provision. But how is the principal going to solve the typical agency problems of writing a contract with the managers that is efficient and which can be enforced? Through reregulation.

Regulatory agencies would be close to the principal, as they are to fulfil the ambition of the government to regulate primarily the private sector. The value of the work of the regulator is, however, very difficult to measure or even estimate. There are two different kinds of benefits – price and quality – corresponding to the main types of public regulation:

- *Restricting competition:* The agency offers licences in order to promote economies of scale, which could reduce price to the consumer.
- *Increasing competition:* The agency pursues competition policy, meaning that it takes various actions to open up entry and thus accomplish a reduction in price.
- Checking quality in various ways.

Regulation may bring much value to consumers, if it works. It may reduce price and/or raise quality, but regulators may also make mistakes. Whether public regulation works or not is a major issue of contention in economics, but whatever school of regulation one adheres to, it remains true that regulators are government bureaucrats who have to be paid (Stigler, 1988). Can regulation become excessive? And who would benefit besides the regulators themselves?

NPM appears to be conducive to an increase in regulation despite its emphasis on deregulation. One may wish to relate the increase in regulation to the emergence of a risk society or to a fundamental change in the preferences for safety (Wildavsky, 1987, 1997). Here I look at the principal–agent implications of reregulation. Reregulation may have positive outcomes if it increases the monitoring of the producers or goods or providers of services. The regulators may function as a cheap monitoring device, not only in relation to the private sector but also in relation to public organisations. On the other hand, reregulation may be the mere reversal of deregulation, resulting in the same problems that beset traditional regulation.

The principal–agent approach and the public sector

Throughout this volume I will analyse central topics in public administration and public management using the principal–agent framework ('the P–A approach'). The basic idea is that governments contract as principals with agents in order to get the job done in the public sector. Thus, the emphasis here, as within public administration and public management, is upon the outputs and outcomes of the political system. I believe that the P–A framework adds new insights compared with the two main approaches to the public sector, namely public administration and public management, as well as public policy and implementation by focusing on the logic of contracting in government, the nature of information and the role of incentives (Laffont, 2003).

In both public administration and public management there are some unresolved questions concerning strategy that limit the usefulness of these approaches. This is not to deny many of the insights reached in public administration and public management, but to add a vital part of the story that is missing. I will pay attention to the essence of public administration – legality – and the core element of public management – efficiency, but the P–A framework allows one to integrate these into a general framework for the analysis of strategy in government outputs.

Generally speaking, a principal undertakes an activity in order to accomplish an objective, or a set of activities in relation to a set of objectives. The objectives are to be achieved through the production of outputs O by an agent A to be paid for his/her work by the principal P. Thus, there will be contract between principal P and agent A, stipulating the remuneration or wage as well as the output aimed at for that wage.

The P–A framework targets the interdependency between the principal P and the agent A. They are both dependent upon each other but they have conflicting interests at the same time. The principal P wants to achieve the objective O while minimising the wage to the agent A, whereas the agent A wants to maximise his/her remuneration for the work done in relation to the objective O. Thus, we have the following equations:

(1) $O = f(e, E)$, output is a function of effort and the random environment.

(2) $w = f(O)$, remuneration depends on output.

(3) $P = O - w$, the principal P's profit is the value of the output minus wage.

(4) $U(A) = w - e$, the utility of the agent is his/her wage minus effort.

The principal P may need a set of agents – a team – but this would only make the contracting problem more complicated. Contracting with agents may be modelled as a two-stage process, where the principal first contracts with a CEO, who in turn contracts with a team of agents.

The P–A problem can be formulated in the following manner given the equations (1)–(4): What menu of contracts is likely between the principal P and the agent A? The P–A problem covers any organisation where one may identify owners and employees. Typical of the P–A framework for the analysis of contracting between principals and agents is that the following restrictions tend to hold upon the set of feasible contracts:

- non-observability of agent's effort
- verifiability of contracts in courts
- participation constraint of the agent

- incentive compatibility restriction for the agent
- risk-neutral principals and risk-averse agents.

These five restrictions normally hold for any principal–agent interaction, in the private sector as well as in the public sector. I will, however, argue that there are important differences between these two sectors of society when it comes to principal–agent interaction. Just as there is a principal–agent theory for agricultural contracts (Bardhan, 1989), so we may speak of public sector contracts as solutions to principal–agent gaming. Asymmetric information is even more difficult to handle in the public sector than in the private sector.

The menu of contracts that are feasible includes both best and second best contracts, depending upon which assumptions one makes about these five restrictions. I shall identify four extreme outcomes of contracting – exploitation, looting, adverse selection and moral hazard – which give the range of contracting possibilities between the principal and the agent:

- *Exploitation:* The principal sets the remuneration at the reservation price of the agent.
- *Looting:* The agent takes the entire profit of the principal in the form of his/her remuneration.
- *Moral hazard:* The contract *ex ante* between the principal and the agent deviates considerably from the contact *ex post*, as the agent does not respect the terms of the contract but shirks.
- *Adverse selection:* The principal is unable to identify the nature of the agent, i.e. whether the agent is a low-effort or high-effort person – pretending.

When the public sector is approached as a nexus of contracts, then I suggest one applies the concepts above in order to understand strategy in the games between government on the one hand, and its service providers or goods producers on the other. Public sector reform may be seen as attempts to handle these contractual difficulties by choosing alternative institutions. Figure 1.1 contains a most general model of the principal–agent interaction, which allows for a statement of both shirking and adverse selection covering both the bureaucracy game and the public enterprise game above.

The principal wants to know whether the agent with whom he/she is contracting will put in effort $e1$ or effort $e2$. If the principal can identify the type or nature of the agent and write a complete contract, then he/she offers either ($W1$, $e1$) or ($W2$, $e3$). However, if there is asymmetric information, then the agent may *shirk*, i.e. promise (*ex ante*) the effort $e3$ but only deliver (*ex post*) $e2$. The risk for the principal is to end up in the *ex post* contract ($W2$, $e2$), where all the gains are eaten up in remuneration to the agent – *looting*. Governance in the public sector is about picking the

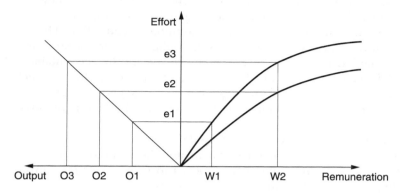

Figure 1.1 Principal–agent interaction: the general picture.

right agents, separating low-effort from high-effort agents, and avoiding the danger of shirking. If the principal acts under asymmetric information, then he/she does not know the type of the agent, whether he/she is high effort or low effort or whether he/she will shirk. If the government faces two agents, one low effort, *A1* and another high effort, *A2*, then it may not be able to distinguish them, as agents may *pretend*. If government only has a 50/50 chance of picking the right agent, then how can it offer a contract like (*W2, e3*)? The principal *P* would search for contractual mechanisms that reduce the risk of shirking and the consequences of pretending.

Management, public organisation and the principal–agent model

Public sector reform in well-ordered societies has resulted in plural government after NPM. Perhaps this organisational variety, which is now characteristic of the public sector, can be called *enlightened public governance* (EPG)? In any case, the task of understanding the present situation, which is neither bureaucracy nor contracting out (Ferlie *et al.*, 1996) remains.

The policy paradigm seems less relevant for the analysis of the post-NPM situation than before, because public sector reform has changed policy outcomes less than the organisational structure of the public sector. It has not significantly reduced the public sector, but it has changed its structure. How can one understand the new complexity of public organisation? Besides bureaucracies, traditional public enterprises and public joint-stock companies, there are public–private partnerships, networks, mere contractual relationships and various kinds of performance units, as well as outsourcing. In addition there has been reregulation, introducing new regulatory agencies. This organisational heterogeneity or complexity can only be captured with a most general approach to public organisation. The distinctive feature of public organisation is the political nature of the whole enterprise behind the public sector, or more specifically accountability. Thus, public teams are accountable to government in various forms, which is what sets them off from private organisations. I suggest the principal–agent framework may be developed so that it captures this feature of public teams or agents.

The principal–agent (P–A) approach models the interaction between two sets of people, the principal on the one hand and the agent(s) on the other (Ricketts, 2002). The interaction is supposed to take some time, involving multiple moves and frequent interplay. Thus, it is a game with many moves which can take a considerable time to be played and can involve replays. To analyse such a complicated game and derive strategic solutions the P–A model assumes that the agent works for the principal in exchange for remuneration to be paid by means of the value of the output that the agent produces. The agent is assumed to maximise his/her utility, which depends on the remuneration and the disutility of his/her effort in connection with the production of the output that the principal wants the agent to provide. The principal is maximising his/her utility in relation to the value of the output minus the remuneration of the agent. The agent is risk-averse, whereas the principal is risk-neutral. These assumptions set up a game of long duration under which there is both cooperation and conflict. Thus, both the principal and the agent want an output that has value marketwise or otherwise, as they both get utility from it. What is conflictual concerns the split of the gain from the output where the principal and the agent have opposing interests. The key question is whether the two actors can coordinate upon Pareto-optimal outcomes, or whether there is a loss of output due to the strategies of the two players.

The P–A model would not have received so much attention in economics if it had not added one critical assumption to the framework, namely asymmetric information. Given full information, the game has the standard solutions in economic theory, which depend upon the type of the market, i.e. the availability of agents, resulting in perfect competition or monopoly. With asymmetric information, the determinate solutions are more difficult to identify, implement and enforce. The game has several interesting applications, as analysed in the economics of information. Asymmetric information games cover insurance, sharecropping, CEOs and stockbrokers (Mudambi and Ricketts, 1997). Why not also apply the P–A model to plural government? I suggest not only that the P–A framework is applicable to public organisation but also that it is highly suitable for analysing relations involving accountability. The two main phenomena in principal–agent interaction – hidden action and hidden knowledge – may be identified in public organisation. In addition, one may speak of the relevance of transaction costs when the state is set up (*ex ante*) and when it delivers public services (*ex post*).

Politicians want two things from the public organisations: competence from a technical or administrative point of view and accountability to the principal. There is literature on the so-called problem of bureaucracy, which is a perceived lack of productivity and accountability within the civil service.

This is the result of an environment where neither the President nor the Congress has well-defined property rights over the federal bureaucracy. The current civil service is, itself, an imperfect institutional response to these conditions (Johnson and Libecap, 1994: 154). The three major groups of bureaucrats tend to be: (1) political appointees, (2) senior career officials, and (3) rank-and-file career employees. Weber's theory of government tried to combine accountability with competence, recommending strongly bureaucratic government where political leadership is to be combined with administrative competence or merit.

The bureaucracy serving the political leaders should score high on both political accountability and merit. In reality one finds all kinds of combinations between political accountability and bureaucratic merit. Political accountability of the bureaucracy will be high when the legislative assembly is strong and active, as with the US Congress or when the premier is strong and surrounded by loyal ministers, as in the UK Parliament. Thus, political leadership over the bureaucracy can be exercised by either the legislative or executive branches of government. It involves the following things from the point of view of the legislature:

- *Legislation:* setting up the rules.
- *Financing:* covering the costs of operations.
- *Investigations:* monitoring policy.
- *Questioning:* finding out what is going on.

Political control over the bureaucracy will be strong when the legislative assembly can set up and fund lots of statutory bodies, make frequent investigations through its committees of oversight and engage in constant monitoring through the questions institution. The political control over the bureaucracy will also be substantial when it faces a Prime Minister who holds his/her cabinet with a firm hand, although this would be executive control rather than legislative control. On the other hand, political control of the bureaucracy is low when either the bureaucracy coordinates to protect its interests and autonomy (*Beamtenherrschaft*) or when the bureaucracy is captured by special interests and split up into turfs fighting each other (*Satrapenherrschaft*).

Merit may be accomplished in various ways in the bureaucracy, as there is a variety of competences that bureaux draw upon. Whether competence is defined in terms of legal skills or medical training or technological skills, it remains the case that patronage is the main cause of bureaucratic incompetence. How, then, can the consequences of political patronage be restricted, which, by the way, increases political accountability in the bureaucracy? This is the crux of the matter. Merit may be established through central examinations. This is the approach from the British Northcote–Trevelyan Reform in 1854 as well as the American Pendleton Reform of 1883. Bureaucrats are accepted while young and they move through the various parts of the bureaucracy accumulating wisdom and expertise. When professionalism could not offer the criteria for advancement, then bureaucracies employed seniority in order to avoid patronage. However, merit may also be established through decentralised recruitment procedures. Public sector reform has in many OECD countries entailed that the various bureaux and agencies may recruit their own personnel. As a matter of fact, under NPM they may decide whether to recruit at all or use outsourcing instead. In an executive agency it is the CEO who decides the basic management policy, including:

- whether to use insourcing or outsourcing;
- which people are necessary in in-house production.

Whereas impartial centralised examinations accomplish the rule of law, it is an open question whether decentralised recruitment will do so. The power of the CEO in an executive agency may constitute a problem for political accountability and the rule of law. However, decentralised recruitment may lead to more of efficiency from the personnel hired. At least this is the implication of the street-level bureaucracy theory, claiming that true competence in public service delivery most often resides with the street-level bureaucrats, or the lower echelons of the bureaucratic structure.

Besides political accountability there is judicial accountability. The difference between political and judicial accountability is that between political guidance on the one hand and the observation of legality on the other. Legal accountability is more easily combined with merit than political accountability. A high level of technical competence in the bureaucracy does not guarantee a strict observation of rules about transparency and honesty in government, but it helps. It is the difficulty of combining merit and political accountability that lies behind the problem of bureaucracy. The more competent the bureaucracy is, the more it strives for bureau autonomy.

Public management and the politics/administration separation

In the rapidly growing literature on public management there is a strong conviction that one has finally identified the missing link in public administration. In traditional public administration there was a strong emphasis on the inputs into bureaux, agencies and enterprises such as laws, personnel, premises, materials and budgetary appropriations in an effort to secure the rule of law and accountability. The policy paradigm added the output and outcome side to the analysis, underlining that inputs should be related to the outputs as they were conducive to outcomes. Thus, rule-of-law requirements have to be complemented by the demand for efficiency. The making of public policy is one side of the equation, comprising intentions and inputs. The other side of the equation is equally valid, namely, the implementation of policy through policy outputs and outcomes.

The policy approach argued that it had located the missing link in the analysis of government, namely, the implementation of policy through the actions of lower-level bureaucrats and professionals, often changing policy completely. Thus, it set up an input–output framework for the analysis of government and its programmes where inputs were matched with outputs. Thus, various concepts of efficiency could be developed for the comparison between inputs, outputs and outcomes, such as productivity and effectiveness, to be further developed by means of various indices. A range of literature followed with a variety of labels such as evaluation study, outcome or impact or efficiency analysis. Yet there remained the puzzle of how inputs are linked to outputs through the doings of the bureaucracy. And this is where public management makes its fundamental point as well as departure, namely that the transformation of inputs into outputs requires management to the same extent in a bureau as in a private firm.

The new literature on public management attempts to show that the black box between inputs and outputs matters. Thus, public management is a new field of study underlining the importance of managing the resources so that they are transformed into productive outputs and effective outcomes. It is yet to be established just how public management matters for outputs and outcomes. It seems that although scholars may be convinced about this relationship, they have made available little firm evidence to that effect. In any case, there is a clear risk that the emerging theory of management will be as ill-structured as the established theory of private management (Mintzberg *et al.*, 2001). Concerning the running of a private enterprise, all agree that the managers play a key role in its achievements, but no one has succeeded in clarifying exactly how. Yet, there is one puzzling aspect in the new literature on public management that one may wish to decide on one way or the other. I am referring to the denial of the distinction between politics and administration that is typical of this new literature. Thus, the public management literature looks on each policy area or public programme as involving management by politicians and officials together without making a separation between the two (Brudney *et al.*, 2000a–c).

The politics/administration separation has been a source of much contention and debate within public administration. Yet I would be inclined to argue that it is vital to the enterprise of analysing how democracies conduct public policy and implement policy. But I would also add that the distinction between politics and administration is best analysed within the principal–agent framework.

There are two aspects to the question about the politics/administration separation in public management:

1   How does one make the distinction between politics and administration? This question has caused a lot of discussion, as it has been difficult to find and explain the demarcation line between politics and administration. Is it values against knowledge, objectives against technology, etc.?

2   How can one analyse the interaction in public management between the central players? In the new literature on public management one looks upon the management function as involving both politicians and bureaucrats without making any distinction between those politically elected and those appointed to the bureaucracy.

These two questions are not entirely independent of each other, as an answer to one has implications for an answer to the other. I am inclined to deny the separation in (1), but model the interaction in (2) with a distinction between the principal and his/her agents.

Conclusion

Looking at the public sector as a nexus of principal–agent relationships from the population over the politicians in a democratic regime to the bureaucracies and public firms that act as agents of government offers a convenient way to model – in a highly general manner – the organisational complexity of modern or reinvented government. The key concepts derive from that of strategy (effort and remuneration) and the social value of output.

The public sector offers a wide range of programmes that deliver goods and services to the population. The benefits that they lead to could be called their 'social value', i.e. what the population would be prepared to pay for them. Government is responsible for the articulation and aggregation of the demand for public programmes, but it must contract with agents to deliver them, and getting the job done with the various agents and their organisations will incur costs for government. This sets up the principal–agent interaction, dealing with how the social value of the public programmes is to be divided among the three parties:

- the population
- the government
- the agents.

Understanding the governance of the public sector involves locating the problem of contracting: how can the principal agree with the agent to deliver an output at a reasonable remuneration? Here the focus is on the contract between government as the principal and its various agents who implement or enforce public policies. The so-called *agency problem*, how to motivate the agent A to work for the principal P in an efficient manner given the institutional constraints in place, surfaces for instance in that most classical state function: budgeting.

The agency problem in politics has been analysed for the legislative setting in the United States (McCubbins, Noll and Weingast, 1987, 1989), with regard to the enforcement of law by the bureaucracy. However, agency problems crop up not only in the autonomy of the bureaucracy and in the amount of freedom in delegation it possesses in relation to the legislative assembly. They are omnipresent in all forms of government implementation where a team of people is contracted to put public policy into effect. The concepts of moral hazard and adverse selection may be broadened to cover not only shirking or pretending but also, as with McCubbins, Noll and Weingast, too much agency independence. In this volume I look at the agency problem from the point of view of public administration and management: how to get the job done.

2 Public principals and their agents

Introduction

Neo-liberalism has rightly emphasised that markets create wealth, the affluence of nations depending critically on whether they have vibrant markets for goods and services as well as financial markets. The dominant economic school – Chicago School economics – has propagated this message without pause through numerous outlets (academic journals, textbooks, television, newspapers, etc.), claiming that markets tend always to be efficient. Yet, as the period of neo-liberalism (1967–2001) has come to an end, it is urgent to reflect upon why it is the case that governments everywhere are involved in the economy in various roles, for instance in providing badly needed stability to the market economy.

The core analysis of government and the public sector in not only Chicago School economics but also the right-wing inspired, so-called Public Choice School was far too negative in its general tone. One cannot simply explain away the public sector by referring to myopia, opacity and the capacity of minorities to combine and defeat the majority by engaging in capture strategies and rent-seeking. The presence of government in the economy is simply too obvious to be explained away by any such theory. When market economies go into recession or face crisis, then the visible hand of government becomes crystal-clear. In addition, the importance of the state to society and the economy was not recognised in neo-liberalism, especially for its role in enhancing the rule of law and justice in well-ordered societies and for allocating social services in Third World countries.

Milton Friedman still delivers newspaper statements to the effect that an advanced country could do with a minimum of government as well as that we still face the threat of socialism destroying the market economy and that government should reduce its stake in the economy by privatisation, deregulation and liberalisation. However, the recent experiences with Enron, WorldCom, Vivendi, French Telecom, British Energy, etc. do not support the position of Friedman. Instead, more and more evidence points at the crucial roles that governments play in the economy, in both rich and poor countries, and it is far from always a negative impact that government has upon the economy.

The study of government and the services provided in the public sector needs to balance the market exuberance that characterised much of neo-liberalist thinking. It can go back to classical political economy, which never left government out of the analysis of the economy. Economics is not only the theory of markets. Government has a profound impact upon the economy, which is not merely a question of perverse behaviour such as rent-seeking, fiscal illusions or social choice paradoxes.

Political economy is the theory of how the state and the market interact in the economy (Persson and Tabellini, 2002). It covers all aspects of economic behaviour: ownership, allocation, regulation and distribution. The role of government may no doubt be negative, hampering economic growth and destroying affluence, but it may be positive as well. Yet its existence is undeniable but not well accounted for in the dominant approaches, such as Chicago School economics and the Public Choice School. There must exist some fundamental positive reasons why governments are present in the economy and provide vital services to society in the public sector. In this chapter I will apply the principal–agent framework to the public sector in order to see how it can help us understand what governments may achieve through their public sectors. The purpose in this chapter is thus to suggest clues as to how the principal–agent framework may be put to use in understanding the public sector, given the fact that it has illuminated contract-making within a wide range of private sector areas, such as sharecropping, insurance and private sector management (Bardhan, 1989).

From public finance to public management

In a very simplified view of society, one may state that it consists of two sectors, namely the public and the private sectors. The public sector would, from an economic point of view, consist of public resource allocation and income maintenance, leaving public regulation outside of this framework as it touches the entire private sector. This classification has been elaborated in the international system of public finance, employed by, for example, the OECD in its comparative statistics (*National Accounts*). The key question here concerns the size of the public sector as a percentage of GDP. The public sector expansion theme has been very much researched in relation to the so-called capitalist democracies, where traditional socialism was discarded, but all the same, government increased in an almost phenomenal manner during the twentieth century – the growth of the tax state argument by Schumpeter from 1918 (Schumpeter and Clemence, 1989).

The search for an optimal macro size of the public sector has driven some scholars to suggest lists of the tasks that should be public and those that should be private (Rosen, 2001; Stiglitz, 2000). Any such list fails, however, to identify the proper size of the public sector, as income maintenance is almost 50 per cent of the public expenditure and there is hardly any limit to how much can be spent on social justice. One may argue that government ought to concentrate its efforts on so-called public goods, but this argument has little practical relevance. Governments allocate semi-public goods as well as private goods. And when income maintenance programmes are added, there is hardly any magic size of an optimal government.

This perspective from political economy or public finance, which is highly political, needs to be balanced with an organisational perspective: Which bodies are active in the public sector? There is general agreement that publicly owned joint-stock companies do not enter the public sector, meaning that the public sector proper comprises all kinds of government authorities, agencies and boards. These bodies correspond basically to the public teams that operate the public sector, including the regulatory agencies. Country-specific institutions clearly impact upon the derivation of the list of public bodies, as public universities, for example, are in some countries independent bodies, but in others, bureaux. The key question in relation to the public organisations is: How can public organisation be managed in an efficient manner, given the requirement of rule of law?

In the public finance perspectives there occur borderline cases whose classification is difficult to resolve with the public–private separation. One may ask where public enterprises with an autonomous position should be placed, or how third-sector bodies which receive public funding are to be classified. The important point here is not to resolve any such item of definition but to insist that the public finance perspective – the relevance of privatisation – is entirely different from the organisational view – the relevance of market mechanisms to public organisation. It is easy to confuse these two perspectives, but in reality they are quite separate. Public sector reform may target the downsizing of government, meaning privatisation, hiving off etc. Or it may restructure the public organisations to make them more like private organisations for instance. Table 2.1 shows this distinction between privatisation reform and public management reform.

Table 2.1 Public sector reform: privatisation and outsourcing

	Political economy	
	Public organisation	*Private organisation*
Traditional public administration	I	II
New public administration	III	IV

In the UK, Thatcher attempted combination IV, but achieved in some areas only III. In the Scandinavian countries it is combination III which has been relevant. In a few countries it is still combination I which prevails, such as France and Germany. Public sector reform may comprise both favour privatisation *and* New Public Management.

Whichever form of organisation is chosen, the public sector in a well-ordered society may be interpreted as consisting of a huge set of principal–agent relationships. The key players are government, the bureaucracy and the public enterprises. Government is the key public principal, setting itself a number of goals to be accomplished in collective action and having an objective function comprising all kinds of goods and services to be provided by the organisations that government sets up purposefully. To do this, government needs to contract with agents, or lots of agents. This sets up principal–agent games in the public sector, the resolution of which will depend upon strategy.

The public principal

Employing the new principal–agent framework for the analysis of key issues in public administration and public management seems worthwhile not merely because this approach has scored a number of successes in economics. It could also highlight aspects that were neglected in traditional political science, such as information and incentives. Of course, strategy in public administration and policy implementation was recognised by several scholars, especially Wildavsky (Wildavsky and Caiden, 2003), but the new tools of game theory have never been put to systematic use in the organisational analysis of the public sector.

I will argue here for the relevance of the principal–agent framework for understanding key problems in the public sector. Although the principal–agent framework has been developed chiefly for the private sector (insurance, agriculture, employment contract) and is now based on a highly refined theory about incentives, the analysis of the public sector with the help of the principal–agent approach is not a mere repetition of a series of private sector models. One must start afresh and ask fundamental questions like:

- *Who is a public principal?* Looking at government as a principal calls for a clarification of the objectives that government pursues. A principal has certain interests that he/she wishes to pursue. We must examine which are the objectives of a public principal.
- *Who are the agents of government?* To get the job done, government may rely upon different kinds of agents working for the principal in contracts under various institutional arrangements. It remains to enquire into this variety of institutions and their contractual consequences.

A principal is a person who instructs an agent to act on his/her behalf in exchange for remuneration. Government becomes a principal when it hires people to do the job for it. However, government is not just another principal. There are many private sector principal–agent relationships, from two-person interactions to the organisational complexity involved in the modern firm, where a CEO directs thousands of employees. Government is a public principal, i.e. the principal for the public sector. The difference between a private and public principal concerns the incentives of the players. A public principal in a well-ordered society targets social objectives which he/she accomplishes in relation to a group or community of people. In a well-ordered society there are at least three main types of goods and services that government would want to allocate: (1) security or law and order; (2) infrastructure; (3) welfare services: education, health care and social care.

These three categories of objectives are broad enough to cover thousands of public programmes, from pure public goods to social insurance, as well as income redistribution. The ambition of the government can be small or large within all these areas. A rich literature has speculated over why government in a well-ordered society always settles upon these objectives. This literature has also attempted to derive some principles that determine how much government should try to accomplish in these three areas, suggesting the criteria of efficiency and justice in public policy (Musgrave, 2000; Buchanan and Musgrave, 1999). Whatever the conclusions from this literature on the proper size of government may be, it remains true that government will need agents to execute its policies and attempt to accomplish its objectives.

It is perhaps impossible to arrive at one criterion on the optimal public sector. Several policy criteria make a programme belong in the public sector. There is nothing in principle which stops a government from going beyond these criteria. And several governments in Third World countries fail to provide programmes that score high on all of these criteria. These contingencies do not reduce the validity of the basic insight that government as a public principal has incentives linked to the promotion of social objectives. Thus, social objectives – affluence, human development, education, health and social care, as well as income protection – loom large for the public principal, who may be also driven by private incentives like money, prestige and power. Here, we face the first major riddle in public administration and public management: How are social and private incentives mixed with the principal in the public sector?

Incentives in the private sector tend to be self-centred, as both the principal and the agent maximise their economic benefits from the interaction. The private principals and their agents have common economic interests in creating an output that is highly valued in the market, but at the same time they have opposing interests in the distribution of the profits from selling the output. The conflict between distribution and allocation may lead the agent to shirk, i.e. not try hard to produce the highly valued output, thus causing an allocative inefficiency, or to loot, i.e. pocket all of the profits.

As emphasised by the Public Choice School, incentives in the public sector are not entirely different from incentives in the private sector. Selfish motives play a major role with politicians, bureaucrats and professionals. However, the public principal does not sell his/her output in the market, looking for a profit. He/she provides an output that accomplishes a social objective, i.e. is valuable to the population of the country. Thus, social objectives play a major role in the incentives of the players in principal–agent interaction in the public sector. The output in the public sector is either provided gratis or it is sold at a subsidised price. The incentives of the public principal are directly and indirectly linked with the quality and the quantity of the output, although no profit maximisation takes place.

The incentives of the public principal include intangibles such as the well-being of the nation, economic growth, community development, peace and prosperity. They are valued directly by the population as well as indirectly for their contribution to the selfish goals of the principal, such as election or re-election prospects, reputation and power. The preferences of the public principal comprise priorities among different outputs related to social objectives besides his/her selfish motives. Politics is to a large extent the decision-making process leading up to a commitment of government to the realisation of these social priorities (Etzioni, 1990, 1994).

Social priorities as incentives

The public principal may be driven by mainly selfish motives such as economic gain, personal power and individual prestige. Probably these incentives occur with all players in the public sector, although their importance becomes overwhelming only with a few of these actors. What matters much in the public sector is the choice between alternative social objectives. Various players have different priorities attached to these alternative social objectives. Voting, for instance is a method for choosing between social priorities.

What the public principal offers is an output that is collective, at least to some degree. These collective goods and services may be provided in relation to different social objectives concerning quantity and quality. The public principal faces a choice of how much of the government resources should be allocated to social objectives and how much should go to the selfish interests of the political and administrative elite. Thus, the public principal faces the budget restriction shown in Figure 2.1.

It is when this trade-off between promoting social objectives and protecting selfish interests degenerates into personal aggrandisement that the public principal is turned into a mere private utility maximiser – moving for instance from EF to GH in Figure 2.1.

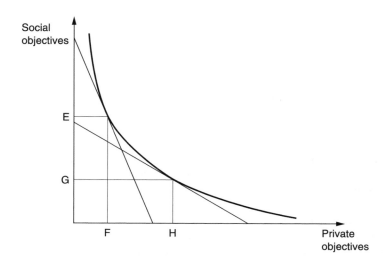

Figure 2.1 Spending on social and private objectives.

We may distinguish between motives – selfishness or altruism – and the provision of goods and services by government – private or collective ones. Thus, we arrive at a 2 × 2 table (Table 2.2), which identifies four theoretical possibilities: government may decide to provide collective or private goods and services for either altruistic or selfish reasons.

When government has set its social objectives, it then needs agents to do the job. Principal–agent relationships arise for transaction cost reasons relating to the need for delegation, decentralisation, division of labour, economies of scale, etc. Government has no or little implementation capacity by itself. Thus, it must contract with agents to get the job done.

Legal–rational authority attempts to institutionalise the interaction between the public principal and his/her agents. As Weber emphasised, the modern state differs from traditional authority, by the leaders not using personal ties with the agents (family or vassals), and differs from charismatic

Table 2.2 The public sector: motives and output

Motivation	Goods or services	
	Private	*Collective*
Altruism	I	II
Selfishness	III	IV

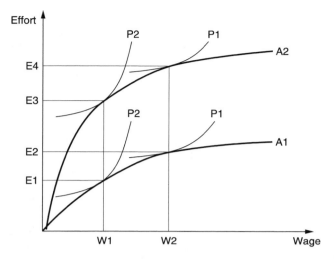

Figure 2.2 Principal–agent contracting (the full picture with convex preferences for principal and concave preferences for agent).

authority by not relying upon religious connections (disciples). The institutionalisation of the interaction with agents can be done in more ways than the Weberian ideal type of formal bureaucracy. Besides, Weber never fully explained why only the bureau would be regarded as the most rational means for the public principal to contract with agents. The achievement of the social objectives requires expertise, but agents will only deliver that if properly rewarded. Thus, we arrive at the typical remuneration–effort problem that lies at the core of all principal–agent interaction. Figure 2.2 depicts the basic utility curves of one principal and two agents *A1* and *A2* for the exchange of remuneration *W* and effort *E*.

If principals and agents had complete information about the curves in Figure 2.2, then contracting would be a rather simple and straightforward task. If the principal prevails in relation to two competing agents, one with low effort (*A1*) and another with high effort (*A2*), then he/she offers two contracts: (*W1, E1*) for *A1* and (*W1, E3*) for *A2*. But if only one agent presents him/herself for a contract in relation to many principals, then the agent will get (*W2, E2*), which is a clear improvement over (*W1, E3*). However, these points in Figure 2.2 will not be the equilibria once one takes into account the possibility of moral hazard and adverse selection in a temporal account of contracting, involving a hiatus between *ex ante* and *ex post*. A high-effort agent may shirk on the contract (*W1, E3*), delivering only (*W1, E1*), or he/she may pretend that he/she is a low-effort agent, forcing the principal to offer the contract (*W2, E3*) or (*W2, E4*) to elicit a higher effort.

The *ex ante* contract (*W2, E4*) would be highly vulnerable to *ex post* contractual opportunism, though.

What makes public administration and public management difficult is the occurrence of asymmetric information, meaning that there is contracting with incomplete information. The principal–agent model suggests that incomplete contracting will be the outcome under asymmetric information. It takes two forms: hidden action and hidden knowledge. The principal–agent framework will only be relevant to the theory of public administration and public management if these two concepts – hidden action and hidden knowledge – pinpoint crucial difficulties in the governance of the public sector.

Delegating power (competences) and handing over resources to the agent, the public principal would like to instruct the agent how to behave in various contingencies, as well as select the agents who are most likely to be responsive to the wishes of the principal. Monitoring *ex post* how the agent fulfils the conditions for the delegation is the response to hidden actions. Screening candidates *ex ante* is the response to hidden knowledge. Contracting involves two stages, the *ex ante* stage and the *ex post* stage. At the *ex ante* stage, promises are exchanged, stipulating the conditions of the contract. At the *ex post* stage, the performance of the relevant actions may fulfil the contract, at least to some extent. A key aspect of contracting is the degree to which the fulfilment of the contract is observable by the participants and verifiable by a third party, such as a court.

In the economics of information literature there is an emphasis on the observability and verifiability of contracts in order to avoid the difficulty of reneging. However, what is observable and verifiable is the performance of the actions as well as the situation. What is not directly observable or easily verifiable is the effort of the agent. Thus, there arises the problem of contracting under incomplete information, as contracts between the principal and the agent typically involve a promise that the agent will try to do his/her best for the principal. But it may turn out to be no more than that: a promise.

It is often emphasised that all contracts are in reality incomplete as it is impossible to foresee all possible contingencies and stipulate all relevant conditions (Milgrom and Roberts, 1992). The principal–agent approach focuses on one cause of contractual incompleteness, namely the ambiguity surrounding the effort of the agent. *Ex ante* this ambiguity takes the form of adverse selection, meaning that only the agent knows his/her type, i.e. whether he/she will put up great effort or not, or whether he/she is efficient or not. *Ex post* the ambiguity takes the form of moral hazard, meaning that the agent disguises or hides the real level of effort or efficiency.

When the public principal contracts with agents to get the job done in the public sector, then *contractual opacity* is general. A theory of public agency must account for how the principal responds to contractual ambiguity, especially in relation to the effort of the agent.

The fundamental agency problem in the public sector

The accomplishment of social objectives is only possible through the work of people working for government. Somehow these people – the agents – will be contracted by government, implicitly or explicitly, and given remuneration for their work. In the modern state the remuneration tends to be either a salary or a fee and the output of the agent may be measured in terms of some physical indicator of performance. What is not observable is the effort of the agent, although the situation may be verifiable.

The parameters of principal–agent interaction in the public sector thus involve the utility function of the principal linked with the output of the agent minus the wage of the agent as well as the utility function of the agent linked with the remuneration minus the cost of his/her effort. Thus, the principal wants to maximise the value of the output minus the costs involved in paying the agent for his/her work, whereas the agent wishes to maximise his/her salary minus the cost of effort. What are the outcomes of this interaction? One may model the relationship between government and a bureau or public enterprise as principal–agent games. One may also model the relationship between the manager and his/her employees within a bureau or public enterprise as such a principal–agent game. We will distinguish between these two games – government–bureau (enterprise) and manager–employee – in the subsequent chapters.

Solving for principal–agent interaction one may assume either complete knowledge or incomplete knowledge. Typical of the principal–agent interaction in the public sector is that the value of the work of the agent is not measurable in money or at market value. However, the principal must pay the agent and thus he/she incurs costs. Can the principal write and enforce a contract that elicits high effort? The agent will not work for free, only participating if his/her utility is at least at some minimum level (reservation price), and he/she will not produce high effort unless rewarded for that (incentive compatibility). Given perfect information about the contract and its enforcement, there is a set of first-best contracts that would secure an efficient solution. The outcome would basically depend upon the availability of agents, meaning that the more abundant the agents are, the higher the gain of the principal in the sense of low salary costs.

However, due to the ambiguity of public sector contracting the agent could choose a contract with high reward, but supply low effort. There may occur suboptimisation due to the behaviour of the agent, who in a sense reneges on the contract. One may also conceive of the possibility that the principal reneges. The basic problem is the occurrence of contractual incompleteness. Thus, we have a game where the principal has a dominating strategy – low pay – and the agent has similarly a dominating strategy – low effort. The logic of incentives in public sector agency according to this representation is thus that an optimal contract is not feasible when there is contractual incompleteness due to unforeseen events or a lack of enforceability of contracts. Ambiguity or incompleteness results in incomplete knowledge, of which asymmetric knowledge is one kind. Two types of asymmetric knowledge have been much discussed in the principal–agent literature, namely adverse selection and moral hazard.

One may conceive of a number of possible contracts between the public principal and his/her agent, responding to the occurrence of asymmetric knowledge. However, the incentive of the public principal would be to arrive at an efficient provision of public services, meaning that he/she must be able to separate a high-effort agent from a low-effort agent, as well as be able to identify and punish low effort in a replay involving either a new contract or some form of retaliation. The incentive of the agent could, on the other hand, be to camouflage low effort as much as possible (hidden action), or to pretend that he/she is a low-effort agent (hidden knowledge). The outcome of the principal–agent game will depend on *strategy*.

Public sector agency: hidden action

When government moves to execute its policies, it relies upon agents to implement its programmes. Instructing, funding and monitoring the agents constitute the core task of public sector governance. The principal–agent framework classifies the governance problems under hidden action and hidden knowledge. Let us spell out what this means more concretely. Several of the major themes in public sector governance refer to either hidden action or hidden knowledge, or both. The traditional mode of public governance is the massive employment of instructions by government to their agents. But how can government be sure that its instructions are followed?

Agents may use a panoply of strategies and tactics in hidden action, increasing asymmetric information. The key parameters are agency effort, agency performance and the environment of the agency. How can the principal correctly assess these parameters when communication is also strategic?

The risk of arbitrariness

The abuse of power is one form of hidden action. It is a primary concern when setting up a public sector agency. If, in theory, government has sovereign power, then it must make sure that the delegation of this power to an agent satisfies the restrictions that are referred to as 'legality' or 'rule of law'. Public administration offers a framework for confining agency to law and its requirements in accordance with the idea of the modern state as legal–rational authority.

We will devote a separate chapter (Chapter 5) to the legal framework for achieving rule of law in public agencies. The key concepts in administrative and constitutional law – accountability, complaint, redress – refer to restrictions imposed by government upon its own agents, especially its bureaucracy.

The risk of appropriation

It is not only power that may be abused in the public sector. Money and government resources may also be employed for purposes not laid down in the instructions from the principal or the agent. There are many forms of agency appropriation of public resources, from embezzlement and corruption to petty daily misuse of the resources of the office.

Lack of information on outputs or outcomes

The agent typically concentrates his/her energy on stating inputs and rather shuns communicating performance, and is especially reluctant about measuring outcomes. Agents talk about the resources they need and detail these with great precision. They speak vaguely about various ambition levels. But they do not voluntarily come up with precise output or outcome data. The transition from input budgeting to performance budgeting has been imposed upon the agent by the principal. Despite much progress in performance analysis there is still no established technique for outcome analysis, as the value of the output remains elusive.

Misrepresentation of costs

The agent looks upon cost estimation as strategy. Thus, start-up costs will be underestimated, whereas follow-up costs will be overestimated. What is crucial is to get a programme started, even if its costs are underestimated. Once initiated, the principal is reluctant to give up his/her investment. The principal slowly becomes hostage to his/her own commitment, which works to the advantage of the agent.

Incremental behaviour

To shield him/herself, the agent may focus on the increment, i.e. the small yearly changes. The bulk of the budget would be beyond discussion, the so-called base. Thus, the agent would be protected from sudden and major changes. Incremental budget procedures are especially favourable to the agent when there is a public sector growth process. A series of incremental positive changes may mean that the agent doubles his/her budget quickly. A process of negative increments could, however, favour the principal if they lead to more efficiency.

Increasing discretion or autonomy

The agent underlines the importance of discretion or decentralisation for competency in handling matters effectively. However, it also increases asymmetric information. The agent tends to prefer a legal position that protects it against incursions from the principal, being a statutory body under parliament rather than merely a department within the ministry of a principal.

Blaming unforeseen events or factors

Although actions and the situation are observable and verifiable, unlike effort, the agent will use his/her information advantage when interpreting what he/she has done as well as what the situation calls for or admits. Since performance is the result of both effort and the situation, any perceived reduction in the first component can always be blamed on unforeseeable forces in the situation that the agent faces.

Collusion

The principal often resorts to one agent to check another agent. Thus, the principal may instruct a special agent to monitor the other agents. Such a bureau of auditing or performance measuring may constitute a powerful tool in order to reduce information asymmetries. However, the use of one agent to check another may have the adverse effect of increasing the search for discretion and autonomy. Worse still, such a move may be countered by collusion among agents.

Public sector agency: hidden knowledge

The public principal became aware early in civilised history of the need to screen potential agents before delegating power and resources to them. Ideally, the principal would like to select the agents with that special Weberian quality: *vocation*. Thus, the Chinese bureaucracy were already employing formal tests during the Han period. Professional criteria were laid down for service in the various offices of the Roman Empire. The modern state could not recruit competent agents without the use of a variety of signals about agent capability. In modern legal–rational authority we find the following screening devices.

Screening: special schools of public administration

In order to inculcate a special motivation with its agents, the principal could set up a formally designed training programme that becomes an entrance ticket to the bureaucracy. Such schools or institutes may prepare students for service as public agents, training them in the special qualities of public service. However, the principal can never fully control these establishments. Often they develop into independent centres for education and research whose messages may deviate far from the rosy picture of the public sector that the principal may adhere to. These schools may (as in France) become the breeding ground for so-called *corps*.

Signalling: training in public law

The principal may screen out two kinds of agents that it can trust in policy execution and implementation. Either it may attempt to recruit agents with a social science background, combining perhaps political science with economics, sociology or psychology. Or the principal may resort to agents with a legal training, preferably in public law. Following the civil law tradition, the principal may underline the special qualities of a public law training, resulting in an ethos favourable to public service. However, a legal training is only appropriate for certain kinds of public service.

Proporz

In strongly politicised societies the principal may acknowledge that a neutral civil service is in theory impossible. The key groups may be allowed to recruit their proper share of the agents, securing some degree of loyalty to the principal. This manner of screening the applicants for public agency is in stark contrast to the mode of selection of agents that focuses on the mastering of language and writing.

Clientelism

A loyal agent may be selected through special mechanisms that circumvent competence criteria. Agents may be chosen on personal criteria in the hope that they can be trusted and remain loyal no matter what. All kinds of personal relationships may be employed in clientelism. However, loyalty may be traded for competence. The American *spoils* mechanism is an interesting device for securing loyalty while also allowing for quick adaptation to a new principal. It is in stark contrast to the main West European practices where few agents leave when there is a change of principal.

Corporatism

An attempt may be made to combine loyalty and competence, as with corporatism. Thus, representatives of interest groups may be chosen as agents when they have the relevant knowledge for implementing a policy. They would also guarantee that the programme has moral backing because it would be linked with the key interests at stake for the agents.

The two main solutions to the agency problems

Thus, the theory of public governance suggests a number of mechanisms that the public principal may employ to handle the problems of hidden action and hidden knowledge. These mechanisms will have to be designed

while taking the key strategies of the agent into account. Different mechanisms may be devised while recognising the rationality requirements of the
agent. Here, we outline the two ideal typical solutions:

1   *The immortal bureau:* long-term contracting.
2   *Tendering/bidding:* short-term contracting.

The classical theory of bureaucracy suggests mechanism (1), whereas NPM
exhibits a preference for a mechanism that adheres to (2). The soft sector
of the public sector used to be structured according to mechanisms of
type (1), whereas the public enterprises or the trading departments mixed
both types of mechanisms.

When faced with such a bewildering organisational heterogeneity in the
public sector, it is not enough merely to describe the key models employed in
various areas. One must seek to understand the basic rationale of a mode of
public organisation, as well as map the performance of each mode, meaning
its outcomes. Government may use alternative modes of public organisation
and one would like to explain why one mode is chosen in one area, whereas
another mode is employed in another. In the literature on private organisation the basic theory argues that transaction costs determine the mode
of organisation, minimising transactions as driving the choice of alternative
institutional arrangements. Thus, for example, the Williamson framework
focuses on the two basic modes of the market and the hierarchy. In public
organisation there are, however, other considerations besides transaction
costs, mainly accountability under the rule-of-law framework.

It is not the size of government which is the key question today, but how to
handle the management of public organisations. It seems as if the size of the
public sector is fairly locked in at between 30 per cent and 50 per cent of GDP,
depending on whether a well-ordered society adheres to the welfare society
model (Japan, US, Australia, New Zealand) or the welfare state model
(Continental Europe, the Nordic countries). A few countries, like Singapore
and the Hong Kong Special Administrative Region, are below the 30 per
cent barrier, but it is a matter of special legacies. Although privatisation
has been an important element in public sector reform, this strategy has
hardly diminished the public sector in a dramatic way. What has changed
dramatically though is the governance of public organisations, labelled New
Public Management (NPM).

Organisational heterogeneity is on the rise in the public sector, as various
modes of organisation are emerging or become mixed: 'plural government'.
Thus, there is no longer one technique or institutional set-up for running a
public organisation, as was the case when the Wilsonian or Weberian ideal
type of a bureaucracy was the dominant mode. There is no longer one
logic of public organisation, but several logics, ranging from pure Weberian
bureaucracy to reliance upon outsourcing and also private–public networks.
As the public sector has become increasingly complex with all the new

forms of service delivery and reregulation, the only way to encompass all this organisational heterogeneity and institutional complexity is to use the principal–agent framework – this is at least the position in this book. I shall make the P–A approach somewhat more concrete by discussing the central problems of budgeting using this framework.

Budgeting: the principal–agent perspective

Budgeting may be looked on from the *ex ante* perspective or the *ex post* perspective. According to the *ex ante* perspective budgeting is bargaining between the policy-making ministry *M* and the policy execution agency *A*. From the *ex post* perspective budgeting is information gathering. Traditional budgetary theory underlined control, whereas the policy network theory emphasised trust (Wildavsky, 1986a,b; White and Wildavsky, 1992; Wildavsky and Swedlow, 2000). Under NPM, budgeting becomes basically public procurement, although it involves interaction over a long time. A principal–agent interpretation of the contract between *M* and *A* captures the strategic aspects of the interaction between the two parties. Budgeting *ex ante* is basically contracting, whereas budgeting *ex post* amounts to accounting. It is the hiatus between *ex ante* and *ex post* which creates the uncertainty or risk in budgeting, the solution of which always comprises a vector of agency effort (e), agency remuneration (w) by a ministry, and agency output (O). Budgeting *ex ante* should be separated from financial management and accounting. It is interaction, i.e. a game. It is also different from entitlements, which are determined by existing regulations (Hyde, 1992).

A number of budgetary systems have been constructed in order to give policy-makers the capacity to steer the organisations that are responsible for policy implementation. The most recent attempt is *accrual budgeting*, but one may mention a long series of efforts such as programme budgeting, zero-based budgeting and three-year budgeting, as well as sunset budgeting. However, the outcomes have seldom or perhaps never matched the ambitions behind budgetary reforms (Schick and Lostracco, 2000). Why is this so? Given the difficulties in introducing and implementing a rational system of budgeting, one may ask whether budgeting is a tool for steering an organisation *ex ante* or whether it is a tool for registering the transactions *ex post*. One theory of budgeting that used to be the dominant one – incrementalism – focused on the *ex ante* side of the budgetary system, limiting government capacity to govern to the yearly increments – plus or minus. Have the advances in game theory made incrementalism or marginalism obsolete? Has NPM made organisational steering *ex ante* easier?

Budgeting from the *ex post* side results in accounting records. They are of course vital for a government which practices the rule of law. However, accounting merely for the sake of keeping track of things – organisational memory – has not been considered sufficient. If an organisation keeps a record of its costs, then what? An accounting system could, when including information about outputs and outcomes, be employed for organisational steering towards efficiency, but this requires monitoring and replay.

I wish to discuss the interaction between a ministry M and its implementing agency A in order to pinpoint the role of budgeting (Schick, 2003). The nature of the interaction, I suggest, is most conveniently subsumed under a principal–agent model. I will employ a few simple diagrams to show how the hiatus between *ex ante* and *ex post* in budgeting invites strategies that make optimal outcomes hardly probable.

Budgeting and risk

Budgeting is the process through which a ministry M arrives at a contract with an agency A about the delivery of a public service at output O with remuneration W, covering the cost or price of the agency putting in effort e. The uncertainty in budgeting derives from the risk involved in the *quid pro quo* between the three fundamental elements: O, e, W. There is a fundamental contractual opacity in all budgeting as the *ex ante* contract may deviate considerably from the *ex post* contract. *Ex ante* budgeting results in an agreement, the expectations contract, between M and A, which must be tested against the fulfilment of the terms of the agreement during the year to come, which results in an *ex post* real contract. The real contract may deviate considerably from the expected contract – this is the source of risk in budgeting.

Contractual opacity in budgeting concerns the *quid pro quo* between agency output O and remuneration W, where the crucial link is agency effort. The ministry M may receive an output that is different from the expected one or it may realise that the remuneration is too high given the output delivered. The strategic component in budgeting is effort e, which is only partly observable and verifiable *ex post*. How to handle the uncertainty in budgeting is the key problem in budgeting, driving budgetary reforms since the 1960s. Either the ministry assumes all the risk (traditional budgeting) or it may attempt to hand over some of the risk to the agency (NPM). To handle the risk deriving from the *hiatus* between *ex ante* and *ex post* in budgeting, M may engage in massive information gathering about A using all kinds of budgetary formulas – the monitoring option. However, it comes with transaction costs that must be covered from the value of the output. The efficiency of monitoring is again uncertain, meaning that it may not decrease the risk in budgeting significantly.

The parameters of budgeting could in one example be identified in Table 2.3. The expected value for low effort is 90, whereas the expected value for high effort is 420. Can M and A arrive at an *ex post* contract that achieves the best outcome? Well, it depends upon the choice of the *ex ante* contract and the fulfilment of this contract. M would be interested in the high-effort output, but only if the remuneration to A does not go too high.

Table 2.3 Effort and output

Agency effort	Probability of output	
	Output = 100	Output = 500
Low	0.8	0.2
High	0.2	0.8

There are two mechanisms available for channelling this interaction, which may be described within the principal–agent framework in the following way:

- *Cost budgeting:* The principal assumes all risk: *M* offers a contract where it pays for the cost of *A*, whatever *A* delivers. *M* tries to steer or monitor *A* towards the best result for *M*.
- *Price budgeting:* The principal and the agent share the risk: *M* offers *A* a contract where *A* may make a profit as *M* pays *A* a price for the delivery of an output *O*.

Traditional budgeting is 100 per cent cost budgeting, as *A* must return any cost savings it may run up. On the other hand, public procurement is 100 per cent price budgeting, as *A* gets to keep the difference between price and cost. In between these two extremes one finds a whole spectrum of possible combinations. Neither cost budgeting nor price budgeting solves the problem with the hiatus between the *ex ante* and *ex post* perspectives on budgeting. I shall point out some of the difficulties in the major forms of budgeting since the quest for budgetary reform was initiated in the 1960s (Forsythe, 2004; Rubin, 1996; Lee *et al.*, 2003).

Budgeting and bureaucracy

Budgeting is the process leading up to the funding of an agency, e.g. a bureaucracy. It is basically a two-person game, one party appropriating resources to another party that is responsible for service delivery and requesting money to cover costs. The budgetary dialogue is the interaction between the appropriating authority and the requesting agency. What makes it interesting from a game theory perspective is that it involves discretion or considerable degrees of freedom on the part of both players. Thus, an appropriation may be increased or decreased considerably and an agency may deliver well or badly.

Budgeting is decision-making under interdependency. It is different from paying for entitlements in social security where the existing regulations present no or little discretion. One may discuss whether the national budget today is more budgeting or more entitlements after the sharp rise in social security costs during the last 20 years in most advanced countries. Moreover, budgeting is the requests–appropriations interaction between a ministry M and an agency A, through which one arrives at a decision about the quantity and quality of the service to be provided by A against a certain remuneration by M covering the costs of A.

Budgeting is not only different from entitlements, but it also constitutes a different process from tendering/bidding, which is the hallmark of NPM. Budgeting by M in relation to A presupposes a long-term interaction with yearly rounds of play where M and A develop expectations and take each other's response into account. Budgeting is funding, and not buying. Even when A engages in procurement, buying from subcontractors instead of producing in-house, M still needs to appropriate resources to A. Thus, there arise the two core problems in budgeting:

- How large should the costs of A be?
- What service quantity and quality should A provide?

Budgeting tends to be institutionally defined to a high extent. Thus, the yearly budgetary process will start at a specific moment in time and end at another specific date several months later. It involves many players, but they may be arranged as either appropriators or as requesters, reducing the complex interaction to a two-person game. Moreover, budget-making is not a one-shot game but a continuous process of *ex ante* decision-making and *ex post* evaluation. Thus, there is replay and repetitive interaction with several rounds of play over a period of several years. What, then, is the basic logic of budgeting? My argument is that the special features of the budgetary game derive from the uncertainty of contracting, as there is always the risk that the contract *ex ante* differs widely from the contract *ex post*.

Budgeting and financial management

An agency A may command vast fixed resources such as buildings, land and premises. Or it may use lots of capital in its service provision. The management of these resources – financial management and accounting – is no doubt of great concern not only to the agency itself but also to its principal, the ministry M or parliament. However, budgeting is not financial management. The internal procedures of A with regard to the use of its resources may be the target of more or less advanced systems of management, based on more or less advanced information systems. Financial management starts where budgeting ends, i.e. when the appropriation has been done, then the agency starts acting within its financial system. Budgeting is a special two-party interaction where a ministry covers the cost of an agency as a *quid pro quo* for the delivery of a service by the agency. And budgetary theories suggest alternative explanations of the nature of this *quid pro quo* in models of budget-making. Financial management is the internal handling of resources within *A*.

The traditional model: budgeting as inputs

In traditional public administration, *M* is supposed to have full information about what *A* should do in various situations. *M* may thus instruct *A* though various channels: legislation, budgeting and regulations. The problem with traditional public administration is that its planning framework was a very rudimentary one, budgeting upon input categories such as expenses of various kinds. The theory of line item budgeting merely outlines the resources a team may employ for the achievement of objectives. But how about outputs and outcomes?

Budgeting as listing the input resources fails for both information and incentive reasons, as *M* cannot predict all relevant situations in which *A* will implement programmes and *M* lacks any instrument to get *A* to try hard. One may debate whether it is the information requirement or it is the incentives which constitute the major hurdle to budgeting as planning. Incrementalism suggests information, starting from its model of bounded rationality. However, the principal–agent frame would suggest incentives, as information may always be manipulated.

The crux of the matter is that within traditional public administration, budgeting can only be used for checking that the rules are obeyed. It cannot be widely employed for steering the organisation towards the accomplishment of objectives, because it is orientated towards the inputs and not the outputs or the outcomes of the organisation *A*.

Budgeting as planning

Input budgeting may be supplemented by a list of outputs that *M* wants *A* to deliver. *M* may try to plan the activities of *A* such that the objectives are accomplished. Again there is the double difficulty of information and incentives. Any centralised system of policy-making will fail because *M* does not possess sufficient information about the service delivery situation of *A*. Even if *M* has this knowledge, which is not likely, then *M* cannot be sure that *A* will deliver in accordance with the plan, which any realistic theory of incentives would entail.

Planning by *M* of the activities of *A* runs up against the omnipresence of asymmetric knowledge. In most cases *A* knows more about the activities and the conditions for service delivery than *M*. Planning is then doomed to fail. *M* must devise some mechanism that will make it interesting to *A* to use his/her knowledge and search for new relevant information. From the problem of information we arrive at the problem of incentives: How can *M* contract with *A* so that an optimal supply of public service is forthcoming?

Top-down implementation is unlikely to succeed if one pursues a principal–agent perspective on the interaction between *M* and *A* with its implications of shirking and pretending.

Budgeting as trust

It is true that in a decentralised approach to budgeting using a bottom-up perspective on policy implementation, the existence of asymmetric information is recognised. *A* knows more than *M* about the conditions for successful policy implementation. *M* puts up a sum of resources for *A* to be employed as *A* finds best. Yet, the two main budgetary problems have not been resolved:

- How much should *M* pay *A*?
- What are the terms of the *quid pro quo* between *M* and *A*?

I would claim that the policy network approach never came up with an answer to these two problems that are central in all forms of budgeting. *M* cannot simply hand over resources to *A* and expect that in all probability things will go right. Thus, budgeting as trust tends to develop into budgeting as evaluation, as *M* attempts to find out what *A* is really doing with the appropriated resources, which means searching for information about outputs and outcomes.

Budgeting as evaluation

The evaluation of public programmes may targets outputs or/and outcomes. It may be done by *A* itself or *M* may hire a special team for the evaluation of *A*, either a permanent one or an *ad hoc* team. Evaluation may be connected with accounting, as both deal with the *ex post* perspective on public organisations. When *M* employs a separate accounting team on a permanent basis, then *M* tends to demand that such a monitor deliver not only the traditional accounting information but also information about efficiency, either the productivity of *A* or the effectiveness of *A*.

Budgeting as evaluation may resolve many problems concerning asymmetric information but it does not address the incentive question of how to get *A* to try hard in policy achievement. Evaluation may give *M* lots of information about *A*, but how is *M* to employ this information when interacting with *A*? The only conclusion possible for the above is that budgeting from the *ex ante* perspective is contracting and expectations, not information *ex post*. Budgeting, however, is interaction, not information. The budgetary game between *M* and *A* has a strong temporal dimension. Budgetary interaction between *M* and *A* tends to go on over several stages of play, as if the game is almost without end. The classical incremental models developed by Wildavsky in accordance with Simon's and Lindblom's model of bounded rationality captured this time dimension in budgeting.

Incremental budgetary models

The incremental budget models predict the size of the increment, allowing for the stability of the base, and investigate whether the increments tend to be stable over time. Incremental decision-making may occur when there is a steady growth process in the public sector, such as occurred in the 1960s and 1970s. When there is no underlying growth or decline mechanism in place, for instance in the economy or in the population, then budgeting is hardly incremental. And marginalist calculations offer very unsatisfactory answers to the two core problems in budget-making discussed above. When budgeting turns non-incremental, then it is the base which is subject to change. If the appropriating authority believes that there is no *quid pro quo* in the present allocation, then the base may be altered in a fundamental way with the occurrence of so-called shift-points. Is, then, comprehensive budget-making feasible?

Rational budgeting

The list of budgetary reforms since the 1960s aiming at rational budgeting is impressive, although many budgetary experts would agree with Wildavsky that it is entirely an abortive idea. Rational budget-making attempts to eliminate risk from budgeting, but this is impossible. It is true that studies of budgeting reveal much that indicates organised foolishness. There are simply too many players involved and the interaction is too complex, given strategies for there to emerge anything like rational budgeting. Yet, this is all macro rationality. Things look different when we examine the budgetary process from the micro perspective. All the players may individually behave according to rational choice requirements, updating themselves in Bayes–Nash sequences of games.

Rational budgeting would lead to optimal outcomes, but how would a technique of budgeting be devised which is strategy proof? Budgeting is a game where there is lots of risk involved, information is not easily or freely available and strategic behaviour may pay off nicely. The impossibility of macro rationality in budgeting does not entail that the players in budgetary games do not search for rational strategies to enhance their interests – micro rationality.

Budgeting as interaction between rational players

Budget-making *ex ante* ends with an appropriation of the ministry to the requesting agency. It may be interpreted as a contract between a principal and an agent concerning three identities which are linked: remuneration W, effort e and the provision of a service at quantity and quality O. I will regard e as a general variable covering the ambition and competence of the agent. W represents the cost of production in this case. O is a function of the effort of the agent, such that a high level of effort tends to result in a high output and a low level of effort tends to give a low output. Once the appropriation is made, budgeting *ex post* replaces budgeting *ex ante*, as the focus is now on what actually takes place – accounting and evaluation before there is a possibility of replay. Budgeting is a game with at least two rounds of play, as the appropriating authority will look at the information *ex post* and take it into account in the next round of *ex ante* budgeting.

Between *ex ante* and *ex post* budgeting there is in the normal case a period of one year. This *hiatus* creates the risk in budgeting, as the contract *ex ante* may not be fulfilled *ex post* or it may be the case that the contract *ex ante* was far more generous than necessary *ex post*. The risk in budget-making arises from both asymmetric information and strategic behaviour. It cannot be eliminated in the models of macro rationality. However, the parties to a budget, the ministry M and the agency A, would, I am inclined to assume, search for the most recently available information and attempt to attain a *quid pro quo* between W, O and e that is as good as possible for them, taken separately. Such a rational micro foundation for budgetary behaviour is to be found in the principal–agent approach to gaming or interaction and it captures the principal difficulty in budgeting, namely risk.

Accrual budgeting

The implementation of so-called OBB systems of budgeting and accounting (output- (or outcome-) based budgeting) is currently in its infancy. OBB systems can provide assistance in the effort to improve public management practices, but, as a result of implementation weaknesses, OBB systems will not constitute the panacea. The Australia Public Sector (APS) has undergone interesting changes in financial management practices. Here there is a shift towards the presentation of public sector budgeting information on an accruals and output basis. As a matter of fact, the adoption of accrual accounting and budgeting techniques has been part and parcel of broad-based public sector reform, including the new managerialism, contracting and market-based activities (Parker and Guthrie, 1993; Alford and O'Neill, 1994; Olson *et al.*, 1998). Thus, there is a marked trend within the APS, whether at Commonwealth, State or Territory level, from traditional cash-based budget reporting towards accrual-based budgeting, facilitating greater focus on outputs and outcomes, to be found to varying degrees in the Australian Capital Territory (ACT), Victoria, Western Australia, South Australia, the Commonwealth and, to a limited degree, Queensland. In fact, New Zealand provided the setting for very early adoption of accrual, output and outcome techniques to the public budgeting problem (Guthrie and Carlin, 1998).

Budgeting is the process by which government funds are distributed amongst competing interests. In a budgetary system the major actors in the process set criteria and discourse as a means to resolve the allocation of funds. The budget process and the annual budget itself are immersed in these political processes. The politics of the budgetary process is central to understanding budgeting. In order to understand the recent transformations taking place generally in central budgeting, one needs to look at the following (Lynch and Lynch, 1997: 22–23):

- Budget formats and procedures influence policy outcomes.
- A major feature of future budgeting is the use of performance measures or outputs and outcomes.
- The use of accrual formulas to replace more traditional public sector accounting.

Accrual budgeting is another means of shifting the emphasis of the budgetary process away from cash inputs, towards outputs and outcomes, in the hope that this will result in greater management efficiencies, and hence, better outcomes for governments and the communities they service. The achievements to be obtained from adapting OBB have been explored in Queensland. Accrual output-based budgeting is a process through which agencies are funded and monitored on the basis of delivery (performance) of outputs which have been counted moneywise on a full cost basis. The following are some of the claimed benefits:

- customer focused;
- based on supply or services/products;
- separates purchaser and owner;
- reflects full accrual costs;
- gives clear choices to the buyer;
- provides a sound basis for internal resource allocation;
- focuses on outputs and outcomes.

The traditional cash-based budgets focused on inputs and processes (Guthrie, 1998). A key feature of accrual reforms in central budgeting is the movement towards a 'resource', 'accrual' or 'funding' system of budgeting. It is hoped this will provide details about the assets held by the agency, the liabilities incurred by it and clear information on the full cost incurred by the government in funding the agency's activities.

Common difficulties in the OBB systems as implemented in Australia and New Zealand surface as a lack of rigour in the definition and measurement of outputs, a lack of clarity and measurability in the choice of outcomes, as well as a lack of reflexive feedback performance measurement systems to provide feedback on the impact of purchased outputs on policy-driven outcomes. A striking feature of many OBB systems was how similar in form the resulting budget paper documentation was to documentation prepared along traditional input lines. One may question the extent to which internal management processes had fundamentally changed as a result of the adoption of accrual systems in the guise of OBB. A difference between budget documentation that suggests that a certain dollar figure has been spent on a particular service, versus a set of budget papers that suggest that a certain quantity of a certain service has or will be purchased at a given cost, is difficult to identify. Significant contributions to improved public management can be made as a result of the adoption of OBB systems, but only if certain preconditions are met. These include:

*   *Appropriately specified and defined outputs:* These should relate directly to the activities of the agency, and conform to the definition of outputs provided above.
*   *Appropriately specified and measurable outcomes:* While the value of a reflexive input–output–outcome budgetary management model rests on its ability to provide accountability for the degree to which public resources are achieving public goals, the linkage is severed if stated outcomes are immeasurable.
*   *Appropriate performance indicators and performance measures:* These provide the link between outputs and outcomes, and if not present, or are inadequate or transient, are a detriment to the delivery of accountability and transparency.

Not even accrual budgeting, however, can transcend the hiatus between the *ex ante* and *ex post* perspectives on budgeting.

Budgeting according to a principal–agent model

Employing the principal–agent approach, the policy-making ministry M is the principal and the policy implementing agency A the agent. The interaction tends to consist of several rounds of play, from the making of a request by the agency at time $T1$ to the making of a new request at time $T2$, as well as a new appropriation after an earlier appropriation has been made in between $T1$ and $T2$. Thus, the game involves the possibility of punishment and retaliation, as well as rewards. The essential elements of the budgetary interaction include the following: the budgetary appropriation by M, the effort of the agent e, his/her remuneration W and the provision of a service O. I will assume for the sake of simplicity that the budget is made up of only the salary W and that output O depends only upon effort e according to the probabilities above.

The budget game I: bureaucracy (one principal and one agent)

*   *Principal's objective:* $\text{Max}(q - w)$.
*   *Agent's objective:* $\text{Max}(w - e)$, where effort is not costless.
*   *Rules:* Two rounds of play between request and appropriation.

I will employ a simple diagram to portray the interaction between M and A in the budget game. Figure 2.3 contains two ideal solutions to the

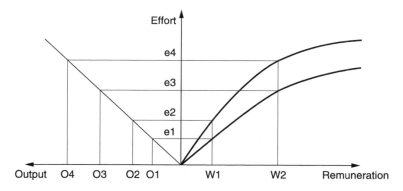

Figure 2.3 Principal–agent interaction I.

interaction between the principal and the agent in the first round of play: (1) low effort – small output (*W1, e2*); (2) high effort – large output (*W2, e4*) with a corresponding difference in remuneration *W*. Given complete information and no strategic behaviour, the players would opt for the second contract, as it would be Pareto superior to the first contract, involving both higher output and larger remuneration. However, will such an ideal contract be put in place by the players?

The solution with a high-effort agent (*W2, e4, O4*) is not strategy proof against the typical forms of strategic behaviour in the budgetary process. The same is true of the solution with a low-effort agent (*W1, e2,O2*). Given asymmetric knowledge and a hiatus between the *ex ante* and *ex post* situation, there may by no gains at all for the principal: (*W2,e3, O3*) and (*W1, e1,O1*), respectively.

One may identify one type of strategic behaviour within a principal–agent framework: moral hazard (see Figure 2.4). The agent signs up for one contract but delivers according to the other. The agent *A* promises *ex ante* to deliver *e3* against a remuneration of *W2*, but *ex post* it is *e2* that is actually delivered. Now, the entire gain for the principal is lost as *W2 = O2*. The principal can now only do only thing: retaliate, offering a new appropriation at *W1*, which would restore part of the gain to the principal.

Conclusion 1: Bureaucracy has an in-built tendency towards an inferior result under a normal or traditional budgetary process.

Budget game II: New Public Management (one principal and two agents)

- *Principal's objective:* Max$(q - w)$.
- *Agents' objective:* Max$(w - e)$, where effort is not costless.
- *Rules:* Two rounds of play between request and appropriation.

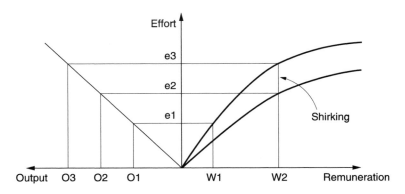

Figure 2.4 Principal–agent interaction II.

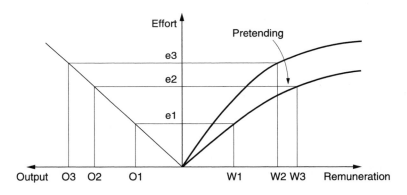

Figure 2.5 Principal–agent interaction III.

Budgeting under an NPM regime becomes a version of public procurement where the contract is neither indefinite, as with bureaucracy, nor a spot-on contract, as with normal public procurement. There will be a tournament or an auction to score a winner for the contract, but the contract will have a longer duration, normally between 1 and 5 years. Now, one may ask whether the principal can separate between two agents, one high performing (high effort) and another low performing (low effort) (see Figure 2.5). One risk for the principal is that he/she pays too high a remuneration to the low-effort agent – adverse selection.

Ex ante the principal would want to sign up with an agent who contracts at *W2, e3* with the prospect of a substantial gain at *O3*. However, the principal cannot be sure whether the agent is a 'Cadillac' or a 'lemon'. To get the

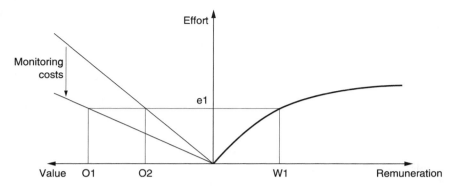

Figure 2.6 Transaction costs.

higher effort the principal could be forced to pay *W3*, which, however, does not give any gain. It would be better to sign up for *W1*, *e1 ex ante* and receive *O1 ex post.*

Conclusion 2: NPM has a tendency to provide agents with economic rents, resulting in the looting of the principal's gain.

Decreasing contractual opacity

Budgetary reform could be interpreted as being driven by the chief aim of minimising the risk of a huge hiatus between the *ex ante* and the *ex post* perspective. The principal may do so by increasing the information about what the agent is really doing or by finding out about the nature of the agent. However, information and monitoring is costly with, for instance transaction costs (see Figure 2.6). In a multistage budgetary game the principal may achieve an *ex ante* contract at *W1*, *e1* with the possibility of an output at *O1*. However, when the costs of evaluation and monitoring have been added, most of the gain has once more been dissipated.

Budgetary reforms keep coming and going. Why, then, is it is difficult to achieve optimal outcomes through budgeting in the public sector? One interpretation of the budgetary process that could explain its elusiveness is through targeting the hiatus in time between the expected budget (*ex ante*) and the achieved budget (*ex post*). The larger the time lag between *ex ante* and *ex post* the more opacity in budgeting as contracting, which makes optimal outcomes difficult to accomplish, given the omnipresence of strategy.

Conclusion

Public administration and public management both deal with contracting in the public sector. The public sector in any society may provide for the achievement of several vital social objectives. Government as the principal cannot get the job done unless it contracts somehow with agents. The key problems in public administration (legality) and public management (efficiency) refer to contractual difficulties between the principal and the agent, resulting from incentives, asymmetric information and incomplete contracts. The main problem in budgeting can be stated in terms of the PAF.

Should one examine power or look at efficiency when analysing the various modes of public organisation? This question appears very relevant when it comes to analysing public sector reforms. Similarly one may ask: Does public sector reform aim at changing policy outcomes or the public organisations? To an institutionalist, public sector reform is first and foremost about power when it is the structure of organisation that is at stake. However, to a rational choice scholar, public sector reform targets or should target policy efficiency and aim at improving performance. I will discuss the basic economic rationale of the state and the public sector in the next two chapters.

3   The economic reasons
for government

Introduction

An economic theory of government would explain why people support and pay for a political authority, starting from their self-centred reasons or pecuniary interests (Ménard, 1997). This way of framing the question of the origin of government sounds much like the old contract school, i.e. the systematic thinking about the government contract that dominated Western political philosophy from Grotius to Rousseau (Skyrms, 1996). But it also links up with the most recent developments in game theory, especially evolutionary game theory (Vega-Redondo, 1996). What, then, would lead rational players to set up and pay for a government in the short as well as the long run?

The basic insight in so-called 'Austrian economics' is that human interaction knows two major systems of institutions, the market and the state. On the one hand, the rules of the market define exchange or symmetrical interaction, i.e. how human beings can trade, buy and sell with one another as well as acquire or hand over assets. Government, on the other hand, involves the exercise of authority, which is an asymmetrical form of interaction where leaders give orders and people obey these orders. The Austrians – von Mises and Hayek – argued that markets are superior to government, because they handle information better. Why, then, is there government at all, and why does the public sector tend to be so large in well-ordered societies?

Von Mises and Hayek posed the questions: State or market? Capitalism or socialism? However, this way of approaching the question of how the market and the state interact in the economy is of little help. All national economies include *both* government and markets. Emphasising the 'either/or' does not enhance the understanding of how the state and the market are present together in all major forms of economic behaviour. *The Driving Force of the Market* by Kirzner (2000) states a modern version of the Austrian message about the superiority of the market. Yet what we also need to realise is the driving force behind government.

In this chapter I argue that the economic importance of government must be identified positively alongside the Austrian recognition of the contribution of markets to affluence. It is no accident that one always meets government when one arrives in a new country and starts examining the economy. The presence of the government in both rich and poor countries is not merely a bare Hobbesian necessity – the Guardian State – or the result of self-centred incentives among public officials – the Public Choice School. Government matters in society in general and in the economy in particular through both its power to legislate (*imperium*) and its possession of resources (*patrimonium*), to employ Roman Law concepts.

Imperium and *patrimonium*

In human civilisation, from as far back in time as we can reliably determine, one encounters evidence of the two main aspects of human interaction: rule and property (Finer, 1999). In several of the ancient civilisations the distinction between ruling over people (authority) and the owning of things, especially land, was known, although never fully institutionalised. Political authority – *imperium* – exists, as Weber clarified, where people obey the commands of a ruler, supported by a group of servants. The opposite of political order is anarchy, where there is no unified rulership (Weber, 1978). *Patrimonium* refers to the way land and things are appropriated and exchanged, especially whether people have full private ownership rights to their possessions, e.g. houses, cattle and land. In the history of the great civilisations we find both separation between *imperium* and *patrimonium*, as in Roman Law, as well as all kinds of mixtures of them, including total fusion.

At one extreme, there is a complete fusion between *imperium* and *patrimonium*, meaning that everything belongs in principle to the rulers and can be disposed of by them, as they find appropriate. This is patrimonialism, or the rule of a country along the idea of a household. The public household is the country. At the other extreme, one finds a complete separation between the property of the state – *fiscus* – and the private assets of people, including those of the rulers. Here public ownership is clearly demarcated and separated from private ownership to such an extent that certain assets of the rulers are also considered their private holdings – the theory of the king's two bodies (Kantorowicz, 1998). This is typical of the modern state in a market economy.

Patrimonialism, or the failure to distinguish between *imperium* and *patrimonium*, is to be found with Oriental despotism, where the hydraulic character of agriculture led to giant imperial possessions of land (Wittfogel, 1981). One finds patrimonialism in all the great civilisations outside of Western Europe, where *patrimonium* in the form of small peasants' holdings was favoured by the orientation of agriculture towards the production of milk by ownership of cattle (Weber, 2001). In Western Europe the distinction between *imperium* and *patrimonium* was blurred by feudalism, under which regime land is held not as property (*allodium*) but as loan – the *fief.* The disintegration of the feudal society in Western Europe paved the way for a clear separation between *imperium* and *patrimonium*, confirmed in the introduction of modern civil law after the French Revolution. In common law, the idea of property was never abandoned in favour of feudal notions, as peasants tended to remain the full owners of land, although under a fiction. Yet the feudal notion that a person cannot own the land itself is still to be found in English land law, the owner having an 'estate' in land, a fiction that entitles him/her to enjoy land as if there was full ownership.

Thus, the process of separating *imperium* and *patrimonium* was a slow evolutionary one involving both early recognition and later reversals. In the Communist regimes of the twentieth century there was a temporary return to patrimonialism, as the state was made the owner of almost all assets. However, it proved economically inefficient. With the separation between *imperium* and *patrimonium* comes the clear distinction between public property and private property, which benefits the operations of a market economy. However, this transparent distinction does not entail that all property will be privately held. On the contrary, one finds lots of public property in societies adhering to a strong market economy. What is peculiar about public property in a modern society is not that it is small but that its governance regime is different from that of private property. The owner is a legal corporation – the state – and its employment should benefit the entire population.

One finds much state ownership in both rich and poor countries today. Government is everywhere the owner of huge assets such as portions of land including parks or national parks, roads, highways, ocean beaches, coastal areas, underground minerals, etc. In the United States one finds immense public ownership of land, as for instance the federal land in Alaska. In Hong Kong all land belongs in principle to the government. This fact is hardly accidental or merely an institutional error that would need to be corrected through privatisation.

State ownership of large territories such as coastal areas or natural parks is not only feasible but also desirable, as private ownership is not naturally forthcoming. Private ownership builds on the principle of fencing in the area, which is not possible here. This does not entail that all land should be owned by the government, which is clearly not efficient or just according to elementary principles of justice, as there are the commons, which belong to each and every person (Ostrom *et al.*, 2002). Farmland is very suitable for private ownership, which is not true of parks, rivers or coasts. The size of state holdings is considerable in any country. Government can run these holdings in a proper manner, meaning that the population at large benefits from their public management.

Whether assets under the soil belong to private persons or to government depends upon the legal system of the country. In some countries mineral assets belong either to the landowner or to the prospector, whereas in other countries government has the first claim on them. When they belong to the state, government can auction them out to the highest bidder, securing efficiency in allocation. Or government can exploit these resources through its public enterprises. The Norwegian government has shown that a public regime can be made operational in the difficult area of oil drilling, providing billions of dollars to the Norwegian population since these off-shore resources were declared exclusive state property in late 1950s (Andersen, 1993), to be exploited under state supervision, as well as first and foremost by public or semi-public enterprises.

Mineral resources are often exploited by the state. Whether public or private enterprises should handle the actual operations is a question of expediency. There are both pros and cons with state-owned enterprises, a question that we will return to. However, most countries have some form of state activities in relation to the production of minerals, which cannot be explained merely as a result of incentives such as corruption or rent-seeking.

Although the private sector cannot in general engage in *imperium*, or the making of regulations for society, the private sector can have a large *patrimonium*. Yet in all countries considerable assets are held by governments. This is not the outcome of Communist endeavours, as public ownership under Communism was taken much too far. However, some degree of state *patrimonium* appears economically both feasible and desirable, just as private enterprises may engage in *imperium* in relation to their own employees, although only by means of internal firm regulations. In reality, the state is a major economic actor in both rich and poor countries holding a variety of assets, including enterprises, banks and financial assets. Such public *patrimonium* may often be too large or wasteful, but it is not wrong in itself.

Thus, the state in a market economy is both *imperium* and *patrimonium*. It is the grand regulator but also the large owner of huge assets, such as costal areas, land, infrastructure, etc.

Crown jewels are not merely regalia

Following neo-liberal recommendations, some governments have been eager to divest themselves of state assets. This may be a perfectly valid ambition when privatisation leads to a larger output or when it brings badly needed cash to the state coffers. However, divestiture may also be driven by ideological reasons, i.e. the mistaken belief that only the private sector can handle resource allocation efficiently. It is difficult to understand why railroads or airports need to be privatised. Some country assets are naturally placed with government.

It is true that the balance sheet of the state is not a true measure of the affluence of a country. This was the classical position of mercantilism and this doctrine was employed to motivate a huge role for government in the economy. The affluence of a nation is a function of its output, which depends critically upon how vibrant the markets of the country tend to be. Yet state ownership of certain assets is not merely regalia or elegant clothes with which government provides the state in order to impress. Crown assets exist in all countries. They tend to be concentrated in certain domains where they complement private ownership. The prevailing theory of ownership among adherents to law and economics argues that state assets can or should be divested to the private sector. Private ownership is superior to public ownership, this argument claims. But is it really true?

Since the market philosophy became the dominant ideology, there have been a few stunning privatisation failures, which should lead to a reconsideration of the pros and cons of keeping state assets with government. The most spectacular example of failed state divestiture is perhaps the British railway system, where an almost bizarre system of multiple owners of railtracks and of operators led to an undersupply of vital services. It is difficult to understand why other European governments would decide to introduce private ownership in their railroad system, given the negative UK experience (Clifton *et al.*, 2003).

It is true that many assets are most effectively held under a private property regime. When transaction costs are low and full appropriability may be ascertained, private property is to be preferred to state ownership – according to the Coase theorem. There is simply no reason to have public ownership when the asset can be exchanged and the fruits from its employment can be appropriated fully. However, there are assets for which this condition is not fulfilled, so that government is the best owner of the asset. Examples are roads, highways, airports, railroads and harbours – essential facilities (Cooter and Ulen, 2003).

In *Governing California's Coast*, Stanley Scott (1975) provides an example of how government can act to protect vital assets through both *imperium* and *patrimonium*. Private land can be separated from public land, to be managed in accordance with a social regime, and environmental regulation can secure protection against abuse of the use of both public and private land, the Alaska oil regime. How about nationalisation: how and when?

Eminent domain

It is true that government may act arbitrarily, engaging in so-called *voluntary takings* of private property. In many countries, property has been nationalised without proper procedures or with little or no compensation. The nationalisation of whole industries may be essentially politically motivated, as when the oil sector was socialised in several Arab countries after the Second World War. However, the fact that government action in takings may be politically driven does not exclude that some assets of a country are best held by the state.

When land is necessary for community development, then the argument about an *eminent domain* is applicable. The eminent domain doctrine has been developed to its limits in the United States, where there is much hesitance about nationalisation and the dangers of voluntary takings. Yet what the doctrine of eminent domain and voluntary takings shows is that government land ownership may be rationally motivated and that private persons can be properly compensated through a predictable mechanism for expropriation (Epstein, 1985).

Government is the proper owner of certain land – this is the essence of the eminent domain doctrine. It is basically a sound one, as land whose social usefulness is larger than its private usefulness should be owned by government. One may identify various criteria, which pushes land from private ownership to public ownership, such as environmental concerns, externalities, non-appropriability, state interests, essential facility or common carrier.

The huge federal land in Alaska – why would one even attempt to privatise it? This may not even be possible or justifiable given the claims of the aboriginal populations there. There is no reason why the United States Federal Government could not be the best owner of this immense land, including its shores and sea areas within the territorial borders of the country. It has been suggested that state land could be held as commons without any defined owner or that it should be parcelled out in the form of private property rights. But why choose these alternative regimes when state ownership could be a handy and efficient governance form?

Public goods and merit goods

Markets create affluence through decision-making mechanisms involving private property, contracts, excludability and appropriability, as well as financial institutions such as the stock market and limited liability companies. Thus, it has been argued that poverty in the Third World results mainly from a lack of institutionalised mechanisms concerning capital (de Soto, 2001). Economists who would not dream of arguing in favour of the planned economy have, however, pointed out that there are goods and services where market allocation is not forthcoming naturally or involves considerable risks and disadvantages. Thus, scholars within the public finance tradition have for a long time pointed out that a society needs certain goods and services, which do not have the properties that market allocation naturally requires or prospers from. These goods and services have been described by different properties including (Musgrave and Musgrave, 1989; Stiglitz, 2000):

- non-excludability
- non-appropriability
- externalities
- economies of scale
- asymmetric information.

Goods and services with these properties are more important in the economy than the market philosophy has admitted (Stigler, 2000; Coase, 1995). They call for state involvement in the economy. One may attempt to create market allocation of these goods and services, but it does not come naturally. Even when one succeeds in putting in place a market-like situation, government will still be present somehow. Perhaps it is just as easy to have the state allocate these goods and services with its bureaucracy or through NPM?

Markets operate well for private goods, but they run into so-called market failures when employed in relation to goods and services that have the properties listed above. Markets rely on individual choice as well as the internalisation of benefits and costs. Goods and services with the above properties are allocated through social choice and they tend to display externalities. Thus, these goods or services require coordination among people so that costs can be covered though individual contributions – 'lumpy' goods or services. Other collective goods and services are such that they suffer from the free rider problem, meaning that their benefits cannot be internalised.

It is an open question how large this set of public or semi-public goods and services is in any economy, poor or rich. One may wish, for instance to list these collective goods and services as follows:

- law and order
- defence
- infrastructure
- environment
- research.

One may discuss whether all items that belong under these headings are truly public, or whether some belong to the private set of goods and services. Technology may push one set of goods or services from one category to another, as has happened, for instance in telecommunications (Eliassen and Sjovaag, 1999). These lumpy goods or services will only be forthcoming if the total willingness to pay of all individuals in a group matches the cost of the public good. Thus, individuals must coordinate in order to allocate these lumpy goods and services, summing their individual willingness to pay into a collective decision.

Yet, the possibility of free riding entails that the proper group is an organisation with state authority and the power to tax, i.e. a government – central, regional or local. Even when free riding is not feasible due to the excludable nature of the goods and services, the necessity of their allocation still favours state allocation, because they cannot be left to the vagaries of the market. They must simply be allocated. As emphasised above, the state budget now contains lots of income maintenance items – how are they to be classified in terms of public–private goods?

Public necessity

The late master of Austrian economics, Schumpeter, developed the emphasis of von Mises and Hayek on information, discovery and innovation into the concept of *creative destruction* as the logic of enterprises in the market (März, 1991; Schumpeter, 2002). However, governmental organisations cannot operate according to this logic, as they cannot be allowed to go under. If one searches for the key principles of government in society, i.e. the rational reasons for why mankind has developed the institutions that we identify with the concept of the state, then they are to be found where the border to the market is located (Baumol, 1997). Thus, the following principles hold for the state–market separation:

- The *complementarity principle* entails that the government should not try to replace markets where markets operate well. Markets constitute mechanisms of interaction that are well suited for economic life, most of the time enhancing efficiency and also sometimes justice. However, the logic of markets is not that of the state. Thus, the state should respect the sovereignty of markets in many areas of economic life, as markets increase affluence and their operations enhance the wealth of nations.
- The *priority principle*, however, implies that markets need the state. Markets can accomplish many things, but they cannot deliver their own presupposition, which is contractual validity. Exchange is the key medium of interaction in markets, and exchange is only possible given an institutional system which transparently clarifies what can be exchanged – rights – and what exchange entails in the form of the enforcement of agreements, including the settlement of disputes. It is often stated that exchange is such a simple and rational form of human interaction – bargaining, contract, enforcement. However, exchange is only possible when there are state operations protecting the contract. The state can handle almost any number of transactions through the standardisation of rules as well as their enforcement.
- The *stability principle* entails that governments cannot operate according to the logic of markets. Markets are based on creative destruction, meaning the competitive mechanism through which winners survive and losers are eliminated. Enterprises come and go in the micro processes of the economy. The macro economy operates under the fluctuations of the business cycle, which underlines the instability coming from creative destruction. The state cannot fluctuate like markets, as government must provide essential public services day and night, year in and year out. Finally, the *constitutional principle* implies that government has a core that is entirely different nature than markets, namely political power. This feature calls for a limitation of government in order to place the state under the rule of law.

Education and health enter the public sector in all countries, although these goods or services are not really public or lumpy ones. However, economists have not launched a convincing argument for their inclusion into the set of public services. One theory focuses on their meritorious nature (Musgrave and Musgrave, 1989). Government in a well-ordered society would wish to allocate goods and services which are in the best interests of the population, as well as make access to non-meritorious goods and services more difficult. In reality, social policy in both a narrow and broad sense has its rationale (see Chapter 6). Meritorious goods as well as unmeritorious goods call for government action, due either to asymmetric information or to concerns about equity or equality. Egalitarian considerations also constitute a rationale for government intervention with social policies – a kind of market failure.

Government as employees, money and law

Government derives its importance to society from its access to three formidable resources of power: employees, money and laws (Rose, 1981, 1989). By employing up to one third of the workforce, government can produce a number of services to societies. Government employment may not be as well paid as private employment, but it offers most of the time a secure job situation. The stretch of government is longer when money is considered, as up to half of the GDP or even more may be collected by government in the form of taxes, social security contributions and user fees as well as loans. Besides paying its employees, government uses its money to pay for all its external contracts, as well as to meet its huge promises of cash payments in the social security system. Finally, as the law maker for the entire society, government is in the possession of an arm which touches everything, as it does not matter whether an activity is organised publicly or privately, whether funded by government or not or whether the owners are public or private.

Thus, government in a well-ordered economy has several economic roles which are of critical importance for society and social well-being:

- government as the owner of large-scale assets;
- government as employer of lots of people;
- government as the setter of rules;
- government as the provider of goods and services;
- government as revenue collector and issuer of bonds.

Not only is it the case that each one of these roles is of great economic significance; it is also the case that these roles may come into conflict with each other, which makes the economic business of government complicated.

Can one find an economic explanation of the omniexistence of government in well-ordered societies, one which lies behind all the roles above?

Mancur Olson's book *Power and Prosperity: Outgrowing Communist and Capital-ist Dictatorships* (2000) outlines his answer to the question of the economic reasons for government: the need for protection. A similar answer in an endogenous theory of government is to be found with Barzel (2002). Using classical contract theory combining Hobbes and Locke, Barzel presents an argument to the effect that the state is a super Hobbes protector whose basic advantage is economies of scale in enforcing contracts:

> Exchange requires agreements, and agreements must be enforced. Initially, all agreements must have been self-enforced, relying on long-term relations. Increases in the extent of social interaction enabled third-party enforcement without the use of force, by elders for example, to emerge. When the state emerged, it provided third-party enforcement by using its ability in violence (Barzel, 2002: 269).

Since societies search for the most efficient institutions following Calabresi (2000), they would wish to have one enforcer, government.

Moreover, this Hobbesian position is combined with another argument of Barzel that the rule of law also emerges in order to protect the protected against the protector, i.e. the Lockean position:

> The need to contain the specialized protectors is never-ending. When subjects control their protectors, we expect them to impose constraints, such as the length of service and on their budget. In addition, we expect subjects to pay wages to the protectors, rather than allowing them to retain the spoils of war (Barzel, 2002: 268).

Let us try to put more substance into these somewhat vague statements, forming parts of a purely economic theory of government, by resorting to the powerful tools of game theory. What would lead utility-maximising players in a society to set up a government with a rule-of-law mechanism to govern it?

Transaction costs and coordination

The basic argument about the state that economists put forward focuses on coordination failures. The ultimate source of government is the transaction costs which human beings incur as they interact in groups. Social existence is impossible without coordination between individuals. Social coordination opens up the possibility of civilisation, i.e. a division of labour and a joint effort between individuals to secure common ends. Human interaction runs the gamut from conflict and destruction to close or intimate cooperation. Coordination is the process of interaction through which individuals learn to cooperate and coordination failure takes place when individuals clash or they fail to develop mutually beneficial interaction. Government would under this economic interpretation basically offer a mechanism which enhances human coordination.

Coordination is the process through which human beings take each other into account, explore the alternatives of action which are of concern to them and choose a strategy that leads to a stable outcome which is in their common interest. It has been rightly stated that markets constitute a coordination mechanism of immense consequences for the economy and society. It is one of the major mechanisms of coordination, which has evolved over time to the benefit of mankind – a *spontaneous* order. Simple markets like the Saturday grocery market build upon the same preconditions as complex markets like futures' markets, namely property rights, trust in exchange and contractual enforcement.

Exchange is a most powerful tool of coordination. Human beings can interact freely and negotiate the terms of a two-party agreement, which they stick to, sometimes enforcing it themselves. However, exchange as a mechanism of interaction has two limitations:

- *Coordination failures:* Here one finds several situations, including that individuals fail to strike a deal, that individuals make an agreement but it is not enforced, that individuals renege, or simply that individuals choose the worst possible outcome. In general, contracts tend not to be self-enforceable, but require a third party for their enforcement.
- *Transaction costs:* When it is no longer a matter of two persons interacting, then transaction costs start running high as when groups of people decide about how to cooperate, negotiating the terms of cooperation endlessly.

Government or the state would, according to the economic approach to the state, resolve coordination failures and reduce transaction costs. These are the basic economic rationales of government in a society. Let us begin with the analysis of collective action, or group decision-making, where a group of people needs to take action in order to safeguard a common interest. Government may resolve collective action problems by operating public programmes and holding public assets.

The enforcement mechanism and groups

When two people have a common interest, then the existence of a mechanism that offers *correlated* strategies entails that they can make an agreement about what to do and that the agreement will be enforced. The enforcement mechanism envisaged here is of a minimum type, as it only provides for contractual verification and enforcement. Such an enforcement mechanism may be called 'government' or 'political authority' when it is made valid for a larger group of individuals or a distinct territory. Again the reason would be economical in nature. An enforcement mechanism would develop economies of scale in providing third-party coordination. Thus, it would be efficient for a society to have one and only one enforcement mechanism that would develop its order to be valid for a group of N persons, i.e. create a legal order.

What may drive the process of enlarging the application of the enforcement mechanism is the search for rents on the part of the enforcer. Drawing upon the economies of scale in enforcement, the enforcer may wish to seize monopoly rents. Thus, he/she may try to eliminate any competitor and charge a high 'price' for his/her services. Among a group of potential enforcers one family may emerge victorious, to be called the 'king' or the 'royal' family. It is in the interest of the enforcer to establish his/her position as firmly as possible. The danger is again economical in nature, namely the monopoly rent.

The enforcement mechanism cannot remain voluntary due to free riding, as it will have to pay for its cost. With economies of scale the unit cost will be lower if many individuals contribute to its financing. However, enforcement being a public good it is not in the interest of any single individual to contribute. The incentives of the individual can be modelled according to the condition of *group rationality*:

$$\frac{\text{Cost of enforcement}}{\text{Group size } N} < \frac{\text{Cost of enforcement}}{\text{Group size } N-1} \tag{1}$$

But for any individual i the condition of *individual rationality* holds:

$$\text{Individual cost } i > \text{Free riding by individual } i \tag{2}$$

Thus, the group will not accept (2) but it will also insist upon (1). It will accept to make the enforcement mechanism *obligatory*, i.e. provide it with the characteristics of public law. Individuals would have to contribute whatever their willingness to pay could be. This is all a static analysis of the economic reasons for government. I shall add a few words about the dynamics of the enforcement mechanism.

How can a group of a large size decide upon and implement a common action like an enforcement mechanism? When groups take action in order to provide for some common interest, then transaction costs surface at once, as group consent requires negotiations among all persons concerned. The group will have to decide about how to decide about collective action. Two-to-two-person bargaining will be too cumbersome: if a group involving more than two people wishes to take a decision about a common project, then striking a series of deals between two people runs up lots of transaction costs. It may be feasible when the group is truly small, but with a group size of $N > 15$, the process quickly becomes unwieldy. Other decision mechanisms than bilateral negotiation become necessary, such as group meetings where all participate, discuss and take a decision at one point in time. Thus, bargaining may fail to resolve an issue: If a group considers a set of alternative projects about what to do, it may not be able to resolve the issue of which one to select by two-to-two person bargaining. Negotiating all projects among all the participants runs up transaction costs. The only viable alternative would be to introduce a quicker decision technique when conflicts emerge within a group: if a group of people has in the past been able to coordinate on common interests, then the group may not wish to dissolve itself. Instead it could employ a formal decision technique, which permits it to resolve the issues, namely, voting within a parliament or a referendum.

Thus, a group may decide to set up a permanent enforcement mechanism – a government, which handles collective decision-making. This would be a mechanism that may be employed for continuous collective action. A government would take action when it has identified a common objective on the basis of some procedure for taking decisions such as monarchy, aristocracy or democracy. The classical Wicksell analysis of group decision-making posits a trade-off between external and internal decision costs (Mueller, 2003). Here we will add legitimacy to the economic analysis of government.

Why would an individual accept the decisions of a government, if he/she had not participated in the making of them or dissents in relation to them after having participated? A person would like to benefit from the enforcement mechanism but he/she may wish that the group engages in many forms of collective action. How is this paradox of collective action to be resolved? Let us look at how this question was resolved by the major theoreticians in the classical contractarian school of government within political theory.

Contractarian schools

Although political authority has existed since the dawn of civilisation, one may still ask why men and women accept it (Weber, 1978; Finer, 1999). Contractarian theories focus on an economical *quid pro quo* between individual people and government, whereas utilitarian theories refer to expediency or total utility in policies (Binmore, 1994, 1998). If the hypothesis suggested above is correct, namely that transaction costs constitute the economic source of government, then minimising transaction costs lies behind both the contractarian and the utilitarian frameworks. It is because people do not find time and opportunity to make and enforce a long series of agreements between them that it is necessary to hand over power to a government or it is convenient for society that a few rule the many. Both the contractarian and the utilitarian approach look upon government and society as a *quid pro quo* relationship under which society accepts to be ruled, i.e. submission or political obligation, against receiving something in return: safety, human rights or the maximisation of average utility. How did the masters of political philosophy conceive of this Wicksellian *quid pro quo?*

Old contractarian theories

The contractarian school flourished in the seventeenth and eighteenth centuries. A number of scholars from Suarez and Grotius to Kant argued that political obligations and rights derived from a contract among men and women living in a natural state, as it were. They differed, though, in how they pictured this natural condition and what rights and duties the basic contract contained. I shall merely exemplify how government could be derived from the idea of consent of individuals.

Hobbes: safety traded against submission

The agreement between government and society for Hobbes concerned the trade-off between life and safety on the one hand and total submission on the other. Without government, people's lives would be poor, nasty, brutish and short. Locke argued that a list of rights could be made binding on government once it had been put in place, namely, life, liberty and property. In his criticism of the contractarian framework, Hume replaced the agreement with considerations of utility, which to him led men and women to favour government ahead of anarchy. The distinction between a contractarian and a utilitarian approach to government may also be found in modern political theory (Kymlicka, 2004). However, common to both approaches is the implicit hypothesis that people cannot make and enforce agreements with each and everyone all the time for the things they value the most such as safety, liberty and property. Transaction costs would be overwhelming.

Hobbes' predicament – the protection of life as the foundation of government – is only a necessary condition for the state and not a sufficient one, as government could itself fail in protecting the lives of citizens, thus itself reneging on the contract. To Hobbes, society needs government so badly that the contract entails the submission of citizens to a Leviathan sovereign. But why would people accept an arbitrary government, which may commit genocide upon them? Even if government or the state is merely a transaction cost-saving mechanism, a government that fails to respect the social contract would violate people's rights and increase transaction costs in society. Thus, the power of government must be restrained through some legitimating device like an institutional mechanism, e.g. a constitution (with Kant) or continuous participation (with Rousseau).

Locke: anticipating principal–agent interaction

With Locke the *quid pro quo* basis of government and political obligation could not be modelled as one-sided as with Hobbes. Thus, the interaction between the rulers and the ruled is conceptualised as a trust. In Anglo-American law 'trust' denotes a relationship of *quid pro quo* between one person who has the power to manage something, e.g. property, and another person who has the privilege of receiving the benefits from that property (McLoughlin and Rendell, 1992). There is no exact equivalent to the concept of a trust in civil law systems, but the synonyms include: custody, care, guardianship, keeping, safekeeping and wardship. This reciprocity between the rulers and the ruled leads Locke to his theory of limited government, revolution and human rights. However, we still have no answer to the question of when political obligation is legitimate as seen from all the members of the polity and not only the gentry. Trust would be a weak or vague definition of the principal–agent relationship between the people and their masters.

Rousseau: obligation derived from participation

It is true that Rousseau did not target transaction costs as the basis of government, but he was not really far off the idea of minimising transaction costs. Man and woman may have lived as peaceful savages before the advent of civilisation, using their natural force as their liberty in society. However, when these primitive people realised the implications of private property, institutions then had to be created in order to eliminate or minimise chaos. What was natural before the great contract becomes institutional after the contract. What people want – rights – are now much more safely protected, as they cannot be violated so easily. Freedom has been turned into law.

In reality, Rousseau is looking at the transaction cost argument from a different angle than the making of agreements. He underlines the implications of the enforcement of contracts, or the difficulty of enforcing agreements without consent. Enforcement is of course a transaction-type cost. When each man and woman enforces their rights, then transaction costs will be high. If a sovereign is erected to enforce the rights of citizens, then all must obey, or be forced to be free, as Rousseau stated. If enforcement could at each time and place be called into question, then how could transaction costs be minimised? Thus, a government once created by the social contract must be obeyed, but there is only an obligation to obey when this contract meets with the consent of all.

Kant: rule of law restrains

Kant looked upon the contractarian idea of one or two great public contracts as a fiction that allowed people to solve the legitimacy question of why a few people would be entrusted with the task of governing the many. Speaking of political power as based on a contract between rulers and the ruled allowed one, argued Kant, to introduce restrictions on government in order that the state would be a *Rechtsstaat*. If there was a contract, then the rational rules people consent to as the foundation of government would be the rule of law. The legitimacy perspective complements the transaction cost approach but does not replace it. Coordination failures with attending losses to the players may be minimised by creating a third-party institution that enforces agreements. Government is the third-party enforcer *par preference* since it may capture the economies of scale in contract protection. The resort to an enforcement mechanism in society leads further to the classical problem in all contract theory of government: *Sed quis custodet ipsos custodies?* (But who shall guard the guards?) It may be argued that a Kantian mechanism of rule of law is the best transaction cost saving device for solving this problem of controlling the enforcers.

New contractarian theories

Contractarian thinking about government and the state received a great stimulus from the publication of John Rawls' *A Theory of Justice* (1999), outlining in a Kantian fashion the two fundamental principles of justice that rational men and women would endorse if they were they in a natural condition under a veil of ignorance. A similar approach was employed by other contractarian theorists such as Nozick (2001) and Gauthier (1987), the first following the Lockean framework of innate rights and endowments and the second the Hobbesian approach of *homo homini lupus*. The Rousseau framework is to be found with two groups of scholars, on the one hand the participationists, claiming that the popular will must be expressed in a continuous fashion (Pateman, 1970, 1985; Barber, 2004) and on the other the communitarians, focusing on the values that a local contract in a community would express (Walzer, 2004; Taylor, 1992).

The principal–agent model, discussed in this volume, may also be seen as a device for pouring new wine into the bottle of old contractarian theory. There would be two basic contracts involved in setting up a state, just as Pufendorf conceived of the social contract. First, the population would, as principal, contract with government as its agent – the electoral contract in a democracy. Second, government would contract with agents to get its job done – the management contract. It is this second contract that will be analysed in the coming chapters from the standpoint of theories of public administration and public management. However, I will continue the analysis of the first contract in this chapter by looking into the economic rationale of setting up a government.

Contracting in the public sector

When one speaks about the public sector, then the key word is 'public'. It is used to make the crucial distinction between two parts of reality, the public and the private. When analysing the public sector, the relevant theories are classified as 'public' policy, 'public' management and 'public' administration. It is a fundamental belief in well-ordered societies that there exists a 'public' domain where there occurs a 'public' discourse which is separate or different from the 'private' domain with its 'private' discourse (Habermas, 1992; Calhoun, 1993). To clarify this distinction one often employs the concepts of state and market, although some scholars may wish to add a third concept, namely the family.

Something is thus called 'public' when it is part somehow of the state. Public policies are the programmes or commitments of the central, regional or local governments. Public management is the steering and monitoring of teams of employees in the state, the regional or local governments, in order to accomplish outputs and outcomes efficiency. Finally, public administration is the institutionalisation of government in all its aspects with a view towards achieving the rule of law.

In political science the public is identified with the obligations for a community of individuals. Thus, the public sector emerges from statute law taking the forms of constitutional law or administrative law, which are both always binding on all citizens. The state is authority, i.e. there is a high probability that obedience is forthcoming towards a command. In economics, the private sector or the markets are analysed as contracting between separate persons. The logic of markets is the making of deals: bargaining, agreement and the enforcement of deals. Consequently, private law results from the mutual regulation of rights and duties between individuals.

Yet, paradoxically, the theme of this book is that the public sector is also basically contracting. Government results from the contracting difficulties among citizens and the state is structured in terms of contracting between principals and agents. To understand why contracting is basic for understanding the public sector, one needs to recognise fully the implications of transaction costs for public organisation.

The two kinds of transaction costs

Transaction cost theory is employed frequently within so-called 'new institutional economics' or neo-institutionalism, which is a new branch of economics attempting to endogenise rules, meaning explain them as resulting from choice, given either full information or bounded rationality. 'New Institutionalism' refers to the variety of schools that seek to explain political, historical, economic and social institutions such as government, law, markets, firms, social conventions, the family, etc. in terms of economic theory. Although the term 'New Institutionalism' is used about the work of Coase, Alchian, Demsetz and Williamson based on the transaction costs and the property rights paradigm, it also embraces some well-known 'economic' theories of non-market social relationships (Becker, Mincer), political processes (Buchanan, Tullock), jurisprudence and legal processes (Posner, Landes), as well as social and economic history (Fogel, North). Here one may also mention scholars within evolutionary economics (Hodgson), the economics of property rights (Dnes) and law and economics (Martin).

Institutional economics has analysed the organisation of markets and firms with great insight, especially when linked with game theory in an evolutionary perspective on human behaviour. A number of textbooks are already available (Vromen, 1995; Mantzavinos, 2001; Rutherford, 1996; Potts, 2001). In addition an International Society for New Institutional Economics has existed since 1997. It focuses on the explanation of the role of rules in restraining behaviour through sanctions, i.e. the consequences of institutions. To quote from its mission statement:

> The International Society for New Institutional Economics (ISNIE) was founded in 1997 to stimulate and disseminate interdisciplinary research on economic, political and social institutions and their effects on economic activity. Topics of interest include the organisation and boundaries of the firm, structure and performance of contractual arrangements, the determinants and impacts of property rights and transactions costs on resource allocation and governance institutions, the causes and effects of government regulatory and competition policies, the structure and effects of legal, social and political institutions on economic performance, the role and response of organisations to innovation and technological change, and the nature of economic development and transition economies. (www.isnie.org/)

The basic tenet is that in the long run only those rules or regimes are forthcoming that regulate interaction and channel behaviour that are transaction cost saving or minimising. The concept of cost used to denote production costs in economics, but the neo-institutionalist revolution has extended the concept to cover also so-called transaction costs. What are these?

'Transaction costs' have a narrow, clear and precise meaning: costs incurred when buying or selling securities, including the brokers' commissions and dealers' spreads (the difference between the price the dealer paid for a security and that for which he/she can sell it). However, in institutional economics the content of this concept has been enlarged considerably. It is now said that total production cost can be decomposed into production costs and transaction costs. And transaction costs can, in a broad definition, be said to cover all kinds of motivation, enforcement and coordination costs. This definition of production costs and transaction costs is found in Wallis and North (1986: 97), although they use the term 'transformation' cost instead of production cost. The division of transaction costs into further items, such as motivation and coordination costs, occurs with some scholars, e.g. Milgrom and Roberts (1992: 29). I will distinguish here between transaction costs *ex ante* (negotiation) and as transaction costs *ex post* (monitoring) the contract. Thus, we have at least the following two kinds of transaction costs besides the standard production costs of payments to labour, capital and land:

- *Ex ante:* the time and effort put into bargaining and contracting.
- *Ex post:* enforcement costs: court action, policing, monitoring, etc.

It should be emphasised that transaction costs constitute costs to the same extent as production costs. In fact, they often show as highly quantified costs for advice, lawyers, meetings and lawsuits in general. Thus, transaction costs are not radically different from production costs, although they may be more difficult to pin down and measure. Transaction costs may be calculated as all three standard types of costs that dictionaries mention: (1a) the amount or equivalent paid or charged for something: price; (1b) the outlay or expenditure made to achieve an object: sacrifice; (2) the penalty incurred especially in gaining something: loss.

Thus, transaction costs stem from prices paid, sacrifices made and losses incurred somehow. They are different from production costs in that they refer to other activities than the production of a good or service, especially to the process through which agreements are made and put into effect. Generally speaking, agreements between two or more parties constitute the foundation for interactions in the private sector. What, then, is the relevance of transaction costs to the understanding of the public sector?

The state and transaction costs

Government was never absent in Manchester liberal economics, which launched the concept of the minimalist state. It is often underlined that Adam Smith devoted much space to underlining the importance of government to the proper functioning of markets. Thus, the state arrives first and markets come second. One may derive this approach from Hobbes and his theory of the natural condition, which tends towards anarchy if government is not introduced through the great covenant.

The point here is that this traditional perspective in political economy makes the market a function of the government in the Anglo-Saxon tradition and the state in the Continental tradition. However, it leaves unanswered the question of the origins of or reasons for government. In the Manchester liberal theory, markets are endogenous and the state is exogenous. What is lacking is a theory of the logic of public organisation in the first place, not deriving the state from so-called market failures and the ambition of government to undo these. Why do people set up or support government in the first place? The night-watchman theory of government focuses on the market as the optimal mechanism for human interaction, but it admits that markets can only flourish if supported by government. After society has erected a state it may proceed to employ markets to provide itself with the goods and services it needs. The role of government is to provide society with the presuppositions of markets, which include *inter alia*:

- guarantee of contracts agreed to;
- punishment of contract violations;
- removal of contract violators from society;
- awarding of compensation for contract violations;
- guarantee of money with which to contract;
- protection of the country against foreign intruders.

The night-watchman government would provide these services to the market after which markets could take on any allocative task. The idea is that the market cannot provide its own presuppositions. This is Hobbes' theory of the state, and it certainly seems valid today.

Contractual validation requires uniformity and efficiency in the application of rules. Citizens would support one enforcer, as the existence of many enforcers would endanger the presuppositions of the market, i.e. it would result in anarchy as in stateless societies in the Third World. Citizens would be prepared to negotiate about the creation of a state e.g. by establishing a constitution and a fiscal regime, but such bargaining could not go on endlessly. Thus, minimising transaction costs would be the ultimate rationale for government. However, the relevance of transaction costs does not end here, as the night-watchman theory entails. The Hobbesian theory of government targets the preconditions of markets, which cannot be supplied by the markets themselves. The reason is in reality a version of transaction cost theory, meaning that the staggering transaction costs in the absence of a state would hurt society tremendously. There cannot be ongoing bargaining about the law and there cannot be several enforcers.

If the night-watchman theory is correct, then why would citizens support a large public sector typical of well-ordered societies? One answer has been that markets may still work badly, even when their preconditions are met. The market failure framework has suggested a number of concepts with which to analyse state intervention in the economy. Thus, public policies would target the following market failures:

- externalities in allocation;
- economies of scale in production;
- asymmetric information in transactions;
- inequalities in distribution.

We will discuss the market failure theory in Chapter 6, where two views on this approach are contrasted, namely the Chicago and Cambridge positions. It is sufficient here to underline that market failure is in reality nothing but the transaction cost argument, as it is certain conditions that lead to various deficiencies of contracting that are outlined in market failure theory, namely:

- *Externalities:* When benefits or costs do not follow the price mechanism, bargaining will fail to give efficient results. If bargaining covered all kinds of external effects, then transaction costs would skyrocket.
- *Economies of scale:* When production costs per unit fall as the quantity goes up, it may be preferable with one single producer, minimising costs and prices. Again, there is in reality a bargaining problem, as negotiations would not find the Pareto-optimal quantity of output, at least not with a minimum of transaction costs.
- *Asymmetric information:* When one player has more knowledge than another player in a market setting, bargaining will not result in efficient outcomes. Removing the asymmetry between, for example, buyer and seller may require huge investments in time and effort, which again leads to staggering transaction costs.
- *Inequalities:* Bargaining tends to produce efficient results, but they need not be just. If the outcomes of market interaction are to be changed in accordance with a principle of justice, then this must be done from outside the market.

Market failure theory claims either that markets fail completely or that they do not lead to acceptable outcomes from either an efficiency standpoint or a justice point of view. Again transaction costs figure prominently in the background of this argument. However, one may reject the market failure approach by means of two counter-arguments:

1 Market failures are not probable.
2 Government failure is even more probable.

Argument (1) is to be found in Chicago School economics. Argument (2) is to be found with the Public Choice School. One may say that Barzel's theory of government as the most effective protector within a rule-of-law frame combines positions (1) and (2). On the one hand, it states that there will be economies of scale in having only *one* protector. On the other, it admits that this one protector must be protected against the temptation to use his/her supreme force for private ends. However, this economic theory of government does not explain the large public sector that well-ordered societies tend to have. Besides transaction costs, one must pay attention to the quest for fairness, especially equality.

Transaction costs and fairness

Transaction costs, fairness and public organisation all point in the same direction, namely the groups that human beings set up and maintain, from local government to nations and international organisations. When groups of people decide to provide themselves with common goods and services, then transaction costs arise immediately. Whether the group provides itself with public or private goods, it must decide on quantities and qualities in the service programmes, thus incurring transaction costs *ex ante* and *ex post*. Besides negotiation and decision costs, there are the enforcement costs in relation to the implementation of the public programmes. Groups in well-ordered societies minimise transaction costs in decision-making by employing the democratic procedure of simple majority voting. And they minimise transaction costs in enforcement by resorting to elaborate mechanisms for public administration and public management.

Groups in action or organised collectivities find government a useful contractual mechanism for regulating their business. By making a common effort public, the probability that it will be adhered to by all is increased (obligation) and it becomes easier to treat all members of the polity in the same way (equality and equity). Citizens cannot bargain endlessly about a mechanism of protection, and competition between protection mechanisms has never worked, as all studies of old feudalism or neo-feudalism show. In infrastructure public supply may again be transaction cost saving as it could decrease both bargaining and enforcement outlays. In relation to social policies, government can guarantee certain standard levels of provision that apply to all citizens. Thus, all parents would wish their children to have a basic training. And nations wish to offer all citizens a basic access to health care and social care. It is when government takes on too much in the field of welfare that transaction gains are non-existent but production costs skyrocket. Social security, for instance, can be handled by the market or by government. Since all citizens seek some form of protection against adversity, the advantage of a public system is universal coverage and egalitarian treatment at a minimum or basic level.

To understand the transaction cost basis of government in a well-ordered society one needs to think through the counterfactual situation when markets fail to deliver vital goods and services. In a market setting, competition entails creative destruction. This leads to large quantities and low prices but also to the possibility of bankruptcy and market collapse. There are services that a group wants where this possibility cannot be accepted because it would lead to staggering transaction costs. Thus, infrastructure and social services cannot be allowed to simply vanish due to private failures. Groups organise themselves as political collectivities in order to guarantee these services. Thus, minimising transaction costs lies at the heart of the creation and maintenance of government. Privatising all infrastructure, security and basic education and health care is not a realistic option in a society which seeks efficiency in service provision.

Conclusion

Economists have sought to explain the existence of government using the *homo economicus* model. The question then becomes: What would lead rational utility maximisers to set up and support an authority? Two kinds of answers have been suggested by economists since Adam Smith, namely:

- *Needs:* There exists a special set of goods and services which only government can allocate and for which people have a strong need (public goods), or should need (merit goods).
- *Transaction costs:* These exists a special set of goods for which transaction costs would become staggering if the market was to be employed (lumpy goods).

This chapter has looked at these two reasons for government, which have a common core in the conception of government as a super enforcer of contracts, decisions and commitments. One must add one more circumstance but it falls outside of the range of the neoclassical decision model, namely, the quest for fairness. Thus, we have a third reason for government:

- *Justice:* Human beings form groups in order to make social arrangements and set up mechanisms of cooperation. Government offers a mechanism for political organisation which may not only handle so-called public goods (social needs) and minimise transaction costs, but it may also promote fairness among the members of a group, or the citizens of a polity.

Yet government must resolve the principal–agent difficulties which arise when the state establishes a set of public organisations for a group. Here, we find the principal–agent approach suitable for the analysis of public organisation involving government as the principal and the various teams it may wish to employ to get the job done. I will focus on the occurrence of hidden actions (moral hazard) and hidden knowledge (adverse selection). Bureaucracy is beset by the former difficulty (shirking), whereas public enterprises struggle with the latter difficulty, especially under the new regime of incorporation and partial privatisation. NPM suggests that government contract more frequently in order to handle moral hazard, but it raises the question of how government can come to grips with hidden knowledge when it outsources the provision of services or market-tests its CEOs or teams, trying to identify which agents it contracts with.

An economic theory of government is thus not entirely satisfactory, as it bypasses the role of norms, especially justice. How, then, is the rational choice approach applicable to government and the public sector?

4 Public organisation, incentives and rationality in government

Introduction

Public sector research has recently been stimulated by the enquiry into private sector organisation, especially the role of incentives and rules, as well as the place for rationality (Furubotn and Richter, 2000). The major advances in the application of rational choice theory in various market settings including the recent emergence of the economics of information and of the economics of organisation (Torres-Blay, 2004) call for an enquiry into public sector rationality along similar lines. Thus, we may ask whether there is rationality in state policy-making (macro aspect), as well as whether the actors in public sector interaction pursue rational strategies (micro aspect).

As a matter of fact, the question of rationality in government has been discussed since Weber suggested that bureaucracy amounted to not only legal but also rational authority. In the literature, we find all possible positions represented, from complete rationality over bounded rationality to complete foolishness. To pour new wine in an old bottle, in the following sections I will distinguish between micro and macro rationality.

The aim in this chapter is to examine a few of the main theories about rationality in the public sector as a foundation for stating a new position, which combines micro rationality with the possibility of macro foolishness. The separation between micro rationality (incentives) and macro rationality (optimality) is crucial if much of the confusion surrounding the question of public sector rationality is to be avoided. If one assumes that the actors in public sector interaction pursue rational micro strategies but the macro outcomes may yet be far from optimal, then one may unravel the logic of public organisation.

Rational public administration

Within the public administration tradition, government rationality was approached basically as a macro phenomenon. Since incentives were almost left out of the equation from the outset, given the assumption that vocation or the public interest drives civil servants, rationality had to be interpreted in terms of a macro perspective. Thus, bureaux and public enterprises were seen as rational when they achieved their objectives in an efficient manner, choosing the most adequate means to accomplish these goals. Many of the so-called proverbs of public administration were guidelines about how to administer government departments in a rational manner in the macro sense.

The concept of macro rationality inherent in the public administration school may be stated in the following way, using the distinction between politics and administration, to which we will return. Table 4.1 presents the politics/administration separation with the concept of macro rationality being defined as clear goals and certain means. According to this conception of macro rationality, it was the politicians' task to deliver clear goals and set priorities among them, including resolving trade-offs when there were goal conflicts. Finding the most effective means with which to accomplish these goals, on the other hand, was to be entrusted to the expertise of either the bureaucrats or professionals. Two kinds of criticism were launched against this macro concept of rationality in government.

First, this concept of rationality in public sector administration was susceptible to the criticism of the politics/administration dichotomy. Thus, it was claimed that policy goals may be set by the bureaucrats or professionals. Or it was argued that the means employed to reach the goals are never neutral and thus not a task merely for technology. This demolition of macro rationality within the public administration school was carried through effectively in classical books by Waldo (1984) and Appleby (1975), after the Second World War. Politics cannot be separated from administration, just as goals cannot be distinguished from means.

Second, the requirement of full information was criticised as unrealistic. The actors in the public sector – government, bureaux and employees – do not come close to fulfilling the assumption of complete knowledge. The requirement is much too demanding of them. An alternative theory of behaviour was developed with the bounded rationality school, where the requirement of complete knowledge was relaxed. Actors 'muddling through' tend to focus on certain goals to the exclusion of others and employ

Table 4.1 Rationality in public administration

Administration		Political goals	
		Unambiguous	*Ambiguous*
Means	Certain	Rationality	
	Uncertain		Foolishness

specific standard operating procedures (SOP), which they know work in most cases. Marginalism or incrementalism replaced rational choice in the organisational theory developed by March and Simon (1993; Gigerenzer and Selter, 2002).

Rationality could be completely done away with, as with the garbage-can model where goals tend systematically to be ambiguous and there is no longer any reliable knowledge about means. Choice is random, leadership is luck and actors have clear solutions to problems they do not understand. Here, the possibility or probability of macro rationality is completely denied (March and Olsen, 1980). Recent advances in game theory cast doubt about the garbage-can model, however. In the rational choice approach, the actors may be modelled as searching for the available information that it is worthwhile for them to acquire. There is no unattainable ideal of perfect information, as actors take into account the search costs of information. In a so-called Bayesian decision-making framework, the players update themselves continuously. Thus, the non-existence at one point in time of perfect information does not rule out rationality in action.

In the concept of bounded rationality, as well as in the garbage-can model, it is not clear whether these schools target micro or macro rationality. One of the great revelations in modern game theory is that the actors may behave micro rationally according to a Bayesian framework but the outcomes may be turn out to be macro foolish – e.g. as in the most famous of all games, the prisoner's dilemma (PD) game. The concept of micro rationality appears far more defensible than the concept of macro rationality. The macro concept of rationality within public administration received its final blow from two angles, one attacking the logic of setting goals in politics and another attacking the logic of goal implementation within bureaucracies. Let us first examine what rationality could mean when it comes to policy-making or the process through which the goal function in politics is established.

Rationality in policy-making: will transitivity prevail?

When people interact in the public sector, if they bring forward objectives that are complex and perhaps often ambiguous, rationality in policy-making becomes difficult. However, the opposite conclusion does not necessarily hold, meaning that when the actors have unambiguous goals, then macro rationality will follow in practice. The social choice literature shows that the choice participants may have clear objectives but the decision-making process could fail to achieve rationality (Nurmi, 1999).

Macro rationality in policy-making must satisfy the criterion of transitivity – this is a necessary condition for policy rationality. Thus, democratic politics can only deliver rational policies if the goals decided upon satisfy transitivity. But will democracies deliver transitive policies? The definition of transitivity reads that a goal function is rational only if it holds that when A is better than B and B is better than C, then A is better than C.

Yet transitivity is merely a logical relationship explicating consistency, as the crucial question is whether it will hold when policies are voted on in a democratic assembly.

Transitivity in policy decision-making may be violated when minorities combine to defeat majorities or when the choice participants engage in log-rolling. Consider the following examples of a choice process involving a set of goals with three groups of players of roughly equal size, the players voting sincerely. The aggregation rule is simple majority.

Example 1: Minorities defeating majorities

Preferences:

- Group 1: $xy, xy', x'y, x'y'$
- Group 2: $xy', x'y', xy, x'y$
- Group 3: $x'y, x'y', xy, xy'$

The majority favours x before x' as well as y before y'. However, if the minorities favouring x' and y' combine, then they can beat the majority. Combining x and y results in the following so-called voting paradox or cycle: xy beats xy', which beats $x'y$, which beats $x'y'$, which beats xy.

The objectives x' and y' are in the minority and thus cannot be accepted in simple majority decision-making, given that separate votes are taken. However, a ticket comprising both x' and y' has a good chance of getting adopted, as it would defeat the counterticket with x and y. At the same time, an objective function consisting of $x'y'$ would not satisfy transitivity.

We now assume the possibility of insincere voting in so-called log-rolling or vote trading games.

Example 2: Log-rolling

- Group 1: x, z, y
- Group 2: y, z, x
- Group 3: z, x, y

Here the Condorcet winner is objective z, which defeats the other objectives x and y in pairwise comparison, given simple majority voting. Yet, group 1 and group 2 may trade votes and secure both x and y, defeating z.

The classical formulation of the difficulty at arriving at transitive objectives in democratic decision-making is the Arrow impossibility theorem (Arrow *et al.*, 2002). It shows that foolishness may be the policy outcome even when the choice participants are rational individually. The theorem states in a powerful manner that there is no policy-making procedure that can guarantee transitive outcomes when all kinds of policy objectives are possible and minorities are not supposed to prevail (Craven, 1992; Mueller, 2003).

The argument about intransitivity in policy-making is a strong reminder against macro rationality; in the public sector minorities prevail in democratic politics but when one explores the possibilities of insincere voting as well as log-rolling, then macro rationality will not be easy to achieve, as it requires restrictions on individual choice and the aggregation mechanism (Riker, 1988). Let us turn to the second kind of criticism of rationality in the public sector, the argument from policy implementation.

Whose rationality in policy implementation?

The book *Implementation* by Pressman and Wildavsky (1984) opened up a new perspective on rationality in the public sector. Its basic finding about the 'implementation gap' – the distance between formally stated goals and real-world outcomes – had important implications for how rationality in government was to be perceived. They argued that policy objectives, whether they were clear or ambiguous, single or complex, easy or difficult to accomplish, tended to be displaced when put into practice at the bottom level of government. Thus, goals that had been decided at the top level of government in a policy could turn out to be far away from what was actually accomplished in society – the outcomes of implementation. It was not merely that policy objectives could be ambiguous or that the technology employed for goals achievement often was unreliable. In between the objectives of top-level policy-makers and the actions of the bottom-level bureaucrats and professionals comes the process of implementation during which new objectives become relevant or existing goals are reinterpreted by the participants.

Implementing Public Policy by Hill and Hupe (2002) presents the intellectual history concerning the rise and fall of the implementation perspective on the public sector. The logic of the story is familiar, as what started out as an entirely new way of approaching the public sector became transformed into a generally accepted and commonplace view on government as consisting of governance. Thus: first an innovative new idea – the implementation gap, then all the additions, refinements and criticisms, and finally the generalisation of the idea.

I shall begin with the idea of implementation, positioning implementation studies within political science. It was the genius of Wildavsky that launched this new approach, which underlines outcomes, not outputs, and asks for substantial evidence of policy achievements. Wildavsky's angle opened up for an immense variety of policy studies aiming at understanding the pros and cons of large government. The implementation perspective initiated by Pressman and Wildavsky contained its own demise, because most public programmes are not one-shot games. They tend to go on, meaning that they evolve more than achieve. Dunsire in the UK once predicted: 'Having been "public administration" in the 1970s, and become "public policy and management" in the 1980s, the name of the discipline may well become "governance" in the 1990s' (Dunsire *et al.*, 1989).

The variety of implementation theory is rich today, covering the top-down and bottom-up approaches, as well as the attempts to reconcile these. Implementation theory developed in a very short time to cover many new aspects of government that were missing in public administration. Thus, the implementation deficit in the top-down approach was discovered and the contribution of street-level bureaucrats was pointed out in the bottom-up approach. Combining these insights, network theory could identify the contribution of civil society to policy implementation and also policy-making. Here at the same time is the riddle of implementation: If different policies can be implemented in a variety of ways, then perhaps one needs a theory of policy implementation that covers all perspectives? If policies evolve over time, then perhaps policy evaluation is a dynamic enterprise, which excludes any specific implementation deficit? Once implementation is interpreted dynamically instead of in a static fashion, then it seems one must arrive at the inevitable but trivial conclusion of implementation as endless evaluation governance. What, then, remains of the implementation idea today?

Implementation analysis after Wildavsky remains an art to which one may devote a craft by political scientists (Wildavsky, 1987). Despite the ambiguity surrounding key concepts such as output/outcome, vertical/horizontal and public/private, implementation remains a distinct research enterprise, analysing what is feasible or what will work in public programmes. It tends towards positivist methodology, speaking of dependent and independent variables and their measurements. Implementation should now be seen as governance, a concept that harbours new ideas about different kinds of steering: authority (top-down), transaction – contracting (public management) and persuasion (bottom-up). Once one accepts that governance comprises alternative implementation models, then one may start using the concept of policy styles in order to characterise how specific countries structure their implementation processes.

When Pressman and Wildavsky initiated the implementation approach, then the hidden target was public sector expansion (Pressman and Wildavsky, 1984). If policies displayed implementation deficit, then why not cut back public expenditures and rely on market allocation of goods and services? Somehow the concept of implementation deficit is to government what the concept of market failures is to the market, namely the so-called caveat *memento te mortalem esse*: always remember that you are mortal. In all kinds of governance research there is the following rationality test: Why initiate policy if markets are available?

The implementation of policy is in reality a struggle between various groups of actors, not only bending the officially stated goals in their favour but also adding new objectives besides the officially stated ones. The implementation gap creating the opportunity for bottom-up implementation makes an implementation deficit highly probable. The idea of perfect administration within the public administration tradition – clear objectives in combination with reliable means – seems a chimera when confronted with the implementation deficit. What, then, about micro rationality?

Micro rationality versus macro rationality

The above analysis implies that macro rationality is a troublesome concept. There really is not much evidence to the effect that policies can be decided rationally or that policy objectives can be rationally accomplished in implementation. The logical conclusion is to deny the possibility of rational decision-making in government, which occurred, for instance, in the well-known thesis of March and Olsen about garbage-can processes in the public sector. If goals tend to be ambiguous and means tend to be uncertain, then the occurrence of organised anarchy in the public sector may be expected, at least sometimes. Yet what the argument about garbage-can processes in the public sector really amounts to is a denial of macro rationality. It does not rule out micro rationality. We have to turn to economics and its neoclassical decision-making model in order to arrive at a strong argument in favour of micro rationality in social life, including the public sector. *Homo economicus* has had such a success in the rapid spread of the rational choice approach in the last decades that we must discuss the possibility of micro rationality in the public sector, despite the difficulties discussed above that surround the concept of macro rationality.

The advances in game theory since the publication in 1944 of von Neumann and Morgenstern's *Theory of Games and Economic Behaviour* (2004) have created a solid foundation for the employment of the rational choice framework within the social sciences, especially in political science and sociology. The usefulness of the key solution concepts in non-cooperative game theory – Bayesian decision-making and the Nash equilibrium – cannot be doubted today. What, however, is contentious is the range of the application of the neoclassical utility maximisation model in various spheres of social life (Etzioni, 1990; 1994; Becker *et al.*, 1995).

The test of a model is its capacity to predict interesting new conclusions, according to Friedman, favouring the parsimony of the *homo economicus* model ahead of more realistic assumptions about human behaviour (Friedman, 1953). And the neoclassical model is truly simple, assuming:

1   Actors have full knowledge about the alternatives of action.
2   Actors have full knowledge about the outcomes of action.
3   Actors have consistent preferences over all the outcomes in order to arrive at the prediction.
4   Actors calculate the expected value of all the alternatives of action, choosing the alternative with the highest expected value.

Only abstract assumptions can have great predictive power and only unrealistic ones can yield truly new insights – this is the methodological defence for the neoclassical model following a Popperian philosophy of science. Whether the model in fact offers new and interesting implications has to be examined empirically, area by area (Blaug, 1992).

Yet, the counter-argument is just around the corner: How can unrealistic assumptions yield true knowledge about a complex reality? The most plausible alternative to the Friedman position was launched by Simon, who outlined an entirely different theory of human decision-making, the model of bounded rationality (Simon, 1997). The model assumptions of bounded rationality are not equally simple:

1   Actors focus on certain alternatives of action.
2   Actors know some of the outcomes of action.
3   Actors focus on certain values and the concluding prediction is much less specific.
4   Actors 'satisfice'.

These model assumptions may appear innocuous and at the same time highly plausible from a realistic point of view. But what in effect do they imply about human behaviour? A theory cannot predict everything, as it must rule out certain phenomena – this is the essence of Popper's falsifiability criterion. What, then, can we predict about public sector behaviour using the model with the assumptions (1)–(4), or – to put the matter differently: What could not be predicted using these weak assumptions?

The Harsanyi innovation in game theory linking the principles of Bayesian decision-making with the Nash equilibrium concept reduces the attractiveness of bounded rationality (Harsanyi, 1976, 1982). Players update themselves using the available information as much as possible. The upshot of the analysis above is that macro rationality is only a normative conception whereas micro rationality has a foundation in behaviour. The relevance of a rational decision-making model for understanding micro rationality in policy-making was stated in several applications of *homo economicus* by Becker (Becker *et al.*, 1995). If actors behave so that they maximise their interests in relation to policies (family, crime, trade), then perhaps also policy-makers can use all the information available when framing policies and similarly policy implementers? Yet the occurrence of micro rationality does not guarantee macro rationality. Consider the basic lessons from game theory below (Dutta, 2000; Gintis, 2000).

Cooperation and coordination failures

I will make the analysis of coordination as simple as possible by only considering two individuals or organisations that have an interest in maximising their gain from interaction in a variable sum game. Thus, these players may wish to cooperate. However, they may fail to do so when coordination problems beset the interaction. Various coordination failures may be identified, arising in different kinds of interaction. Cooperation is merely one strategy in the games that will be analysed below. What is crucial is whether cooperation is a Nash equilibrium, meaning it is the best response of a player towards another player? The distinction between cooperative and non-cooperative game theory is crucial here. Cooperation will only be pursued if it is part of a non-cooperative strategy that is Nash. This distinction makes it possible to analyse how players may bypass Pareto-optimal outcomes and end up in coordination failures (Nash, 2001).

Coordination failures with pure strategy Nash equlibria

Here we have two situations: (1) PD situations, i.e. the two players defect from the Pareto-optimal solution; (2) chicken situations. i.e. the two players may push for their best outcome and thus bring about a Pareto inferior result. The PD game is the most dismal type of coordination failure, as both players have the dominating strategy of defection against cooperation (see Table 4.2).

The value of the game is 6, but the players only achieve 2, which amounts to a clear and expensive *strong* coordination failure. Two solutions are conceivable:

•   *Correlated strategies:* Communication between the players could lead to a new strategy (cooperation, cooperation), but it will not be self-enforced. Actually a number of correlated strategies could be devised to arrive at the value of the game through side payments, but they all require a third party to police the agreement. Where does this third party come from and how is he/she to be paid, reducing the value of the game?

Suppose that the PD game is played two times consecutively. Then the value of the game is 12 but the players only achieve 4 due to the chain store paradox. Communication and a cooperative solution involving, for instance, alternation between cooperation/defection and defection/cooperation would be Pareto superior. But how is such a correlated strategy to be enforced?

Table 4.2 The PD game

Player A	Player B	
	Cooperation	*Defection*
Cooperation	3, 3	0, 6
Defection	6, 0	1, 1

- *Meta-strategies:* If the game is played several times without a fixed time horizon, then the discount rate of the players will lead them to coordination only if they discount future cooperation little. The discount rate d in an infinite sequence of PD games would have to satisfy the following condition in order to favour cooperation ahead of defection:

$$3/(1 - d) > 6 + 1/(1 - d)$$
$$3 > 6(1 - d) + 1$$
$$2 > 6 - 6d$$
$$-4 > -6d$$
$$6d > 4$$
$$d > 2/3$$

If one player has a discount rate lower than $2/3$, then cooperation is not going to be the outcome of coordination. The chicken game is less dismal from the point of view of coordination. Let us look at its structure (Table 4.3).

The value of the game is 6 but brinkmanship may bring the game to the dismal solution of -8. However, this negative outcome is not Nash and thus may be avoided by the players. Typical of both the PD game and the chicken game is that communication does not help. In fact, agreements *ex ante* based on communication may trigger the negative solution.

One way to handle the risks in the chicken game is to employ a mixed strategy. However, it entails that sometimes there will occur the coordination failure of 'macho, macho'. Thus, we have:

$$3p + 0(1 - p) = 6p + -4(1 - p)$$
$$p = 4/7$$

We also have:

$$3q + 0(1 - q) = 6q + -4(1 - q)$$
$$q = 4/7$$

Thus, coordination failure may occur as frequently as $3/7 \times 3/7 = 9/49$.

Table 4.3 The chicken game

Player A	Player B	
	Wimp	*Macho*
Wimp	3, 3	0, 6
Macho	6, 0	−4, −4

Communication is a vital strategy in the other two games of cooperation, bargaining games and assurance. Here, it is in the interest of the players to communicate truthfully and treat agreements as binding. However, these games are still basically non-cooperative games. And the players may fail to coordinate on the Pareto-optimal outcomes, although coordination should be rather straightforward in these two games. Let us see how coordination failures may arise despite communication.

In bargaining situations the two players may fail to arrive at the best outcome because they can not arrive at the division of the cake. If bargaining ends with no solution, then there is a *strong* coordination failure. It is in the interest of all players to extract the entire value of the game (6), but the players may prefer solutions that are inside the negotiation set if it provides an acceptable solution from a distributional point of view.

In the game battle of the sexes (Table 4.4) a mixed strategy has no sense, as the players should coordinate on pure strategy pairs, but which? Both players would be tempted to push for their best outcome at the risk of arriving at a Pareto inferior solution. The coordination failure (0,0) is, however, not as likely in the battle of the sexes as in the PD or chicken games, because any negotiated settlement is always better than no agreement at all. Yet coordination failure can result from a first-mover advantage strategy under which both players try to force the other towards his/her best outcome.

If the battle of the sexes is played several times, then a mixed strategy involving a combination of the negotiated solutions (5, 1) and (1, 5) is feasible. The problem of finding this mixed strategy is in reality the same as the cake-splitting problem of how two players can agree to divide a cake into two pieces that add up to 1, or 100 per cent. A number of different solutions has been suggested to the bargaining problem – cooperative as well as non-cooperative solutions (Binmore, 1994, 1998). Determinate solutions to the bargaining problem can be had, but only by assuming complete knowledge.

Cooperation in human affairs appears difficult when it is modelled with the above-mentioned games. Thus, the PD game entails defection undoing agreements, the chicken game favours threat, which may destroy mutual gain, and the battle of the sexes models bargaining as a struggle that may lead the negotiators to nil. Let us look at the assurance game (Table 4.5), which models human cooperation as basically peaceful and capable of attaining

Table 4.4 The battle of the sexes

Player A	Player B	
	Dinner	Tennis
Dinner	5, 1	0, 0
Tennis	0, 0	1, 5

Table 4.5 Assurance game

	Player B	
Player A	Floppies	Hard discs
Floppies	1, 1	0, 0
Hard discs	0, 0	2, 2

Pareto-optimal outcomes. Yet even here there is a minor coordination problem.

Coordination may appear innocuous in assurance situations. However, there may be a failure to coordinate, as communication disturbances may lead to one player to choose floppies, while the other opts for hard discs. Suppose that one player has a special preference for floppies and is known to be stubborn. Then the other player should settle for the Pareto inferior outcome, but will that occur?

Coordination failures with mixed strategy Nash equilibria

When there is no pure Nash equilibrium strategy, then the players will fail to coordinate, one chasing the other. Consider the game known as the Samaritan's problem (Table 4.6). Here there is coordination failure in the *weak* sense that no pure strategy exists, each strategy pair being dominated by another strategy pair. The only way to break the infinite regress that is contained in this game is to play a mixed strategy.

Player A:

$$2p + 1(1 - p) = 3p$$
$$p = p + 1 = 3p$$
$$1 = 2p$$
$$p = 1/2$$

Payoff: $(1/5) \times 3 + -1 \times 4/5 = -1/5$.

Table 4.6 The Samaritan's problem

	Player B	
Player A	Work	Loaf
Work	3, 2	−1, 3
Loaf	−1, 1	0, 0

Player B:

$$3q + -1(1 - q) = -1q$$
$$3q - 1 + q = -q$$
$$5q = 1$$
$$q = 1/5$$

Payoff: $(1/2) \times 2 + (1/2) \times 1 = 3/2$.

Again we may establish that a cooperative solution (3, 2) is Pareto superior to the mixed strategy Nash solution. But how can the players coordinate on this cooperative solution? Consider a version of the chicken game in Table 4.7, the civic duty game, or who is to call the fire services when they smell smoke. If the two players choose mixed strategies in the civic duty game, then they cannot always avoid the worst outcome (0, 0). A correlated strategy such as always one player calling would be a Pareto improvement, but how is such an agreement to be struck between two players who both would prefer not to call? Side-payments? And who would enforce the agreement?

Table 4.7 The civic duty game

	Player B	
Player A	Ignore	Telephone
Ignore	0, 0	10, 7
Telephone	7, 10	7, 7

To sum up

The most elementary forms of human interaction, besides conflict – which, as a zero sum game, will not be considered here – present the possibility of several forms of coordination failures. The loss to the players involved could be so substantial due to coordination failures that they would seek cooperative solutions to their interaction problems. But cooperation is only generally feasible when the players accept so-called correlated strategies, meaning that there would exist a third-party brokering an agreement. Government, Hobbes suggested, is the best candidate available for constituting this third-party mediator and enforcer. I will call this third party the 'enforcer'. Employing the insights from game theory, how would one model government, policy-making and implementation from the perspective of rationality?

The state: arena and organisation

The public sector may be conceptualised as both an arena and a set of organisations. To a certain extent the public sector has a structure similar to that of the private sector, where markets constitute the arenas and the firms are the organisations in action. In a democratic political system this distinction between arena and organisations becomes more relevant than in an authoritarian regime, where choices are made by some dictatorial mechanism. *Arena* and *organisations* – this is the distinction, the relevance of which I will pursue here.

The distinction between arena and players has been well researched in the private sector. Thus, the equilibrium theory of the market according to a Walrasian framework has been complemented recently by a new theory of the firm, or economic organisation theory (Ménard, 1997). Understanding the market is one thing; explaining why economic actors organise themselves as firms is another. Firm organisation relies upon hierarchy, which is a different principle from the guiding idea of the market, namely competition. The market is an arena for firms to act upon according to the principle of the Walrasian auctioneer, but firm organisation derives its logic from contracting, especially principal–agent interaction (Mudambi and Ricketts, 1997; Ricketts, 2003).

The public sector, or the making and implementation of policy in a democracy, may be approached by means of the same distinction: arena *versus* players. Thus, the democratic polity offers the rules of the democratic game or an institutionalised arena for competition between policies. Democracy offers a process of decision-making through which policies are selected or enacted. The system of public administration is responsible for the implementation of policies. Corresponding to markets and firms in the public sector there would be democratic politics on the one hand and public organisation on the other. This way of looking at arena and players breaks with the traditional and much criticised distinction between politics and administration.

The distinction between arena and players is different from the traditional separation between politics and administration. When politics was separated from administration, this distinction was translated into the following opposites:

1   values against technology;
2   preferences against information;
3   enactment of decisions against execution of decisions;
4   subjectivity against value neutrality;
5   goals against means.

Scholars who, like Waldo, rejected the politics–administration separation, argued that distinctions 1–5 presented two difficulties when applied to politics and administration. First, these distinctions themselves were analytical at best and practically useless at worst, as any radical separation between ends and means, values and knowledge, and enactment and execution is likely to be impossible in real life. Second, even if these distinctions could really be upheld, these scholars would simply argue that there was no valid reason for equating politics entirely with values, preferences, enactment, ends and subjectivity, whereas administration would be made up of technology, information, execution, neutrality and means. There was no way the politics–administration separation could meet with acceptance among these scholars, regarding the distinction as a Weberian aberration into rationality. Either there was no foundation for these separations, or distinctions 1–5 could not be applied to politics and administration.

Politics as the arena of policy-making

In a democracy, politics works like a decision-making arena where players meet and exchange policy proposals or ideas. The basic rules of the democratic game guarantee competition and openness. Participation is not restricted to political parties, as civil society may be involved, as well as the bureaucracy. The key question when politics is conceived as an arena is whose preferences in relation to policy-making will prevail.

Politics can deliver stable policies according to spatial modelling, meaning policies which are backed by a sufficient majority (Tsebelis, 2002). Politics can also stage a policy process where policies come and go, i.e. cycling. Politics tends to deliver stable outputs when policies can be placed according to one single dimension, such as left/right in legislation or more/less spending in terms of budget-making. When there is no single dimension involved or perhaps more than one dimension involved, then policy outputs will be far less predictable (Shepsle and Bonchek, 1997).

In democratic politics or decisions about policies there could exist so-called Condorcet winners; these would be the first-best winners, as they could not be defeated by any other proposal. The party system and lobbying may enhance the making of first-best policies. When the party system is based on the left–right scale, as with a two-party system, then Condorcet winners should be identifiable. Lobbying may actually help identify Condorcet winners, as interest groups can only bring pressure if they have muscle, meaning broad-based support. In a multiparty system, Condorcet winners are more difficult to pick or identify, especially under log-rolling. The political arena in a democracy operates like a competitive market where political parties look for support for their policies and interest groups correct the outputs in accordance with their economic weights. However, policies also need to be implemented, thus some form of public organisation is necessary.

Public organisation as the implementation of policy

Implementation starts when policies have been decided upon. The policy-makers need to put together many teams of people to get their policies implemented. This sets up the principal–agent games which form the core object of analysis of this volume. Nothing could be more erroneous than labelling the implementation of policies an apolitical business or mere administration. The implementation of policies is not a value-neutral task where only technology matters. Actually, public organisation for the provision of services includes political deliberations concerning a number of alternative forms of service production.

The public sector is populated by many organisations implementing the decisions of the political authorities. In the business part of the public sector, financed with user fees, one encounters the traditional public enterprise as well as the new public joint-stock company. In the soft sector, mainly financed with taxes, the general mode of organising people and resources has been the bureaucracy. However, one finds increasingly alternative forms of service provision to the bureaucracy, namely the policy network and the tendering/bidding model (NPM). In public regulation, the agency or board has been employed as a form of organisation. Each of these modes of public organisation involves two things:

- selection of CEOs – a principal–agent problem;
- putting together of a team under the CEO – again a principal–agent problem.

Logically, one may approach public organisation as a two-stage game: first, the choice of a CEO and second, his/her selection of a crew doing the job involved in service provision. In reality, the crew may come before the pilots. In any case, public organisation has two principal–agent problems that must be resolved, one CEO problem and another team problem.

Public sector reform in the 1990s and early twenty-first century has shown much ingenuity in solving the above two problems with many experiments with public organisation. The problems of public organisation appear in all forms of government: central, regional and local. They have to be resolved under the restriction of a rule-of-law framework in a constitutional democracy. Typically, the judicial organisations of the state (courts) adhere to a strict bureaucratic form of organisation. It is in the field of the provision of services under the executive branch that the experiments with new forms of organisation are to be found. I shall mention the basic types of political organisation in a well-ordered society before I analyse the two main problems of public organisation stated above.

Political organisation: three basic types

Political organisation tended towards legal–rational authority in the modern age, according to the classical Jellinek–Kelsen analysis of the state. The state is the legal embodiment of legal–rational authority. It proved to be superior to other forms of authority such as traditional or charismatic authority.

Thus, the world harbours a large number of political organisations built upon the basis of legal–rational authority, often institutionalised in a formal constitution that is more or less enforced. We will distinguish three different kinds of such political organisations.

Unitary states

First, there is the set of unitary states. This is a large set of political organisations, comprising more than one hundred states, including a few very small ones, e.g. Iceland and Luxembourg, but also a giant state, mainland China. Unitary states may be either centralised or decentralised, depending on the structure of competences, as well as the allocation of financial powers. Although there is a great emphasis on equality under the law in unitary states, one finds many examples of special administrative decentralisation or the devolution of powers to special areas – home rule.

It has been argued that extensive devolution or regional autonomy within a unitary state implies a federal or semi-federal organisation of the state. This is a very questionable hypothesis, as decentralisation regionally or locally can be quite in agreement with a unitary framework. The basic difference with a federal organisation is that the status of the regions and the provinces are derived from central government decision and not from a theory of states' rights. The regions and the localities, however much autonomy they may possess in terms of decisions and finances, derive their existence from the centre, as in Spain.

Federal states

Second, we have the smaller set of federal states, which may be delineated in somewhat different ways, depending on how a federation is identified. The federal set of political organisations is also very heterogeneous, consisting of some of the largest states in the world but also a few extremely tiny states. The borderline between unitary and federal states is clear when legal criteria are employed, but becomes fluid and rather imprecise when behavioural criteria are used, such as financial decentralisation or the existence of semi-autonomous regions.

It is apparent that some federal states perform well according to standard performance criteria, such as democracy or democratic stability. But it is also true that quite a few federal states underperform (Nigeria, Argentina) or are to be regarded as politically unstable (Pakistan) or even authoritarian (United Arab Emirates). Could one explain this riddle of federalism, or that federal states perform so extremely differently, with the simple distinction between real federalism and paper federalism?

Federalism outlines a special discourse in which politics is discussed among a set of players. Thus, its legal discourse consists of a set of distinct notions which mark federal states off from unitary states and confederations.

Yet the crucial question is whether this discourse is merely words or also a political reality. Thus, the key distinctions of federalism must be enforced, which would at least, as far as federalism entails, guarantee that the country performs well. But why, then, do some federal states manage to put federal institutions in place, whereas others fail miserably in enforcement, although they have a written federal constitution?

In the set of federal states the key distinction is between those states which respect their written federal constitution and those states which are mere paper federalist. Paper federalism occurs quite often, as when the real constitution emerges through practice that is in flat violation of the written federal framework. The formal constitution may outline a logical distribution of public competencies onto the federal government and the state governments. Or it may set up a scheme for collaboration between the federal government and the state governments. Yet the reality may be that power is monopolised in a hidden mechanism that transcends the federal distinction between the federation and the states, such as a ruling party, or a ruling family, the army or a charismatic leader.

Federalism claims in its most radical version that a federalist framework operates best for any political organisation. Thus, it offers a basic explanatory model of how a political organisation can work or should operate in an optimal manner. The advantage of federalism is derived from its contractual basis, meaning that two or more parties can federate through a pact and define what goals they wish to promote through rational endeavours. If one believes in rational choice, then federations offer an attractive choice opportunity in relation, for instance to war and peace or with regard to economic integration or social heterogeneity. Thus, Australia was federated partly as a function of the growing Japanese threat, and Western European federalist efforts have been driven by the promise of economic gains through customs union, the internal market and the monetary union. Switzerland harbours the pure type of a dualist federation based on excessive heterogeneity.

The disadvantage of a federalist framework derives from the tensions it inserts into the political system. At least one of the following three problems tends to be found in a federation:

- *States' rights:* When will the constituent parts of a federation feel that they want it no more and what can they do about it?
- *Cultural heterogeneity:* Is a federation between two or more nations or peoples really sustainable in the long run?
- *Money, benefits and costs:* Can a union achieve an equitable distribution of benefits and costs, given the ever-mounting pressure from regional inequalities?

Some federal states have shown that they can handle the uncertainties that derive from these tensions. Other federations have succumbed to them or responded with non-federal practices emerging in a hidden fashion.

IGOs or confederations

Third, there is the set of international organisations, the intergovernmental organizations (IGOs) or confederations. One may raise the question of what kind of political organisation they amount to, but it is clear that they do not qualify as states. Political organisation covers a large number of these intergovernmental bodies, which may be characterised as clubs or as coordination mechanisms. Confederations are often described as less capable of action than states, unitary or federal ones. However, a few IGOs have proved to be very capable of action, for instance the North Atlantic Treaty Organisation (NATO), the International Monetary Fund (IMF) and the World Bank (WB).

It is the development of the EU that has made the borderline between federations and confederations all but transparent and precise. The concepts of flexibility and variable geometry developed with the Union have shown that political organisation may comprise elements from entirely different logics. International organisations have become increasingly relevant, as states set up coordination mechanisms to which they delegate decisions and resources. Some of these coordination mechanisms are global (WB, IMF, WTO), whereas others are regional (EU, NAFTA, ASEAN – Association of Southeast Asian Nations). The many non-governmental organizations (NGOs) are placed in civil society.

The basic logic of public organisation

According to the economic theory of the private firm, the key organising principle is the minimisation of transaction costs, given the objective of producing a product or service. Acknowledging all the difficulties in conceptualising and measuring transaction costs, this Coase–Williamson approach to private organisation as transaction cost minimising has accomplished a deeper understanding of how entrepreneurs put together teams of people to work for them. Transaction costs affect the choice of alternative forms of contracting, from the simple work contract to the complex forms of contract in the joint-stock companies (Ouchi and Barney, 1987; Buckley and Michie, 1996). What, then, accounts for the basic forms of public organisation?

In a well-ordered society the population is to be regarded as the principal of the state. This democratic principle implies that government in all its forms must be capable of being held accountable to the people in various forms. Using the principal–agent framework in the analysis of the public sector, the focus must be on how the norm of accountability is translated and inserted into all the forms of public organisation.

Public policy is the hallmark of the state, as government is called upon to deliver in relation to its principal, the population, in a democratic system.

Governments receive legitimacy in elections by promising to conduct a range of public policies. To fulfil the terms of the electoral contract, government must turn to agents who implement the policies. The central question in public management and public administration is how to organise these teams of agents. One key concern is accountability, especially for a democratic regime, whilst another chief concern would be merit and efficiency, or the competence of the teams.

Public sector reform during the last 20 years has changed public organisation fundamentally. One may raise the question of whether policies have changed to the same extent. In any case, the interest in public organisation has been manifested in the search for efficiency, either internal (productivity) or external (effectiveness). It is believed that the traditional forms of public organisation are not productive or effective enough. Thus, there has been a strong search for alternative modes of organisation in order to improve upon how public teams work and what they accomplish.

The present situation displays so much organisational variety that it is almost impossible to find any common denominator among all the kinds of organisational forms now employed for public service delivery. Government in the post-modern society displays organisations' heterogeneity and little of organisational isomorphism. However, there is one core aspect of public organisation that cannot be changed, namely that accountability must be satisfied by any and all forms of public organisation. Hence, public organisation in a rule-of-law state is driven by the principle of accountability maximising, whether it is a matter of political, legal or financial accountability.

Public organisation is institutionally embedded. Various countries have had different legal frameworks in place to guide the public teams operating in their public sectors. Yet, despite all institutional variety, one may speak of two classical public organisations, namely:

- the bureau
- the public enterprise.

Public sector reform has shattered these two ideal-types, replacing the simple structure of a division between authorities and enterprises with a complex carpet of organisational forms and mixtures. The new organisational forms have been introduced together with changes in funding and budgeting. It is an open question whether these new organisational structures perform better than the above two classical models. This is a question for evaluation in relation to the implementation of various policies under alternative organisational forms within public sector reform.

Scholars examining the organisational reforms of the 1990s use a variety of labels to describe what has taken place, but they all agree on the managerial bias in the reforms. The new managerialism has meant that the traditional forms of public organisation have been abandoned in the search for more flexible arrangements. Thus, public organisation now displays a variety of other structures:

- networks
- public–private partnerships
- public joint-stock companies
- purchaser–provider teams
- trusts
- executive agencies
- independent commissioners.

Nowhere has this organisational heterogeneity been pushed further than in the UK, where the state has been almost petrified since the advent of Thatcherism – plural government. The reinventing government (Osborne and Gaebler, 1992) message in the United States was influential in directing public sector reform towards market mechanisms and it did change the bureaucracies towards a flatter structure.

Public sector reform has tried to change the governance mechanisms in government, especially in the provision of services, but also within social security. The guiding principles include:

- market testing of public teams;
- outsourcing;
- separation of policy and implementation;
- removal of hierarchy;
- contracting in;
- individual salaries;
- performance or outcome measurement;
- incorporation.

No country in the OECD set has been spared from reforms inspired by these ideas about the necessity and desirability of public sector reform, often labelled 'NPM'. But there are major country differences in how con- sistently these ideas have been pushed through. One may speak of an Anglo-Saxon model that harbours these new ideas, as they were put in practice in New Zealand, Australia and the UK with particular consistency. But they have also received much attention in other countries, e.g. the Scandinavian ones.

One may debate whether there is one coherent model of public sector reform to be labelled NPM. Perhaps it is more accurate to speak of alternative governance models, where NPM is merely *one* model and not *the* model for the provision of public services. In reality the public sector now comprises several models of organisation and often mixtures between these. What needs to be discussed, however, is how various forms of public organisation perform with the key rods of measurement, namely accountability and merit. What, then, is public or political accountability?

Accountability

A state in a Rawlsian well-ordered society faces the fundamental principle of accountability, without which no democracy or rule of law is possible. Dictionaries give the key meaning of accountability as being called to answer for what has happened or what goes on. The *Oxford English Dictionary* states:

1   The quality of being accountable; liability to give account of, and answer for, discharge of duties or conduct; responsibility, amenableness.
2   Liable to be called to account, or to answer for responsibilities and conduct; answerable, responsible. Chiefly of persons (to a person, for a thing).

When one accounts for something, then one has responsibilities, which constitute the bedrock of holding someone accountable. *The American Heritage Dictionary* mentions as synonyms 'responsible' and 'explicable':

1   Accountable: Liable to being called to account; answerable. That can be explained: an accountable phenomenon.
2   Unaccountable: 1. Impossible to account for; inexplicable: unaccountable absences. 2. Free from accountability; not responsible: an executive unaccountable to anyone.
3   Responsible: 1. As of one's actions or of the discharge of a duty or trust. 2. Involving personal accountability or ability to act without guidance or superior authority.

The opposite of accountability is arbitrariness or irresponsibility, which is completely unacceptable in any public organisation in a well-ordered society. Herein lies the difference with the private sector, where accountability has a limited range of application. After all, a person has the right to conduct his/her own business. Thus, he/she is accountable to no one.

Public organisation maximises accountability, whereas private organisation minimises transaction costs. However, accountability is not the sole concern in the public sector, when the implications of rule of law are spelled out. Besides accountability, merit counts in public organisation. It is not enough that the public teams – the agents – as well as the government – the principal – act under a variety of accountability norms, be they political, legal or economic norms. They must also be capable of producing outputs in relation to the population – merit. Whatever balance is stuck between accountability and merit, it still holds that the principal–agent nature of public administration and public management captures the requirement of both accountability and merit.

Macro and micro rationality and the non-profit organisations

The argument presented here is basically that questioning the possibility of comprehensive or holistic rational policy-making as outlined by, for instance Dror (1971), which does not entail the rejection of the rational choice model when it comes to the understanding of the behaviour of the choice participants. Micro rationality seems much more plausible than macro rationality. Employing the neoclassical decision model, how is one to explain the voluntary sector, for example?

The voluntary sector in the economy and in society, however difficult it may be to pin it down and locate its borders with the private sector and the public sector, needs to receive attention when public management is examined. Dollery and Wallis's *The Political Economy of the Voluntary Sector* (2003) makes a very ambitious attempt to answer the key questions about this not so well-known sector, including: What is a voluntary organisation? How does such an organisation operate? What functions does it fulfil? If one starts from a clear set of parsimonious assumptions about human beings – the economic decision model – then one may ask the perfectly legitimate question: Why voluntary organisations in the first place?

Voluntary organisations can only exist or be forthcoming if some people want them and other people supply them – this is an excellent starting-point for theorising the behaviour involved here. Voluntary organisations would handle goods or services that markets or governments do not provide – the failure theory. The search for a theory of non-profit organisations (NPOs) is part of the extension of economic analysis in two directions: (1) Explanation of non-economic or non-market organisations; (2) Inclusion of non-egoistic motivation such as altruism and social capital. Dollery and Wallis's own contribution to understanding the NPOs is an emphasis on the relevance of leadership. They thus complement the economic approach underlining asymmetric information and public goods. Applying Schumpeter's concept of the entrepreneur, NPOs flourish with the quality of their leadership, which is conducive to trust in the work of such organisations as well as in the willingness of donators to support them. Leadership is what makes NPOs work, undoing market failure and supplementing government services. But it is a leadership of a special kind: inspirational leadership or the leadership of hope and altruism in relation to stakeholders' commitments, the understanding of which leads from the narrow economic model of choice into the sociology of social capital and the politics of managing people, stakeholders and relationships. Despite all the economic imperialism and economic revisionism there is more to political economy than utility maximisation. Public policy towards NPOs can only be understood through an interdisciplinary study combining economics, business administration and political science. Following the research by Coleman (1988a,b) on education and by Putnam *et al.* (1994) on civic participation and institutional performance, there has been a burst of research during the last decade by mainstream economists, political scientists and sociologists into the link between various definitions and indicators of social capital and regional and national variations in economic, social and political performance. The emerging body of theory links the fields of economics, sociology and political science toward the view that economic activity does not occur in a vacuum, but rather within a broader social and institutional environment. Social capital theory, along with the leadership theories augments the basic framework that has shaped economic discussion of the role the voluntary sector plays in a mixed economy. The theme of voluntary associations in the public sector may be linked up with the idea of associational democracy (Hirst, 1994).

The political economy of the voluntary sector is one of a range of subject areas enriched by social capital theory – along with families and youth behaviour; schooling and education; work and organisations; democracy and governance; collective action; public health and environment; crime and violence; and economic development. Network interaction reinforces the norms of reciprocity and social trust, which constitute civic social capital, and exerts a strong influence on the relationship government agencies have with the voluntary sector. The strength of governance in a particular locality depends on the quality of the relationship government agencies can forge with voluntary agencies. These agencies have demonstrated a capacity, in certain cases, to function as effective bridging organisations that can facilitate the formation of network linkages between local communities and external agencies in countries with relatively weak institutions of governance.

Conclusion

Public organisation in a well-ordered society is chosen when the society wishes to maximises accountability. The overriding concern is not minimising transaction costs as with private organisation, but the maximisation of accountability. Many of the typical features of public organisation – legality, separation of power, rights, redress and complaint – originate in this fundamental requirement of public organisation, the accountability norm. However, there is one major restriction upon accountability, as public organisations are also supposed to deliver goods and services – the efficiency norm.

The great puzzle in the theory of public organisation is how accountability and merit interrelate in the public sector. Speaking generally, one may argue that the public administration tradition emphasises the relevance of formal accountability as the organising principle in the public sector, whereas the public management school underlines the implications of efficiency for public organisation. One may conceive of the relationship between accountability and merit in three ways: supporting, conflictual and restraining. I will argue that accountability and merit support each other up to a certain level when a further increase in the accountability of the organisation decreases the efficiency of the organisation. Merit increases the capacity of the public team to deliver but also makes it less accountable to the political principal.

The distinction between politics and administration has been a dogma that has long hampered the analysis of public organisation. It is impossible to separate out politics and restrict it to some part of the public sector. Instead, one should speak about *arena* and *player*. Thus, policy-making in a democracy takes place within the state as the arena for competition between various players such as politicians, parties, civil society, interest organisations and the bureaucracy. Policy implementation on the other hand requires public organisation, which boils down to solving two principal–agent problems: (1) selecting the CEOs; (2) setting up a team. These two main problems in public management have to be solved by respecting the restrictions derived from the rule-of-law framework. Whatever form of public organisation is chosen:

- classical bureaucracy trading department;
- traditional public enterprise – regulatory agency or board;
- joint-stock company;
- outsourcing;
- internal market – executive agencies;
- public–private partnership;
- statutory agency;
- policy networks,

it has to satisfy the norm of public accountability in a well-ordered society. At the same time the public organisation must score high on merit in order to be capable of delivering goods and services effectively. But accountability and merit cannot be jointly maximised. Let us look at the trade-off outlined within public administration. The basic point underlined in this chapter is that alternative institutional arrangements are best analysed with the PAF. Public organisation differs from private organisation, as it evolves under the successive accomplishment of its two core norms: accountability (rule of law) and merit (efficiency). Whereas private organisation may be analysed as an evolution towards the minimisation of transaction costs, the logic of public organisation is a different one entirely, which is to be modelled as a series of principal–agent games below.

5 The essence of public administration: legality and rule of law

Introduction

The most well-known and concise analysis of public administration is Max Weber's theory of authority or legitimate domination. It comes in two versions, both reprinted in his *Economy and Society* (1978). Thus, there is one short version and another long version, both eminently worth reading and both adhering to the special Weber style of arguing, i.e. a parsimonious set of ideal-types as theory, and collecting around these pure models massive empirical information about rulerships in various civilisations.

The basic hypothesis in Weber's theory of authority is that modern states tend to be based on legal authority. All systems of authority require legitimacy, and the modern state derives its legitimacy from the notion of legality. According to Weber, this is the same as rational authority. Legal rules creating a framework for political authority may be enacted in a formally written-down constitution, which requires an enactment, i.e. a rational action. Weber's opposite of legal–rational authority is traditional authority, which could not possibly be rational. The third kind of authority – charismatic authority – is the transitional stage between irrational and rational authority. It can only be a temporary phenomenon, but it breaks once and for all the spell of tradition and opens up the possibility of installing rational authority once the charismatic leader is gone.

The purpose of this chapter is to discuss more specifically what legal–rational authority amounts to. Approaching the states of the twenty-first century with Weber's framework consisting of only three major categories, one faces the question of how to separate between democracies and authoritarian regimes. The problem is the specification of legal–rational authority, which may mean only legality. Or there could be much more content packed into this notion, such as the rule of law and democracy. Given a strong preference for a 'thick' concept of legal–rational authority, interpreted as the rule of law, I will end up discussing the Hayek argument that the rule-of-law regime always derives from so-called spontaneous orders.

A thin legal concept of legal–rational authority

In fact, Weber had very little to say about modern states as they appeared when he did his research, i.e. around 1900. To him, bureaucracy was the core of the modern state and he presented his famous ideal-type of the bureau as the incarnation of modern government. But could not the modern authoritarian or totalitarian government also employ the model of the perfect bureaucracy when governing their countries? We have here a basic puzzle in relation to understanding Weber and how he looked upon classifying various modern states.

When one reads a number of expositions on Weber, one gets the impression that many commentators believe that Weber identified legal–rational authority with democracy or rule of law. Thus, modern government would be to Weber not only rational but also constitutional government, meaning a kind of democratic regime. However, this is hardly a plausible interpretation of Weber. It also fails to do justice to the variety of modern governments in the world where constitutional democracies make up less than 50 per cent of the states.

A key principle in public administration is the notion of legality or rule by law, meaning the requirement that government action is based upon rules empowering governments to act. There must be a law that either permits the government to act or obliges the government to act. Without such a law, government action would be arbitrary. This may seem highly plausible, but what, more precisely, is contained in the principle of legality? The principle of legality may be related to Weber's theory of authority. One of his three categories – legal–rational authority – focuses on the employment of rules in government. Political authority is modern or rational, according to Weber, when its legitimacy is based upon a belief that it is exercised in accordance with rules that are laid down in laws of one kind or another. It has been argued that legal–rational authority is the same as rule of law, or the *Rechtsstaat*. However, I will argue that one needs to add more to the principle of legality in order to arrive at the constitutional state.

Weber argued that the modern state will be based upon legal–rational authority. However, this does not imply that he predicted somehow the victory of the constitutional democracy. An authoritarian regime can be based upon legal–rational authority, like for instance China today or like a semi-democratic regime such as Singapore. Discussing what Weber meant by legal–rational authority brings us back to his notion of legitimacy as the only foundation of stable government authority. Perhaps Weber underestimated the capacity of the modern state to sustain itself on the basis of naked power, as with Iraq? In any case, Weber's legal–rational authority is not the same Kant's *Rechtsstaat*.

What is legitimacy?

Weber anticipated modern institutionalism as he underlined the contribution of rules to channelling the actual processes of behaviour. However, formal or written rules in themselves do not determine anything. It is when they condition behaviour that institutions become crucial for the operation of social systems, e.g. government. Rules exert an especially strong influence upon behaviour when they are considered to be legitimate. Legitimacy was to Weber simply a moral feeling that things move according to rules that are binding. Naked power could not possibly be considered binding. Only tradition, charismatic belief or legality could afford legitimacy. What needs to be discussed here is the basis of legitimacy in the legal order. Will legality always result in constitutionalism, or the limitation of power in accordance with a formally enacted constitution? Why could not the constitution sanction an authoritarian regime?

I wish to separate various elements in the concept of legal–rational authority. It is like a multi-element rocket where the basis is merely the existence of formally introduced and enacted rules that are considered binding. Could these rules deviate from constitutionalism or the doctrine of limited government? The institutionalisation of political life would be transaction cost saving, but the general rules guiding behaviour need not endorse a liberal state in a wide sense of liberalism (Rawls, 1993). Without rules, political authority would become arbitrary. There would have to be constant decision-making in relation to each new case, which would destroy predictability in social life. And power would have to be concentrated to a junta. Here is the first point of Weber: political authority must be based upon rules.

Governance without institutions would not only become arbitrary rule. It would also defeat itself. The most telling evidence for this insight is the Solzhenitsyn story *One Day in the Life of Ivan Denisovich* (Solzhenitsyn, 2000, 2002) about the Gulag, the prison camps in Siberia during the Soviet Union period. When the guardians harassed the prisoners, Ivan successfully filed complaint after complaint for these violations of the rules. The guardians had to be punished because otherwise the system, however inhuman, would not work.

Weber's second point is that the governance rules will only direct behaviour if they are considered binding, i.e. legitimate. Norms that are legitimate are more easily enforced – this is the idea. Using sanctions all the time to enforce norms would again be too time-consuming or transaction cost heavy. Although I have already stated a reservation in relation to this second point, Weber probably underestimating the role of the political repression (naked power) as well as its contribution, I will accept the point here.

Finally, Weber's third point was that the legitimacy of governance norms could only have three possible sources: tradition, charismatic belief, legislation. This is not the place or occasion to dispute this elegant theory, which embraces the history of human civilisations in its entirety. It is in effect an extremely parsimonious framework for classifying a wide variety of ruler-ships. The key question here is whether the third source of legitimacy – the rational enactment of a legal order guiding the exercise of political power – must generate a liberal constitution, democracy and the rule of law. Could there be something like rational authoritarianism?

A repressive regime need not be based upon tradition or charisma. It could be rationally instituted. The twentieth century has witnessed numerous authoritarian constitutions, enacted by representative assem-blies. It may well be the case that these regimes sooner or later degenerated into naked power or blunt repression by the police and the military, meaning that these regimes became arbitrary and thus unstable. But it still remains true that rational authoritarianism could be legitimate as, for instance, in the Muslim world.

Only half of the states of the world adhere to constitutionalism, or the doctrine of limited government. The other half display a mixture of politi-cal regimes, some of which have degenerated into naked power or civil war. Yet, we also find countries with stable authoritarian government, such as China, Arab countries and Cuba. One may argue that these countries are in reality not politically stable and that they are based upon the threat of naked power. However, denying any legitimacy to these regimes would imply that the concept of legitimacy has been restricted already from the outset.

'Legitimacy' may mean merely the same as 'considered binding'. Or it may also connote 'morally binding' in a systematic ethical sense. Perhaps authoritarianism is never ethically justifiable, but the point here is merely that people have as a matter of fact regarded rational authoritarianism as binding upon them. In fact, authoritarian regimes with a basis in legal–rational authority are to be found in several countries in the Arab world and in Asia. One may, however, question whether they are truly legitimate, as it is not entirely easy to distinguish between *actual* legitimacy and *ethical* legitimacy.

Let us now attempt to unpack the notion of legal–rational authority, using the multi-element rocket model, beginning with mere legality in order to add more and more elements before we arrive at the model of a complete constitutional democracy. Weber had a thin conception in mind – rule by law – but nothing prevents one from launching a thick conception.

Legality

Possibly the clearest exposition of the principle of legality in systems of political authority is to be found in *The Pure Theory of Law* (Kelsen, 1997). The legal order underlying legal authority may be approached as a rationally constructed system of norms, which as an ideal-type is logi-cally coherent. Kelsen showed that such a system is possible, given that one assumes the existence of a basic norm, from which the validity of all other norms flows downward in a hierarchy of norms, from the constitution over the ordinary statute laws to the executive regulations and internal instructions of bureaux.

The Kelsen model of the legal order is an interesting explication of the idea of legality. It may not be a realistic model of the legal system of a country, which tends to display inconsistencies and multiple bases, thus flatly denying the Kelsen idea of one basic norm (Harris, 1997; Simmonds, 2002). It is very much at odds with prevailing conceptions of law stemming from the common law tradition (Posner, 1990, 1999, 2001). We cannot enter here into the debate about the pros and cons of the two major approaches to law – the common law and the civil law frameworks – but we may use the Kelsen model, which is anchored in the civil law tradition, to clarify the concept of legality in the state (Kelsen, 1999).

Kelsen's model of pure law focuses on the hierarchy of norms, or that specific logical relationship which obtains when one higher norm validates another lower norm (Kelsen, 2000). Take the example of administrative law. At the lowest level of the administrative hierarchy one finds the internal regulations issued by the local authority. These regulations are sanctioned by a special administrative law, which in turn is validated by the legislative powers of the national assembly. Finally, there is the constitution or basic norm, which confers legislative powers upon this assembly. Legality is this logical entailment between two norms. That is basically all there is to this notion. It follows that an authoritarian regime may satisfy the criterion of legality. A constitution may introduce a basic norm which is authoritarian, according to which the country in question may then be governed. It may be the case that such a regime will sooner or later deviate from its own legality and start using naked power, resulting in arbitrary rule. But one cannot in principle deny legality to an authoritarian constitution like the one-party state in Africa, the Arab state, or government in mainland China.

One telling example is Iran. The first modern constitution in this country was introduced in 1906 in an attempt to create a constitutional monarchy that would replace traditional rule with the Shah. However, political turmoil and foreign intervention worked against any stable solution. The last Shah made an attempt to rule in a patrimonial manner, leading to the revolt of the Mullahs. Khomeini took power under charismatic legitimacy, which, however, can never be transmitted from one person to another. Thus, the Mullahs wrote a formal religious constitution inspired by Shiism. Yet, the legitimacy of the present regime must be considered as based upon legality, at least in combination with charismatic legitimacy derived from Shiism.

The concept of legality is the foundation of the modern state. It introduces legal–rational authority with Weber and creates the hierarchical link between norms as in Kelsen's theory about norms. The basic norm would be the country constitution, from which would flow the variety of statute law, i.e. special administrative law harbouring the public policies of the country, as well as criminal law plus general administrative law governing the bureaucracy and the civil servants. Private law could be influenced by statute law but it always expresses to a large extent judge made law, especially in the common law tradition. Such a modern state may be democratic or authoritarian, depending on other things than mere legality.

Thus, legality as rule *by* law is the first element in building a modern state. I shall move on to analyse the next element, which builds upon legality, namely rights. When rights are enshrined in the constitution and are not merely a façade, then legal–rational authority would restrain the power of the state. The enforcement of rights is a crucial step towards the creation of rule *of* law. When the legal order recognises rights, then the first real limitations are laid down upon the possibility or probability of an authoritarian state. Rights are highly conducive to law's empire (Dworkin, 1998).

Rights

The concept of rights has been much discussed in legal theory. Given the fact that rights figure strongly in legal and political discourse, this is hardly astonishing. Yet the debate over rights concerns deep philosophical problems about the nature of the legal order. Thus, some scholars claim that rights exist like ideals to be implemented in the legal system of each country, whereas other scholars would wish to limit the existence of rights in a country according to some rule of recognition. Finally, one group of scholars looks upon rights as a language that judges or lawyers employ to get things done (Kramer *et al.*, 1998).

It is not only the nature and existence of rights which are debated. Also the kinds of rights that occur in the legal order are discussed. Here we will follow the well-known Hohfeld system of oppositions, outlined in the Appendix. Hohfeld created his system of rights in the early twentieth century by distinguishing between the following four types of rights:

- claims
- privileges
- competences
- immunities.

Hohfeld's argument about rights was that the concept of rights is highly complex as it covers entirely different forms of rights (Hohfeld, 2001). His scheme included both opposition and entailment between these types of rights – see Appendix, Table 5.2. Thus, not only did Hohfeld show that these four kinds of rights are different in nature, but he also disclosed how they relate to each other by opposition and correlates. The theory of human rights covers claims, privileges and immunities. Competences figure prominently in theories of decentralisation, devolution and autonomy, dealing with the rights of public offices in relation to each other, federalism for instance being one such example of a theory of competences. The core of human rights is the set of negative immunities, covering the right to religious freedom, political association, expression and thought, as well as conscience. These rights are inalienable, meaning that government must all the time respect them at all times. One key element in rule of law is the protection of immunities by the courts, such as the *habeas corpus* rights. An immunity as a protected right is the same for all citizens or inhabitants. A privilege is a special right for a person, such as the right to dress as one may wish and to grant benefits to certain people. Human rights also cover the protection of privileges, for instance a libertarian state would have a government which grants lots of privileges. One major part of human rights is positive rights, which constitute claims against the government in a country. Here one may mention education, health and social care as well as income maintenance. Positive human rights cannot be immunities, as they always depend upon the financial capacity or willingness of government to provide these services or resources. Sometimes income maintenance rights are treated as if they were immunities, i.e. they are regarded as entitlements.

A state moves towards the rule of law when government operates under a list of rights, covering all four kinds according to the Hohfeld scheme. A set of immunities, basic human rights and entitlements is often stated in the written constitution, which also outlines the competences of various branches of government. It is, however, an entirely empirical question whether the government really respects the rights in the constitution. A country may practice the rule of law even when it lacks a formally enacted constitution and a bill of rights, like the UK or Australia. Yet, the rule of law entails more than a bill of rights, protected by the Supreme Court (US model) or a Constitutional Court (European model), as there must be separation of powers institutionalised.

Separation of powers

Constitutional government is always and everywhere based upon the doctrine of Montesquieu, stating that political power must be separated along three distinct powers: executive, legislative and judicial. Whenever this occurs, then there is political freedom, predicted Montesquieu. The so-called *trias politica* doctrine may appear as self-evident in relation to the rule-of-law ideal, but the doctrine may be implemented in very different ways.

Presidentialism offers one version of *trias politica*, where the three powers, in this case the national government, the national assembly and the courts, are separated as much as possible; but their competencies tend often to be mixed (Miller, 1994). Thus, executive power may be shared between the president and the legislature, and the president may wield legislative power – 'checks and balances'. Finally, the courts may have the capacity to test legislation and acts of the president for constitutionality – legal review.

Parliamentarism contains a more limited version of *trias politica* than presidentialism, at least in theory, because executive power is linked with the legislature. Thus, no government can persist unless it is at least tolerated by parliament. In reality, many parliamentary systems follow the Montesquieu recommendation to separate the people in executive positions and the people holding legislative positions. For instance, many countries require that parliamentarians who become members of the cabinet leave parliament, or at least that they be replaced by a temporary stand-in. It is true that many parliamentary countries do not recognise the political power of the judicial branch of government to test laws and administrative acts. Where the doctrine of the sovereignty of parliament is strongly entrenched, there the Montesquieu principle of *trias politica* is not that firmly institutionalised. However, there are many examples of countries which combine parliamentarism with an acceptance of legal review.

A constitutional monarchy in Europe was often the first step from despotism towards the rule of law. It put in place a constitutional monarchy where the head of state ruled together with a cabinet and a premier, who depended upon the approval, tacit or active, of parliament. Constitutional developments led to the restriction of the role of the head of state and the confirmation of the power of the premier to govern with the cabinet. Thus, the King or the Queen became a nominal figure besides the Prime Minister. The monarch reigns but does not rule.

Presidential systems came in all shapes, of which only one is close to the *trias politica* model of Montesquieu with a complete separation of powers between the three branches of government (Miller, 1992). The opposite model of true presidentialism is parliamentary presidentialism, where the president is only the head of state with ceremonial functions and the Prime Minister exercises the real executive powers with the confidence or investiture by parliament. Finally, there is mixed presidentialism, where executive powers are shared between the President and the Premier. Following Montesquieu closely, one would be hesitant about calling strong parliamentary regimes based upon the notion of the sovereignty of parliament, where all government members must be members of parliament, systems with a *balanced* separation of powers. The same is perhaps also true of systems where the judicial branch of government becomes a super umpire in politics.

Publicity and redress

Rule of law entails the possibility of correcting mistakes by government agencies. Thus, these agencies must state their decisions publicly so that the people concerned can file a complaint. There must be a reason for a decision, stated officially. Ordinary people have the right to consult their dossiers and must have specific avenues of redress available when the decision is taken. In the philosophy of the *Rechtstaat* with Kant there is an interesting motivation for the requirement of publicness in relation to all actions and doings of government. Kant suggests, interestingly, that a decision that cannot be made public could not possibly qualify as just, since it is probably so bad that it must be hidden. Thus, rule of law and justice requires publicness (Kant, 1994). Publicness is also entailed in the whole approach with citizen complaint and redress, as citizens would need to know the decision as well as its motivation before they could file a complaint or seek redress.

However, countries have different practices in relation to the openness of public decisions, as well as the need to state a motivation for them. The Scandinavian practice of almost complete openness and access to public files stands in stark contrast to the Southern European practice of a lack of publicness. This confrontation between two philosophies of government had to be resolved in the European Union, which settled for the Scandinavian practice.

Public administration has traditionally been very occupied with questions of complaint and redress. Thus, it has focused on the dossier mechanism, i.e. to ensure that all relevant information for the handling of a case is assembled and kept in one file. Whether the file should be accessible to citizens may be debated between different philosophies of government. Certain files (military, espionage, etc.) are classified, meaning that they cannot be opened to the public within a certain time frame. One may view the confrontation between Northern European and Southern European practice as a question about which type of files and how many files should be classified. There are other concerns than merely openness, but the problem is to make a trade-off between the basic principle of publicness on the one hand and other concerns like the protection of state secrets, of sensitive information, etc. on the other.

Legal review

Rule of law does not require legal review, as it only presupposes that citizens or inhabitants have access to procedures for a proper complaint, as well as to the real possibility of redress and compensation, when government has wronged them. Legal review is strong or perhaps even excessive judicial power, as the judicial branch becomes the ultimate umpire concerning the constitutionality of all politics. Thus, the Constitutional Court is turned into a Chamber of Parliament where the final decisions on objectives are laid down. What rule of law imperatively requires is the impartiality of the judges as well as the possibility of stating a complaint or grievance seeking redress against a decision by the public administration. Thus, one needs to distinguish between administrative review and legal review, where only the latter is a strongly politicised procedure where all judges, or a Constitutional Court, test policies or decisions against constitutional documents or a bill of rights, given a certain manner of judicial interpretation.

Setting up administrative review is a complicated business, as a number of different mechanisms are useful. In the civil law tradition one favours the employment of special administrative courts, whereas the common law tradition always underlines the use of ordinary courts, at least in the final resort. When a system of special tribunals is employed, then one may find a rich carpet of various tribunals. When, on the other hand, a system of administrative courts or public law courts is used, then a simple three-level division is often employed, ending with the highest administrative court, often considered as the apex of the whole legal system *(Conseil d'état)*.

Tribunals may be employed in a system of administrative review, which does not recognise a fundamental separation between ordinary courts and administrative courts. This is the case, for instance, in the UK, with its common law tradition, where tribunals are employed in the first instance, but it is the ordinary courts that rule in the last instance. The legal system of the UK also exemplifies the possibility that a common law country does not recognise legal review (Stoner, 1992). Germany exemplifies the other possibility, namely that a civil law tradition with separate civil law and public law courts can be combined with legal review.

The Ombudsman is a special mechanism for administrative review coming out of the Scandinavian legal tradition. It allows far-reaching control of the executive branch of government, although the Ombudsman is not a court. Two versions of the Ombudsman have conquered the world, the Danish version and the Swedish version. In the Copenhagen and Oslo version of the Ombudsman, he/she is chiefly an investigator and reporter to parliament, restricted to the central government and its programmes at the regional or local levels. The Stockholm and Helsinki version is a stronger one where the Ombudsman is a prosecutor besides an investigator and he/she can examine the entire public administration, also the courts. The Ombudsman office has spread around the world and it may occur in both civil law countries and common law countries. There may exist a special Ombudsman for the military branch of government or for gender matters, checking, for instance sexual harassment or discrimination. Wherever the Ombudsman exists, it tends to strongly promote the rule of law.

Within public administration the emphasis is on achieving a high level of rule of law. We will not enter into all the mechanisms that can used for that purpose, as they are well developed within administrative, criminal and constitutional law. The aim in this chapter is to discuss the rationale for emphasising the rule of law in public organisation as within classical public administration. To Weber, legal authority entailed rational government. Rule by means of rules is more effective than rule based upon tradition or religious belief. Does rule of law also enhance policy efficiency? Rule of law or *Rechtsstaat* has been hailed as one of the great institutional achievements of mankind besides democracy and the market economy. The reason is, of course, the value that men and women attach to liberty. Rule of law is conducive to freedom, if not democracy. One may argue though that government should promote equality as well as freedom and that too much rule of law restrains the fulfilment of social objectives such as happiness, well-being and total utility, i.e. efficiency in government. How, then, can one motivate rule of law? Can it at all be rationally fabricated?

The Hayek argument about law and rule of law

Although this book offers a far too limited space for discussing issues in political philosophy, I will bring up one theory of the importance of rule of law and examine it in detail, namely the argument of Friedrich A. Hayek in *Law, Legislation and Liberty* (1982). Here Hayek proposes a full-scale endogenous theory of rule of law, meaning an argument about why men and women would be led to introduce and enforce the institutions of rule of law. If correct, it would explain why rule of law has been given such a pre-eminent place in modern democracies.

It may appear self-evident that a country should opt for rule of law in its legal institutions. After all, it must be the best solution from a normative point of view, recommended strongly by, for example Kant. The modern state would act in conformity with general rules and be bound by these rules which restrict its power – government under the laws. Government under the laws would fulfil strong moral demands for predictability, impartiality and publicity, as Kant conceived of these maxims in his *Die Metaphysik der Sitten* (1994). However, one may approach the question of the nature of the state and rule of law in an entirely different manner, which is actually what Hayek did in his legal–political writings.

Hayek examined rule of law by asking how it emerged and what would guide men and women to adopt it. The tenet of his argument is that rule of law emerged as a 'spontaneous order', or as the result of collective wisdom and not individual rationality. This is an evolutionary theory which Hayek used with success in accounting for the spread of the market. But it is really equally applicable when accounting for the orientation of the modern state towards the ideal of rule of law? I shall quote a typical section from Hayek and ask if the argument suggested here also applies to rule of law:

> Man is as much a rule-following animal as a purpose-seeking one. And he is successful not because he knows why he ought to observe the rules which he does observe, or is even capable of stating all these rules in words, but because his thinking and acting are governed by rules which have by a process of selection been evolved in the society in which he lives, and which are thus the product of the experience of generations (1982: 11).

With Hayek the basic concepts or opposites are *rules* against *purpose* as well as *experience* against *reason*. The rules of society are embodied in the legal order which the state enforces. How, then, does Hayek look upon law? His view on law is to be found in his theory of social order. By 'order' Hayek means rules that achieve coordination between human beings, and the key question concerns the origin of these rules. How does an order emerge in society and for society? Hayek employs a sharp distinction between spontaneous order *(kosmos)* and organisation *(taxis)* depending upon whether the order has emerged from within the social system in question or whether the order has been imposed from the outside through design or intention. Hayek regards the market as the best example of a spontaneous order, whereas the planned economy is the worst example of a created order. Now, what is law – spontaneous order or organisation? According to legal positivism, law is mostly organisation but is legal positivism correct (Golding and Edmundson, 2004)? Furthermore, what about the rules which define rule of law – do they follow the logic of spontaneous order or organisation?

Hayek observes spontaneous orders in both nature and in society. He characterises them in the following way, corresponding to the distinction between *taxis* and *kosmos*:

> Most important, however, is the relation of a spontaneous order to the conception of purpose. Since such an order has not been created by an outside agency, the order also can have no purpose, although its existence may be very serviceable to the individuals which move within such order. But in a different sense it may well be said that the order rests on purposive action of its elements, when "purpose" would, of course, mean nothing more than that their actions tend to secure the preservation or restoration of that order (1982: 39).

What is crucial is the absence of purposiveness in the sense of the design of a social mechanism, where there is a goal behind the organisation, a plan of action. Since our focus is on public organisation, especially the legal order, we must now ask whether parts of law establishing the rule of law, like public law or a legal mechanism such as the Ombudsman can be designed or whether they emerge as a spontaneous order. Hayek's basic point is contained in his idea of law as *nomos*, which is entirely different in his view from law conceived as legislation by an authority, for instance parliament. He says about this sharp distinction:

> In the last resort the difference between the rules of just conduct which emerge from the juridical process, the *nomos* or law of liberty . . . and the rules of organisation laid down by authority . . . lies in that the former are derived from the conditions of a spontaneous order which man has not made, while the latter serve the deliberate building of an organisation serving specific purposes (1982: 122–123).

Thus, the legal order of a country has two parts, only one of which constitutes a spontaneous order. This part is basically the same as the common law in the Anglo-Saxon legal tradition, i.e. judge-made law in accordance with the natural precepts of justice laid down in centuries of legal reasoning. But does rule of law show up in *nomos* or in legislation? The principles embodying rule of law could of course stem from either judge-made law or statute law, which is roughly the same distinction as Hayek's separation between *nomos* and legislation. Thus one piece in the argument is missing, namely the conclusion that rule of law belongs to *nomos*. The rules of rule of law accomplish liberty, but how are they to be introduced and enforced? Hayek is led to emphasise that only one kind of law can harbour the institutions of rule of law:

> It has resulted in a frequent interpretation of law as an instrument of organisation for a particular purpose, an interpretation which is of course true of one kind of Law, namely public law, but wholly inappropriate with regard to the *nomos* or lawyer's law (1982: 114).

There is a clear risk here of a mere deductive argument: rule of law accomplishes liberty and only *nomos* secures liberty, thus rule of law must enter *nomos*. We must ask whether this sharp distinction between law that amounts to the discovery of a spontaneous order and law that is the intended invention of an authority or organisation is really applicable to rule of law. To Hayek the equality between public law and lack of freedom is so tight that it must lead to great difficulties for him when it comes to interpreting that part of public law which deals with the rule of law, namely constitutional and general administrative law. To Hayek it is a basic truth that when public law regulation increases, freedom is threatened.

Although Hayek's main aim is to argue against state interference in the economy, he outlines an ideal constitution which can be put in place also in countries without a rule of law tradition. Hayek launches a model constitution which contains institutions that are far from existing written ones and deviate considerably from constitutional practice. It follows through his basic idea of a radical split between law (private law, criminal law) and organisation (public law). Thus, there would be two completely different representative assemblies, one dealing with long-term questions of law and other handling short-term matters of public policy. Besides the general impracticality of this proposal, suggesting that the Upper Chamber would be restricted to special persons, it may be pointed out as a matter of principle that the implementation of the Hayek ideal constitution would require exactly what he wants to undo, namely public law. Actually, the enforcement of the Hayek constitution would require massive public law creation and juridical vigilance in order to maintain it. How, then, could public law be conducive *sui generis* to the kind of authoritarianism that the author of *The Road to Serfdom* from 1944 (Hayek, 2001) always warns of?

Hayek's solution involving two entirely different chambers would require a vigilant court to be enforced. He writes:

> The whole arrangement rests upon the possibility of drawing a sharp distinction between the enforceable rules of just conduct to be developed by the Legislative Assembly and binding the government and citizens alike, and all those rules of the organisation and conduct of government proper which, within the limits of the law, it would be the task of the Governmental Assembly to determine (1982: 120).

One may ask whether Hayek is not contradicting himself now. To construct a juridical system on the basis of this distinction – rules of proper conduct against rules of organisation – would require considerable effort, not least the clarification of the difference between these two rules. How could this be done without the employment of public law?

Public law grew tremendously during the twentieth century in the advanced democracies. Hayek's counter-argument against this expansion of the state fails to convince the reader of his ultra-liberalism that none of the rules of public law is conducive to 'rules of just conduct'. Positively, I wish to emphasise that public law – constitutional and administrative law – can be employed for the purpose of enhancing the status and validity of 'rules of just conduct', e.g. the institutions of rule of law.

Public sector reform need not be restricted to the search for efficiency. An equally valid goal is the strengthening of the rule of law. And it can certainly be done through the use of public law and the institutions of administrative law, including the Ombudsman. It is true that the American model of legal review developed less out of a public law approach, being based upon the juridical interpretations of the Supreme Court of the American constitution and its amendments (Padula, 2002). On the other hand, the Austrian-German version of legal review follows a consistent public law approach underlining the design of a special constitutional court (Kelsen, 1999). I will not enter into the question of the advantages or disadvantages of the American and the Austro-German models of legal review here. What I wish to point out is that rule of law can be accomplished by less spectacular means, for instance through the use of administrative law, or the Ombudsman.

Hayek actually suggests that rule of law can be introduced into societies which do not have a strong common law tradition. He writes about the prospects of constitutional democracy in societies lacking the special Western tradition:

> If such attempts to transplant democracy are not to fail, much of that background of unwritten traditions and beliefs, which in the successful

democracies had for a long time restrained the abuse of majority power, will have to be spelled out in such instruments of government for the new democracies (1982: 108).

Following Hayek's separation between private and public law, one would like to search for these instruments of government in constitutional and administrative law. This is not only a logical possibility. It is also an institutional reality in many countries outside of Western Europe, where attempts are being made to put in place rule of law. In fact, the successful introduction of rule of law in countries that were under what the major sociologists called 'Oriental despotism' depends critically upon the introduction of a series of institutions that bring about this four-stage rocket that has been analysed above. Each element in building rule of law is equally essential:

- legality
- human rights
- separation of powers
- publicness, complaint and redress.

When a country has institutions that safeguard all these four pieces, then it is a constitutional democracy. Countries with rule of law are still to be preferred to countries without rule of law. Distinguishing between democracy as party contestation and constitutionalism as the rule of law, one may easily imagine that a country like, for instance, Singapore would opt for the latter but display hesitance towards the former, given its social heterogeneity. Introducing and enforcing the rule of law requires new institutions and procedures wherever this takes place, also in Anglo-Saxon countries despite their common law tradition. Thus, we find also in the USA and the UK that the Ombudsman mechanism has widely been made use of on the basis of new statute law.

Whenever and wherever the rule of law is to be promoted, it requires the massive use of public law in opposition to the Hayek argument. Thus, constitutional law and criminal and administrative law are the only means to create the institutions which, when enforced, promote procedural stability, predictable outcomes, equality under the laws and accountability. Public law is a necessary but not sufficient condition, as the failure to achieve rule of law in many countries shows. Merely legislating does not produce rule of law, as civil servants who implement the rules have to be trained. This also requires the bolstering of the courage of those judges who constitute the ultimate guardians of rule of law.

Democracy and rule of law

A state that is devoted to respecting rule of law is not necessarily a democracy. A democratic regime requires rule of law, but the reverse is not true. Thus, rule of law was introduced long before the implementation of universal suffrage, for men and women. In a democracy there must be real competition for political power. This is the gist of Schumpeter's approach to democracy as basically identical to the market. Without contestation for power there is no democracy, although there may well be rule of law. A democratic regime requires more than legality, rights, separation of powers, legal review, namely political competition on the basis of the principle of one person – one vote (Posner, 2003). If most states of the world constitute rule-of-law governments, that would be a great advancement, even if they are not Western democracies.

When democracy as real contestation for political power – free and fair elections, political parties, universal suffrage, open entry, free mass media – is combined with the requirements of the rule of law, then there is constitutional democracy. It may be regarded as the restrictions derived from law upon popular sovereignty. Thus, the elements of the *Rechtsstaat* restrain the exercise of popular power. Historically, rule of law emerged before the introduction of universal suffrage. The chief philosophy of the *Rechtsstaat* – Kant's writings on law – aimed at securing a constitutional monarchy in Prussia but it rejected the idea of universal suffrage, or democracy as participation along the lines outlined by Rousseau.

One may identify three key elements in the rule of law. If a country is governed in accordance with the notions of rule of law, then its state respects law according to the following:

- *Publicness:* All government decisions at any level in the political system or the public sector, whether political or administrative, must be rendered public and accessible by the citizens as well as communicated somehow to the mass media. A decision which cannot be scrutinised publicly cannot claim to be just.
- *Generalisability:* A government decision must have the capacity of being applied to all cases similar to the one decided upon. This idea of universalisation is often said to constitute the core of law, meaning that government first and foremost establishes rules and regulations applicable in the same way to all people. This is at the heart of the notion of predictability under the laws, or the absence of arbitrariness in the state.
- *Complaint and redress:* Citizens need not only to know and understand the decisions of government and its officials. They must also be able to take action in relation to such decisions, reacting with the ever-present possibility of a complaint. The entailment is that each and every decision in the public sector must have a procedure attached to it whereby a citizen may initiate a process of complaint in order to possibly reach redress in some form or other.

For government to rule in accordance with the requirements of the rule of law there must be at least these three elements institutionalised in the state. The demands derived from law upon a democracy have been well identified and analysed within public administration, which targets the consequences for the structuring of the state derived from basic principles of constitutional and administrative law. The rule-of-law implications for democracy must include administrative review and may also cover legal review. I shall explain the fundamental difference between those two forms of rule-of-law check on government and its authorities, boards and agencies.

Growing demand for rule of law: judicialisation

Public sector reform is most often analysed as the reduction of the size or the role of government. Thus, among the key words in public sector reform one finds 'deregulation', 'privatisation' and the 'hollowing out' of the state. Although this trend towards a reduction in state tasks and government employment is undeniable, one must point out that there is a quite opposite development. In relation to the demands for rule of law, we observe an expansion of government, especially its juridical branch.

The term 'judicialisation of politics' is more and more often used to describe the increasing role of courts, judges and the Ombudsman in politics. Individuals and minorities have increasingly turned to the judicial mechanisms in order to uphold their claims upon government and society. Rights have become the language of politics, competing with votes as the software of politics. Rights constitute trumps according to the new natural law theory of law (Dworkin, 1977, 1998). And people expect courts, tribunals and the Ombudsman to validate these rights when they are played out as trumps in the political game.

Several trends converge on the growth of judicialisation. First, there is increasing political activism on the part of judges. Judicial interpretation is more and more used for interference of the judicial branch of government into society and the state. The doctrine of legal positivism, which restricted the role of judges to finding and implementing the intentions of the lawmaker, has been abandoned for a conception of the judge as entrusted with the task of bringing forth natural justice and right reason. Courts are not necessarily confined by the peculiar statute law of a country, but they may refer to international law with its strong human rights entrenchment. And courts are no longer always bound by national borders of jurisdiction. Second, the judicialisation of politics is bolstered by the expansion of human rights to include also group rights or collective rights besides the individual rights, negative or positive. Group rights seem especially promising for historical minorities to correct injustices in the past. Minorities constitute often such a small group that their votes do not offer them leverage in politics. Court action may be more promising than entering the political arena (Dworkin, 2000).

It seems almost as if there is no limit to the expansion of judicial interpretation of rights. Judicialisation may be expanded from the public sector to include also the private sector, meaning that the business of private organisations can be checked in the courts. Similarly, the scope of the Ombudsman control may be enlarged from the state to the regional and local governments, as well as to private firms. Finally, citizen groups may find litigation a more promising strategy than political action to change legislation. For instance, improving the environment and working conditions may be done through litigation against tobacco and asbestos firms (Olson, 2003).

The judicialisation of politics increases the role of government in society, especially its juridical branch, as well as the costs of citizen complaint and redress. In certain parts of the public sector there is a clear conflict between efficiency and rule of law. Take the case of health care where the threat of or actual use of litigation has pushed up costs considerably, especially in the United States. Documenting all measures taken in relation to a patient results in substantial costs in keeping records etc., but the fear of litigation for malpractice carries with it additional costs of doctors doing too much in terms of tests and treatments. Such costs may go extremely high.

Although the legal system is the same in the US and the UK – common law as against civil law in much of continental Europe, the two countries developed different procedures for the rule of law. In the US there emerged the combination of administrative and legal review with Chief Justice Marshall after 1800 (Hobson, 2000), whereas in the UK only the requirements of administrative review were enforced. However, the great English jurist Edward Coke outlined the possibility of legal review to the British in the well-known *Doctor Bonham's Case*, but it was never put into practice due to the basic idea of the parliamentary sovereignty (Stoner, 1992).

This separation between administrative review and legal review is to be found also in the civil law countries, where some practise the Kelsen model of a constitutional court with heavy judicialisation of politics, whereas other countries only adhere to administrative review. It is administrative review which is fundamental to the enforcement of rule of law. It can be done with special administrative courts as in civil law countries or with tribunals and ordinary courts, as with common law countries. In a complaint there are often three roads open: administrative complaint, criminal investigation and civil law suit or litigation. Finally, there is the most vital institution of the Ombudsman, i.e. the Scandinavian contribution to constitutional democracy and public administration.

Public administration and reregulation: a principal–agent perspective

Public administration also covers the operations of regulatory agencies that check legality within the private sector. Many scholars have noted the growth of regulatory agencies in terms of both employees and jurisdiction

(Lowi, 1979; Moe, 1987; Kiewiet and McCubbins, 1991; Majone, 1996). Increasingly, government or parliament hands over the regulation of enterprises to special agencies at arm's length from the executive or the legislature on the basis of a principal–agent theory of a link between agency independence and agency competence. Thus, public regulation and regulatory boards are employed in the field of monetary affairs (central banks), industrial organisation (anti-trust), price surveillance (competition policy) and natural monopolies (quality and price in energy, water, etc.).

The emergence of regulatory agencies is fuelled by changes in one part of public administration, namely public resource allocation. When government outsources the supply of public services or privatises it, wholly or partially, then public administration in the form of regulation tends to increase, compensating for the reduction of the role of government. It has even been claimed that much of what government did traditionally through its bureaucracy can be done by a combination of outsourcing and regulation. Thus, the rise of the regulatory state reflects the policies of downsizing traditional public administration through New Public Management (Majone, 1996). When public sector reform turns out a host of suppliers in competition, replacing a monolithic bureaucracy, then questions about fairness and quality are bound to arise. The creation of regulatory bodies is regarded as the most transaction cost minimising device to handle them. But can the regulator be trusted? The same problem arises in relation to the theory that certain government tasks are too important to be entrusted to government, as only an independent agency could achieve high standards of impartiality and neutrality, pursuing a long-run commitment to a clear set of objectives and rules. But who controls the controllers?

A number of recent theories of government support the creating of strong regulatory agencies. Firstly, in the conception of plural government in the UK (Ferlie *et al.*, 1996; McLaughlin *et al.*, 2001), there is a strong emphasis upon regulatory agencies as controllers of the suppliers of public services. Secondly, in the idea of a Citizen's Charter for the public services, a strong role is given to the possibility of hearing the consumer and providing him/her with a voice in the delivery process via the regulatory agencies. Thirdly, there is the idea of agency integrity which is posted against the image of a confused principal that is the target of strategic behaviour on the part of political groups or minorities. By protecting the agency against continuous interference by the principal, public administration can be saved from pork-barrel politics, politico-economic cycles and log-rolling. Finally, the emergence of regional coordination mechanisms above the nation-state, as with the EU, focuses on the economies of scale in making public regulation similar for a larger set of countries, especially if there is uniform and efficient implementation of one single body of law. Again EU law can be mentioned as the prototype of regulation through an intergovernmental or federal mechanism. At the same time, the emphasis upon public regulation has a long standing in political economy, where the relevance of governmental oversight of the private sector has always been underlined – *Ordnungspolitik*. Without some sort of state control of the fundamentals of private sector operations, especially of a business nature, legality will be jeopardised. Thus, government controls the profitability of joint-stock companies and conducts surveillance of the operations of the stock markets.

The regulatory state is confronted by the principal–agent difficulty of eliciting effective actions on the part of the agent, however much one underlines the advantages of public regulation. There is the ever present danger of agency capture by strong interest groups, as emphasised in the Chicago School of regulation (Stigler, 1988, 2003). When government sets up an agency for regulating the supply of public services or the control of legality in the private sector, then it becomes dependent on agents to do the work, with the ensuing problems of shirking and adverse selection. How can the government protect itself against agents who promise much but deliver little? The answer from game theory has been the so-called trust game (see Table 5.1) (Kreps, 1990a).

The game has been invented to show the principal difficulty in the interaction between the government and an agency entrusted with much independence. The Nash equilibrium of the game is (0, 0), but if the interaction is not a one-shot game, then the two players may coordinate upon a different strategy than 'not trust' and 'abuse trust'. If *A* can retaliate in a credible manner, then *B* may choose to honour trust, allowing for the Pareto-optimal outcome of (10, 10). However, the government must sometimes show that it does not trust the agent, engaging, for instance in a reshuffling of the structure of agencies from time to time. From the point of view of the agent, it is the extent of future orientation that is decisive for the choice of strategy: the less the agent discounts the benefits from future collaboration with the government, the more the agent will choose to honour his/her commitments.

The problem of agencies in public regulation – will they be effective? – can be restated in terms of the basic principal–agent framework, involving both moral hazard and adverse selection. Consider Figure 5.1. High-profile regulatory agents may sign a contract with the principal, promising (*W2, e4, O4*), but in reality, regulators are only capable of effort *e3*, resulting in *O3*, where benefits only equal costs. If it is very difficult to estimate

Table 5.1 The trust game

		B	
		Honour A' trust	Abuse A's trust
A	Trust B	10, 10	−5, 15
	Not trust B	0, 0	0, 0

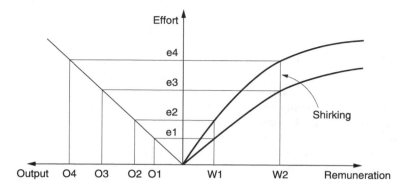

Figure 5.1 Principal–agent interaction: the agency regulatory problem.

the value of regulatory output, then the principal would might opt for a smaller regulatory agency, where he/she prefers the combination (*W1*, *e2*) to the combination (*W1*, *O1*). Perhaps the principal cannot tell whether an agent is high effort or low effort? He/she should then offer *W1* and hope for *O2*. Thus, principals may well be advised not to trust public regulation imprudently or engage in it massively.

Conclusion

Thin legal–rational authority with Weber is not the same as thick rule of law with Kant. Thus, one should distinguish between these two conceptions, as well as not equate them with a democratic regime. How precarious constitutional government appears when one looks at the states of the present world. Only half of the governments of the world acknowledge the rule of law and even fewer practise it. It seems that Weber underestimated the lingering relevance of traditional authority and religious power, as well as the possibility of framing authoritarianism with the help of legal–rational authority. This observation about the difficulty of enforcing constitutional government in several countries leads to the final conclusion in this chapter, namely that a variety of mechanisms has to be employed in constitutional engineering to this objective. It is only feasible if administrative law is employed fully in enforcing the basic requirements of legality and rule of law. And the instruments exist in the civil law tradition where statute law is employed to the utmost in launching institutions such as tribunals, administrative courts and the Ombudsman. The developments in well-ordered societies show that a negative assessment of Hayek's theory of law is correct.

In general, there is often a trade-off between efficiency and rule of law. The classical theory of public administration favoured the rule of law in such a trade-off, whereas the theory of public management gives the highest priority to efficiency. Since the requirement of a constitutional state is a *sine qua non* in a well-ordered society, the key notions inherent in public administration can never be done away with. Constitutional government is a value that requires a number of mechanisms for its attainment. The relevance of rule of law to public management is apparent. Thus, the principal when instructing the agent to implement policies will wish to have efficiency maximised in policy outputs and outcomes under the restriction that rule of law is observed. Thus, the concerns of public administration are far from irrelevant in public sector reform.

One should also criticise the theory of human knowledge launched by Hayek in *The Counter-Revolution of Science* (1991) in order to pin down the crucial differences between micro and macro rationality in social life. Hayek developed a theory of rationality, knowledge and institutions which in effect denied both macro and micro rationality. He is most well known for his denial of the possibility of macro rationality, meaning the conscious direction of whole societies by governmental rational policy-making – this is theme of his *The Road to Serfdom* (2001). However, Hayek also rejected the concept of individual rationality, emphasising the cognitive limitations upon men and women. Yet, he salvaged the notion of evolutionary rationality in the development of human civilisation by his concept of spontaneous orders which evolve towards collective rationality (Hayek, 1996). Let us look at a few quotations from Hayek:

> It is because the growth of the human mind presents in its most general form the common problem of all the social sciences that it is here that minds are most sharply divided, and that two fundamentally different and irreconcilable attitudes manifest themselves: on the one hand the essential humility of individualism, which endeavours to understand as well as possible the principles by which the efforts of individual men have in fact been combined to produce our civilisation, and which from this understanding hopes to derive the power to create conditions favourable to further growth; and, on the other hand, the hubris of collectivism which aims at conscious direction of all forces of society (1991: 91).

Hayek does not only oppose collectivism to individualism but also humility against hubris. He denies the possibility of government rational policy-making, especially economic planning and the direction of the economy towards macro objectives by arguing that not even single individuals can behave in a fully rational manner. How could a collective of individuals do better than each individual alone? He states:

> The individualist approach, in awareness of the constitutional limitations of the individual mind, attempts to show how man in society is

able, by the use of various resultants of the social process, to increase his powers with the help of the knowledge implicit in them and of which he is never aware; it makes us understand that the only "reason" which can in any sense be regarded as superior to individual reason does not exist in any sense apart from the inter-individual process in which, by means of impersonal media, the knowledge of successive generations and of millions of people living simultaneously is combined and mutually adjusted, and that this process is the only form in which the totality of human knowledge ever exists (1991: 91).

Hayek here presents his evolutionary theory of human rationality according to which traditions and institutions which survive contain wisdom – the spontaneous orders. Thus, he accepts a kind of macro rationality – evolutionary practices – but rejects the rationality of collective decision-making, such as government or a political authority. Let us look at a final quote:

The collectivist method, on the other hand, not satisfied with the partial knowledge of this process from the inside, which is all the individual can gain, bases its demands for conscious control on the assumption that it can comprehend this process as a whole and make use of all knowledge in a systematically integrated form. It leads thus directly to political collectivism (1991: 91–92).

Advances in game theory call into question the Hayek theory of rationality. One would be inclined to give him credit for his criticism of comprehensive, holistic planning and policy-making. But the meaning of micro rationality is now better understood. Also, evolutionary game theory starts from micro rationality (Potts, 2001). Several results from game theory, both in two-person games and *N*-person games, indicate that the players participating in policy-making and policy implementation may very well behave rationally but the outcomes are neither rational nor optimal.

Appendix

Table 5.2 Hohfeld's fundamental legal conceptions

Jural opposites

Right	Privilege	Power (competence)	Immunity
No right	Duty	Disability	Liability

Jural correlates

Right	Privilege	Power (competence)	Immunity
Duty	No right	Liability	Disability

6 Public policy criteria: the Cambridge and Chicago positions

Introduction

It is often stated that the destruction of the New York World Trade Center on 11 September 2001 ended the neo-liberal era, meaning the termination of neo-liberalism as the dominant paradigm for the interpretation of the ends and means public policy. Since then, the number of articles and books stating the end of neo-liberalism has proliferated. And the call for government intervention as well as for deficit spending has been raised much more frequently, testifying to the new need for active government and state intervention in the economy.

Neo-liberalism or market conservatism had a flourishing period of about 30 years when it figured prominently behind the policy-making of parliaments and governments, as well as in the thinking of international organisations such as the World Bank, the International Monetary Fund and the World Trade Organisation. Actually, the emergence of Chicago School economics and its ascent to a policy dominant paradigm could hardly have been predicted after the Second World War, when economics and policy were firmly in the hands of the Cambridge School. However, from 1968 when M. Friedman crushed the theory of the Philips curve in 'The Role of Monetary Policy: Presidential Address to AEA,' published in the *American Economic Review* (Friedman, 1969) the initiative was slowly but firmly transferred from Cambridge to Chicago.

The arrival of Chicago School economics in the driving seat of economics, with a long series of famous pilots (Stigler, Peltzman, Posner, Coase, Demsetz, Lucas), several of whom were awarded the Nobel Prize, shattered the Cambridge gospel hegemony (Stigler, 2003). Not only did the gospel of Chicago question the micro teachings of Cambridge, but it also destroyed the high credibility of Keynesian macro economics typical of post-War policy-making up to 1970. The purpose of this chapter is to examine the Chicago School revolution with an eye towards its impact upon policies.

Did it change the ends of policy or merely the means of implementing policy?

Social policy-making remains a huge set of items in public budgets. Although the simple model of a welfare state – universalism, unity and uniformity – is no longer practised among the welfare states, social policies continue to be highly relevant politically, and they pose major managerial problems about efficiency in service provision.

The Chicago revolution: the ends or means of policy?

Just as one may ask the question of how governments get the job done, i.e. the administration, implementation or management problem, so one may pose the question whether some policies are typical of government, in the sense that all governments tend to conduct these, or that they at least ought to. In principle, governments can do almost anything. There are so many examples of policies that should never have been made or tried that one almost cannot state one single policy which no government has ever embarked upon. Designating a proper set of government policies is more difficult than one may perhaps believe. Yet it has been suggested that some policies are more genuine state tasks than others. Let us look at a few of the criteria suggested to separate out the best policies or the most suitable policies for government from all conceivable policies by confronting the Chicago School position with the Cambridge School solution.

It must be underlined that the Chicago revolution had an enormous impact upon policy in well-ordered societies. Perhaps the impact was felt more in policy implementation – deregulation, contracting out, market testing – than in policy formulation? Governments in well-ordered societies seem to be doing much the same things today as in the 1960s.

The derivation of a set of proper state tasks requires the identification of some criteria with which to evaluate policy objectives. Here the question is not the means of policy execution or the techniques to be employed in programme implementation. Thus, for instance it is not the pros and cons of deregulation and privatisation that are at stake. But the key issue is the objectives that government should pursue, meaning: Which goods and services should the state be responsible for?

The standard approach in political economy to the identification of the proper set of policies is the classical *market failure* framework, which examines the nature of goods and services in order to derive conclusions for policy. Another approach employed in political science targets the preferences of citizens, searching for the set of policies they would enact with the democratic method, meaning a majority voting scheme. The crux of the matter is that there is disagreement within political economy about the separation between the tasks of government and the market, between the public sector and the private sector, as manifested in the collision between the Chicago School and the Cambridge School of economics.

In a constitutional democracy or a well-ordered society the menu of public policies will be decided ultimately not by systematic criteria derived from contested economic theory but from the voting procedure. Thus, the impact of economic theory upon policy will be transmitted through the choices made in elections and in parliament. To explain the real policy mix in a democratic country one would need to know the policy preferences of the electorate and the political parties or politicians, which may be affected by theories in political economy in an ambiguous manner. Thus, major changes in policy thinking in economic theory will be translated into actual policy change in a far from clear-cut manner.

Adding voting to the basic problem in political economy of separating between state and market makes the problem of the conflict between efficiency and equity most acute. Government could use its Hobbesian power to legislate for distributional purposes, even if such policies hurt overall economic efficiency. In a democracy such policies would, however, be self-defeating in the long-run, if voters are rational. The gains to be captured through maximising economic efficiency could be shared between the voting groups, but myopia is omnipresent in politics. Simple majority and its relation to the efficiency – equity trade-off presents a set of unresolved and vexing problems for social science analysis (Okun, 1975). What policies should public management attempt to implement according to the respective Chicago and Cambridge positions?

The world according to the Chicago gospel: the key hypotheses

The many Nobel Prizes given to Chicago School economists reinforced the Chicago lead, but from 2001 the spirit of the times has been different. Many events besides the 11 September attack contributed to the shattering of the Chicago message and its three key points, namely:

- the market efficiency hypothesis
- the rational expectations hypothesis
- the Coase theorem.

With these three hypotheses, which constitute the core of Chicago School economics, a large number of policy implications were spelled out during the 1960s–90s. When carried over into the public sector these core assumptions with their policy implications would change the distinction between the public and the private sectors not only in the set of rich OECD countries but also in the Third World through structural adjustment policies. The purpose here is only to discuss these three core assumptions of the Chicago gospel in relation to the making of public policy.

Market efficiency

Public policies are often motivated by the efficiency concept. Thus, governments should promote macro and micro efficiency in the economy by conducting a variety of public policies, all aiming at increasing output or production. However, if markets are at any point in time efficient, then why not trust the market mechanism to allocate all kinds of goods and services? The range of application of the market efficiency hypothesis is not limited to financial markets but can just as well be applied to the real economy (Fama, 1976; Goss, 1991).

If the market efficiency hypothesis is true, then one must ask what is left for government to do. Governments can of course deviate from efficiency and conduct policies for other reasons, where redistribution especially is a strong and always relevant basis for government action. If redistributional policies hurt efficiency in the economy, then governments may prefer to live with such efficiency–equity trade-offs (Okun, 1975). Thus, one cannot conclude that the market efficiency hypothesis must limit the public sector to a minimalist state.

The logic of an efficiency–equity trade-off is that government may accept a lower level of allocation of goods and services in order to get a distributional profile of these goods and services which it accepts as just. Efficiency is a mere aggregative notion, meaning that an allocation is efficient when it cannot be increased. There are two interpretations of efficiency in economics, one according to the cardinal scale and another according to the ordinal scale interpretation: Marshall efficiency and Pareto efficiency.

Under Marshall efficiency an allocation must maximise the difference between total benefits and total costs according to a utilitarian framework. Such an allocation could be inequitable as much of the benefits could be concentrated with one group of rich people, while the group of poor people would receive little. It is conceivable, however, that concentrating more goods and services with the poor group at the expense of the rich group could lead to even higher levels of total utility in society (decreasing marginal utility of money). Such efficiency improvements are ruled out under the interpretation of efficiency launched by Pareto. Pareto's definition of efficiency is well known, namely: An allocation is Pareto efficient if it is impossible to improve for one person while not worsening for any other person. Thus, there is a veto mechanism built into Pareto's concept of efficiency which is altogether lacking in Marshall's.

If one group gains much by a new allocation while another group loses somewhat, then a Pareto improvement is only feasible if the first group compensates the other group. Adding compensation to the equation entails that Pareto changes can accomplish Marshall efficiency. However, one would wish to know when this compensation will take place. It has been argued that theoretical Kaldor–Hicks compensation is enough, but this is not the case following Pareto efficiency. One method of compensation is of course democratic voting with the simple majority principle, but this opens up a Pandora's box of redistribution with the efficiency–equity trade-off.

Rational expectations

The notion of rational expectations strengthens the market argument very much. If true, the rational expectations argument creates a solid foundation for micro efficiency, or the efficiency of incentives. Each actor would, in a market setting, search for the best available information and continuously update him/herself. How could there be a gap between existing and available knowledge on the one hand and complete and full information on the other? Given rational expectations in a market setting, the actors would immediately acquire this knowledge and put it to their use – the principle of arbitrage. The Muth innovation of rational expectations, together with the Harsanyi idea of Bayesian decision-making in a dynamic perspective, seems to undo the confrontation between the rational choice model and the bounded rationality model. Thus, the rational expectations argument reinforces the relevance of assuming rational choice with market participants (Miller, 1994). The rational expectations hypothesis further backs up the claims of the market efficiency argument, as government could not possibly be more informed than the participants in the markets. The Keynes argument that markets are driven by so-called 'animal spirits' causing them to fluctuate in an unpredictable manner is completely destroyed. There is every reason to suspect that markets are more informed than government.

The rational expectations hypothesis may appear extreme for a naïve realist used to human error and miscalculations. Yet it accounts for many diverse and sometimes stunning facts such as the extreme volatility in financial markets (Fama), the elimination of inefficiencies through institutional change (North, Demsetz) as well as the tendency of interest organisations to acquire the legislation they need for their business (Olson, Becker) (Ménard, 2000; Hodgson, 2004; Sheffrin, 1996).

Coase's theorem

Markets can exist for anything if bargaining is allowed to operate freely. Thus, markets emerge naturally from the innate tendencies of man and woman to trade and exchange. When people exchange, then they have bargained *ex ante* to the utmost, meaning that they maximise the total gain from negotiation; however, they divide this gain between them *ex post*. This is the Coase principle, considered as the 'eureka' of Chicago School economics (Stigler, 2003). Its exact meaning has been much debated since it was launched in 1961. To some its import is strictly limited to the non-market setting where people should employ bargaining instead of planning or government authority, for instance in environmental policy.

Yet the Coase theorem – 'If transaction costs do not overwhelm gains, saleable property rights bring social resources to their socially efficient uses, even when there are externalities and total social welfare will be maximised' – could be interpreted in a broad manner as a basic vindication of the market. It restricts government to the control of transaction costs and underlines the role of the judicial branch of government to clarify and enforce property rights. Some have claimed that Coase's theorem is basically empty, stating the truism about the logic of bargaining that people tend to share the whole cake when they divide it up. Others see the Coase principle as one of the great insights comparable to the Hayek argument about spontaneous order. Political economists from Adam Smith to Leon Walras had always emphasised that the state must guarantee the market and monitor its operations – what was called *Ordnungspolitik* in German economics. Coase gave a short and handsome interpretation of this insight by mentioning two very important presuppositions of markets, namely enforceable property rights and low transaction costs (Cooter and Ulen, 2003; Wenin, 2003).

At the same time as one recognises the fundamental validity of the Coase theorem one may raise the question of its range of application. Here things are far less clear. It is extremely difficult to measure transaction costs and practically impossible to identify when they start going up dramatically, calling for the abandoning of bargaining and its replacement by government intervention. Moreover, the creation and enforcement of property rights is no small thing, calling for policies of various kinds. When property rights are not defined, then any government decision has distributional implications which concern the parties more than the assurance that efficiency would be forthcoming, however the property rights are identified.

Coase's theorem that bargaining always leads to efficient allocations no matter how the gain is divided may be interpreted in a narrow or a broad manner. The narrow interpretation is linked with the economic theory of externalities and whether these are to be handled by the market or government (legislation or a Pigouvian mechanism). In a broad sense, however, the Coase theorem touches upon the fundamental nature of law and can be related to the Calabresi idea about tort law, namely that common law judges tend to take the economic concept of efficiency into account when ruling about torts and compensation.

The narrow interpretation concerns the 'internalisation' of externalities. In the Pigouvian solution, firms internalise the externality through the tax (or subsidy) they face. With Coase the parties negotiate an efficient solution, meaning that they maximise their joint welfare, because that maximises the size of the possible transfer and individual side payments. The broad interpretation would have to explain why statute law has increased tremendously at the expense of contract law. Is this because transaction costs tend always to be huge in society, or that property rules are difficult to enforce, or that enforceable property rights are not just? Law and economics argues that private law tends to reach efficient solutions to practical problems, whereas public law is often captured by special interest or distributional coalitions (Posner, 1990, 1992). If true, this would support market solutions unfettered by public law intervention.

Law and markets: what is the role of the state?

The classical delineation of the various branches of law into public and private law as well as civil law and criminal law has been the target of economic analysis within *law and economics*. One may engage in a comparison of the efficiencies of treating certain problems in one area of the law rather than in another, if we assume, as Calabresi did, that law is related to efficiency and not merely justice. Legal scholars would hardly accept this starting point, as they would insist that law is more about justice than efficiency (McLeod, 2003; Harris, 1997; Simmonds, 2002; Friedman, 2001; Coleman, 1988a).

Policy-making would involve considerations on how administrative law, criminal law, property and contract law, as well as tort law, relate to each other when it comes to handling harm, risk and their social consequences. The crux of the matter is that these bodies of law overlap to some extent, meaning that one course of events may be approached in terms of several frameworks of law. For instance, the stock manipulations within the French multinational *Vivendi* could in principle be judged from administrative law, criminal law, private law and in a class action law suit. Thus, one is led to ask: Which kind of law – public or private – is most effective in preventing crime or punishing it? This basic problem of the efficiency of law in enhancing sound economic operations arises not only under a civil law framework with its strong separation between public and private law, or statute law and contract law. The same question surfaces, for instance in the handling of the Enron disaster and the prosecution of Kenneth Lay, who could be charged with violating criminal law or federal regulations, or be made personally responsible for the mismanagement of the company in relation to its shareholders. The US Federal Government unsealed an indictment charging him in a wide-ranging scheme to deceive the public, company shareholders and government regulators about the energy company that he founded and led to industry prominence before its collapse. The federal criminal indictment adds 11 counts against Lay to charges already filed against CEO Jeffrey Skilling, and accountant Richard Causey, accusing Lay of participating in a conspiracy to manipulate Enron's quarterly financial results, and of making public statements about Enron's financial performance that were false and misleading and omitting facts necessary to make financial statements accurate and fair. In a separate action, the Securities and Exchange Commission filed civil charges against Lay, accusing him of fraud and insider trading and seeking recovery of more than $90 million in what the agency said were illegal proceeds from stock sales.

Civil law is a private affair, a dispute between two (or possible more) parties arbitrated by the state. Criminal law is a public matter, because a crime is viewed not simply as an injustice against a single individual but against society. The plaintiff in a criminal trial is the state, not the victim, and remedies are aimed at society, not at restoring the victim. In civil law legal remedies are the norm and punitive damages are rare, whereas the aim of the criminal justice is to punish. The object of criminal law is to protect rights, whereas the object of civil law is to protect interests. Administrative law is the regulation of the state of its organisations when they act towards society and the markets (Martin, 2003; Partington, 2003). Private law, or that part of the law that deals with aspects of relationships between individuals of no direct concern to the state, includes the law of property and of trusts, family law, the law of contract, mercantile law, and the law of tort. Public law is that part of the law that deals with the constitution and functions of the organs of central and local government, the relationship between individuals and the state, and relationships between individuals of direct concern to the state. It includes constitutional law, administrative law, tax law, and criminal law.

A contract is a legally binding agreement, arising from offer and acceptance. There must be consideration unless the contract is by deed. The parties must have an intention to create legal relations in order to prevent a purely domestic or social agreement from constituting a contract. The parties must have capacity to contract and the agreement must comply with any formal legal requirements. Tort is a wrongful act or omission for which damages can be obtained in a civil court by the person wronged, other than a wrong that is only a breach of contract. Tort law is concerned with providing compensation for personal injury and property damage caused by negligence to protect reputation (defamation), personal freedom (assault; false imprisonment), title to property (conversion; trespass), enjoyment of property (nuisance), and commercial interests (intimidation; conspiracy; passing off). The wrong must be done intentionally or negligently, except for torts of strict liability. Most torts are actionable only if they have caused damage, but torts that protect rights rather than compensate for damage (such as trespass) are actionable without proof of damage. The tortfeasor, or the person principally liable, is the one who committed the tort, although under the rules of vicarious liability one may be liable for a tort committed by another person. The chief remedy for a tort is an action for damages, but in some cases an injunction can be obtained to prevent repetition of the injury. A crime is an act or sometimes a failure to act that is deemed to be a public wrong and is therefore punishable by the state in criminal proceedings. Every crime consists according to law of an *actus reus* accompanied by a specified *mens rea* (unless it is a crime of strict liability), and the prosecution must prove these elements of the crime beyond reasonable doubt. Some crimes are serious wrongs of a moral nature (e.g. murder or rape); others interfere with the smooth running of society (e.g. parking offences). Most prosecutions for crime are brought by the police, although they can be started by ordinary people.

Contract law versus tort law

One may employ the concept of transaction costs to analyse the distinction between tort law and contract law. Contract law concerns relationships between people for whom the *ex ante* costs of bargaining are low. Tort law deals with relationships between people for whom the *ex ante* costs of bargaining about the harms are high and who cannot, therefore, enter into a contractual relationship. If there were no costs to bargaining, i.e. to identifying the parties with whom to bargain or to the bargaining itself, then contract law would be an efficient means of allocating the risks. Transaction costs explain how tort law complements contract law. The court assigns liability for harm done after the fact, rather than requires risks to be allocated before any possible harm. If contracts could be fully rational, anticipating all risks or contingencies, present and future, only then could one do without tort law in the legal system of well-ordered societies (Polinsky, 2003; Wenin, 2003).

Tort law versus criminal law

Tort law protects the interests, generally monetary, of those who have been harmed, by 'making the victim whole'. A tort involves (1) 'breach of a duty owed to the plaintiff by the defendant', (2) 'harm suffered by the plaintiff,' and (3) 'the breach being the immediate or proximate cause of the harm'. Criminal law, on the other hand, protects the rights of individuals by preventing the criminal from harming other members of society in the future. Tort law and criminal law parallel each other in their focus on the concepts right/duty and harm. Harm in criminal law is considered as 'public', whereas harm in tort law is regarded as 'private'. The criminal injures society by destroying the security of society, whereas a tortfeasor harms a private person. In criminal law the beneficiary is public rather than private. Criminal law recognises attempts at harm, whereas tort law does not. Criminal law punishes people for attempts to harm, because the danger to members of society by a criminal who attempted to murder but failed is just as great as the danger posed by a criminal who actually succeeded in the attempt to murder another person. If the purpose of tort law is to compensate the victim for harm done, then attempts to harm cannot possibly result in any award of damages (Medema and Mercuro, 1998).

If the harm done by criminals is public rather than private, then that would allow the state to justify outlawing violations of traditional moral codes, i.e. to create 'victimless crimes'. In a victimless crime, a certain activity is outlawed on the grounds that it destroys the moral fabric of the community. In the drugs trade, the price of the outlawed drugs is inflated by the government's attempts to reduce the supply of those drugs and by the dramatically increased risks of life and liberty to dealers. The inflated price may well then only induce greater criminal activity on the part of those who must steal to support their habits. Government, from police to the courts to jails, prosecutes users and dealers. Can it be defended on a theory of law along Calabresi's line of thought, i.e. law as enhancing economic efficiency? Crimes are generally considered such because of a violation of the personal rights of an individual, which results in harm or which could have resulted in harm. In both tort and criminal law, an obligation was breached that caused harm. The distinction between tort law and criminal law stems from the differing purposes when the law reacts to harm. See http://plato.stanford.edu/entries/tort-theories.

Administrative law versus contract law and tort law

Private law offers the parties a wide range of opportunities to define and enforce rights. Yet the immense growth of administrative law indicates that private law regulation is not considered adequate in all circumstances. When the state regulates society through an agency, then there are two advantages:

- uniformity, reducing transaction costs;
- obligation, reducing enforcement costs.

Private law regulation offers flexibility but cannot guarantee egalitarian treatment. It may prove extremely costly to enforce for a single individual. Take the example of pensions which could be provided either through private law or through public law. It is far from self-evident that private law regulation by means of contract law is superior to administrative law. First, citizens may wish to have one pension that is not variable but expresses their belonging to a nation. Second, citizens may doubt whether private law offers a sufficient protection against contractual difficulties or sheer opportunism. It is often argued that administrative law is too inflexible. Yet there is no need for one single solution in pension systems regulated by administrative law. Thus, for example, the Swiss pensions constitute obligatory schemes under public law but they provide for an immense variety of solutions with a multiplicity of pension funds (public and private), responding to the needs of different groups of employees.

In law and economics, inspired by Calabresi and Coase, there is a strong preference for private law regulation corresponding to a belief in the infallibility of the market. The Coase theorem entails that people can solve difficult social problems by negotiating and contracting. The Calabresi argument about common law entails that judges rule on issues in tort law by taking economic efficiency into account. Thus, choosing private law must be efficiency enhancing. Yet the enormous expansion of public law tells a different story (Loughlin, 2003). Administrative law has developed into the main type of statute law, and there are economic gains to be realised in public law. Administrative law is the core of public policies, so that there seems to be little reason to limit the scope of the latter by arguing that administrative law is somehow generally inferior to private law, as with, for example,

Posner (2001). For example, risk as a concern for government regulation appears clearly in the introduction of the so-called precautionary principle in environmental perfection. Here, administrative law prevails over tort law, providing government with the competence to act ahead of a tort. It has raised a huge debate about its pros and cons, especially among scholars favouring environmental law as a complement to tort law.

The precautionary principle aims at the shifting of the 'duty or care' or 'onus of proof' from those who oppose change to those who propose change. It encourages government to err on the side of caution, even when there is no evidence of harm. The Wingspread Statement, produced by a gathering of scientists, philosophers, lawyers and environmental activists in the USA in 1998, pronounced that: 'When an activity raises threats of harm to the environment or human health, precautionary measures should be taken even if some cause and effect relationships are not fully established scientifically.' The problem is that most scientific and technological developments do raise possible 'threats of harm', exposing people to new and often unpredictable risks. An excessive preoccupation with hypothetical risks is detrimental to scientific and technological progress. The rapid incorporation of the precautionary principle into law, such as EU law, is not Calabresian.

The precautionary principle goes back to the German *Vorsorgeprinzip*, which in the 1970s became a principle of German environmental law. It has since been recognised in the World Charter for Nature, and adopted by the UN General Assembly in 1982 as well as in the First International Conference on Protection of the North Sea in 1984. The UN Conference on Environment and Development in Rio de Janeiro in 1992 adopted Principle 15, stating that: 'In order to protect the environment, the precautionary approach shall be widely applied by states according to their capabilities. Where there are threats of serious or irreversible damage, lack of full scientific certainty shall not be used as a reason for postponing cost-effective measures to prevent environmental degradation.' Since the precautionary principle was adopted in the Treaty of Maastricht in 1992, it has been extended from environmental issues to developments related to human health.

One needs to explore cultural assumptions about human vulnerability in order to understand the application of the precautionary principle to ever more spheres of life. The precautionary principle incurs the cost of 'false positives', meaning foregoing many social benefits which tend to make our lives safer rather than less safe. Scientific and technological progress may introduce new risks, but its general trajectory has been to reduce more serious risks, through the development of vaccinations, organ transplantation, blood transfusion, the chlorination of drinking water, the use of pesticides, and much more. The precautionary principle is obsession with risk, meaning that one lives in a state of anxiety concerning almost everything, from food to terrorism (Sunstein, 2005).

The precautionary principle is not merely confined to the spheres of health and science, as every sphere of life, from business to parenting and health, is organised around the notion that it is better to be safe than take risks. Why has the precautionary principle become so influential? One may look for an answer in the growing literature on risk and risk perception (Wildavsky, 1988; Slovic, 2000; Beck, 2001). An increasingly technological society brings with it risks concerning human health and environmental disruption. Science and technology are advancing at an ever-increasing rate so that many people have anxieties about the pace of change and the potential for major adverse consequences if new developments are not appropriately controlled. If science has greater power to do good, it also has greater power to do harm. But scientific and technological advance often enhances a safer world, rather than a more risky one.

What is more effective against risks, administrative law or private law? Take the case of fraud in the stock market, for instance the WorldCom disaster in 2002, involving accusations of an alleged \$4bn (£2.62bn)[1] accounting fraud. When telecommunications company WorldCom declared that it would have to restate its financial results to account for billions of dollars in improper bookkeeping, the market realised that things were wrong. But how are they to be corrected? The US Securities and Exchange Commission charged the US telecommunications giant with fraud, but does it really bite? One way to seek correction would be to employ administrative law, leaving the initiative to the New York Stock Exchange or to the Securities and Exchange Commission. A different method would be to employ private law and focus on contract, tort and negligence. Thus, the owners of WorldCom received compensation for their losses through a class action litigation against a large US Bank, Citigroup, that attempted to buy WorldCom, paying \$2.65bn to investors in WorldCom. Citigroup, the world's largest financial services company, roughly quadrupled its reserves for pending lawsuits to \$6.7bn in addition to the settlement with WorldCom, the telecommunications company now called MCI that recently emerged from the largest bankruptcy in history.

Here is the gist of the preference for tort and contract law with law and economics: private law regulation bites, as well as possibly bringing compensation for damage and negligence. Public law regulation is slow and may merely put people behind bars for some time. People who have been wronged do look for more than punishment, especially financial compensation.

Chicago School implications

One may argue that the teachings of Chicago School economics has had three main practical consequences, one for the First World, another for the Second World and still another for the Third World. This is not the place to enter into a profound analysis of these kinds of impacts. It suffices to indicate that they were indeed very different in nature.

First World impact

Here we have the revitalisation of markets: deregulation and privatisation. The rich countries no doubt benefited from the gains in efficiency due to deregulation and privatisation. Thus, many markets were revitalised by increasing supply and falling prices. Old monopolies were challenged and the two Cs were put in place: choice in demand and competition in supply. Lots of public enterprises were sold off and transformed into competitive firms, operating in a deregulated economy where the role of government was more than ever focused on that of umpire. Thus, output has risen in the rich countries since the ascent of Chicago School economics, which entails that the efficiency goal was achieved. These efficiency gains are chiefly the pros of the extensive policies of deregulation and privatisation during the 1980s and 1990s.

Yet there are some cons in the rich countries from the practice of Chicago School inspired policy-making. Here, one would wish to mention the following:

- increasing inequalities between and within countries;
- the looting strategy in private firms;
- declining public services;
- misguided deregulation.

Let us take a few examples of market failures: the growing social exclusion problem, the Enron or WorldCom disasters, the worsening access to higher education and the California electricity market collapse (Stiglitz, 2003; Krugman, 2003).

'Social exclusion' is the new term for poverty in the rich countries. This kind of poverty is different as it is a predicament which is very difficult to get out of. Thus, social exclusion is permanent poverty and dependency upon help. What several studies show is that the group which is socially excluded has grown during the last two decades when neo-liberalism has ruled as the dominant ideology in the capitalist democracies. Somehow the market economy leaves one group of people permanently behind. Recent figures indicate that as much 5 per cent of the population is stuck in the terrible predicament of exclusion. Conventional social policies seem helpless in relation to the difficulty of not leaving this predicament.

Besides the new social exclusion problem, fuelled by the international drug trafficking, there is a noticeable rise in income inequality in all rich countries, whatever measure is employed. The market economy favours people with high income and inherited wealth, which calls for a redistributional policy of some sort. However, redistributional policies on a large scale as in the European welfare state are extremely costly and far from effective in achieving the desired outcome, namely a more egalitarian income (Tullock, 1997; Lambert and Lambert, 2002). Moreover, it is argued that state intervention presupposes that government is some kind of benevolent dictator, maximising an unknown entity called 'the public interest'. The public choice critique that politicians and bureaucrats seek their own interest, some even with guile, had a profound impact upon the growing scepticism against government and the public sector in the 1980s and 1990s. To Buchanan and Tullock within the Public Choice School, coming out of an intellectual tradition entirely different from Chicago economics, it is a self-evident truth that the public interest is non-existent and that politicians and the public sector employees are in the game for their own selfish interests (Buchanan *et al.*, 1980). The policy conclusion seems obvious, namely that the size of government must be limited through a fiscal constitution that limits rent-seeking behaviour, especially the pressure from lobby groups (Brennan and Buchanan, 2000, 2001). If incentives are a source of difficulties in government, then how about the firm?

The revelations about the internal affairs of some major private companies around 2000 indicate clearly that the joint-stock institutional form for an enterprise has not solved the incentive problem. Oceanic groups of shareholders have seen their assets reduced to zero while the chief managers have pocketed enormous salaries, bonuses and pension benefits. The 'Percy Barnevik' syndrome shows that the institutions of capitalism, to speak against Oliver Williamson's positive argument (Williamson, 1998), have not resolved a fundamental principal–agent problem in the firm, namely how CEOs are to be prevented from looting an enterprise. Barnevik, the CEO of ABB, was designated the best manager possible, year in and year out, yet he left behind a giant enterprise in total disarray while pocketing total benefits worth more than 100 million dollars. The collapse of Enron and WorldCom proved even worse than the reduction in value and size of ABB, because it showed that chief managers would not hesitate to engage in criminal activities against their principal, the shareholders of the firm, if they could benefit in the short run and the probability of detection was low. There is no clear or obvious game solution to the principal–agent problem in a giant or global firm of instructing and monitoring CEOs as agents for the principal that could be added to Williamson's positive evaluation in *The Institutions of Capitalism* (1998). The decline in confidence for CEOs and board members of huge enterprises has hurt financial institutions and the real economy but there is no remedy in sight except eternal vigilance on the part of the principal.

People need public services. This truism may be easily substantiated with reference to infrastructure and social services besides the basic income protection that government typically provides against personal disaster or misfortune. However, with neo-liberalism came the unintended outcome that often public services were not replaced by corresponding and cheaper private services, as the argument for deregulation and privatisation claimed would happen. Instead, either public services declined in quality or sometimes simply vanished. *Qui bono?* The worst example is perhaps the British railways.

Finally, deregulation in many instances brought about the intended outcome – economic efficiency – but there were examples of stunning mistakes and dismal outcomes. A much discussed case is the electricity industry in California. The explanation, it has been argued, was not deregulation *per se*, but wrong deregulation. The California energy crisis was the consequence of a flawed regulatory design and of misguided decision-making at the time of the crisis, rather than the result of any inherent inability of electricity markets to work. Thus, economists have urged a market-based restructuring of California's electricity industry. In 2001, electricity rates were about 40 per cent higher than at the start of the industry's restructuring, state reregulation was increasing, and once-vibrant generators and utilities were struggling for solvency. Since the 2001 electricity crisis, two California utilities have become insolvent, the state has entered long-term contracts to buy electricity at exorbitant rates and the electricity trading industry has gone into near collapse. Meanwhile, the confidence of electricity reformers around the world has been shaken, and initiatives to introduce competition outside California have been delayed. In response to severe electricity price hikes and rolling blackouts in January 2001, the adherents of improved deregulation strongly recommended against the employment of long-term procurement contracts. California could have taken the following market steps toward recovery:

- develop competitive markets;
- reassemble a set of electricity oversight rules and policies;
- limit regulation to those functions the market cannot perform efficiently;
- allow unregulated producers to provide electricity generation;
- rebuild the commodity market for power;
- allow consumers and suppliers to enter into long-term contracts;
- implement real-time pricing of electricity.

If deregulation cannot be trusted, then the conclusion must be that one would start asking for reregulation. In the United Kingdom, for example the deregulation process has been followed by massive reregulation policies.

Second World impact

Whatever killed the planned economy, the fall of the Berlin Wall confirmed not only Hayek's critique on the planned economy but also the call from Chicago School economics that government be reduced. Incidentally, one may point put that Hayek's position has little in common with Chicago

School teachings, proceeding from an entirely different basis, namely Austrian economics (incomplete information) with Hayek and Walrasian theory (complete information) with Friedman and Stigler. The rationale of the planned economy was to outperform the capitalist system. When outcomes indicated that it could not be done, then why would countries cling to an economic theory which scholars had proven wrong from a theoretical point of view? Perhaps this is the ultimate explanation of why the Second World gave up their institutions so easily in the 1980s when the failure of the command economy became obvious? Several of the planned economies have managed the transition to the market economy well with rising output as a result, which is a positive outcome of the market philosophy taught by Chicago economists. Things are, however, different when the outcomes for the poor countries are examined.

Third World impact

It is difficult to point out several successful examples of the so-called *structural-adjustment policy (SAP)*, inspired by the Chicago School. The recommendation by the IMF and the WB to cut the public sector in poor countries did not make the economies flourish. Instead it worsened the situation by reducing much-needed social policies, as well as hurting infrastructure. Some countries have been pushed towards complete collapse by the failure of government to perform vital public sector tasks, as in West Africa, but also in the Caribbean. Perhaps one could mention Ghana and Zambia as successes of the SAP? The hard lesson to be learnt from the SAP is that government cannot be reduced to a minimalist state. Poor countries cannot have economic development unless there is also social development, which is what the SAP denied these countries. Reducing education, health care and social care have proven disastrous, especially for the 49 very poor countries of the world.

The world according to the Cambridge gospel: the relevance of social policy

For 30 years the market philosophy reigned as the dominant model in political economy. It overemphasised the contribution of markets to societies and failed to appreciate the immense contribution of government to the economy in the form of vital services. The world recession of 2000–03 has shown that markets are unstable, that contractual validity is a major problem in markets, that CEOs may loot their own companies, that privatisation of public enterprises is not a simple solution and that people tend to rely upon the state when markets fail or run into difficulties. Within a few months, Kenneth L. Lay turned from being a Wall Street hero into public enemy number one, transforming an unspectacular natural gas pipeline company into a financial powerhouse, and winning himself a place in the Texas Business Hall of Fame and several surveys of the world's top management, before falling into disgrace.

Perhaps market exuberance was necessary to balance the strong preference for a large role of the state in the economy as with the theory of the planned economy and the welfare state model. However, the theory of the efficient and omnipotent market linked with Chicago School economics missed one fundamental feature of any economy, namely the positive role that government can play in social policies. The Chicago School basically denied the policy relevance of market failure, stating that there was hardly any limit to what the market can handle. This is an exaggeration which must be pointed out not only by means of a critique of the main policy positions of Chicago School economists but also through a positive argument of where the necessity of government surfaces in the economy.

Not only was the role of the state in the economy minimised during the reign of the market philosophy, but there was the extremely negative analysis of government presented in the Public Choice School. Thus, even when the state could contribute positively to the economy, it was always described as a mechanism prone to degenerate into waste, favouritism and cronyism. Against the long-standing notion of market failures the new idea of state failure was launched by public choice scholars in order to again minimise the role of government in the economy. This is where we stand today in political economy, i.e. we need a new theory of the role of government in the economy. Such a theory must surpass the market exuberance of Chicago School teachings, as well as balance the fundamentally negative view of the state within the Public Choice School. Can such an argument be presented? It would have to include a principal–agent theory of government outlining how government can get the job done.

Perhaps the discussion in this chapter should have started with the Cambridge School, since it preceded the Chicago School in time. However, the Cambridge School was far less coherent, making it more difficult to pin it down. Here we will focus on the Cambridge ideas which have retained their relevance. Markets have proved that they can deliver huge output and that they tend to be competitive unless government intervenes with too much regulation or ownership. The idea of imperfect competition or the notion of monopolistic competition as alternative types of markets have fewer adherents today, as the basic choice is between competitive markets or government sanctioned monopoly. However, there is one Keynesian insight that has not been undone by Chicago School economics.

Keynesianism implied a positive evaluation of social policies, because they would contribute not only to expanding demand in the economy but they could also promote equality in distribution. Education should be more or less free, as well as health care and social care. A highly educated workforce that has access to modern health care and social care would both stimulate demand and thus economic growth, as well as enhance equality. This basic

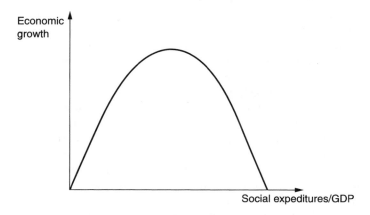

Figure 6.1 Social policy and economic growth.

insight of Keynes may appear naïve today when the costs of the welfare state have reached staggering proportions in relation to GDP and it may not be in accordance with the theory of incentives. But the key challenge is not to dismantle social policies but to make them incentive compatible and provide them with a sound financing. This is true of both rich and poor countries.

In rich countries there is little support for transferring social policies to the marketplace. Almost the entire population wants a basic level of social protection by government. The unresolved problem in social policy-making is how to make a welfare state compatible with economic efficiency. It may be analysed as the hyperbola of social expenditures (see Figure 6.1). The relationship between social policies and economic growth takes the shape of a hyperbola, meaning that at low levels of expenditures social policies enhance growth strongly. However, the impact from social expenditures peaks at a certain level and then it becomes negative when social expenditures skyrocket. The crux of the matter is for each country to decide upon the maximum level of social expenditures that are supporting economic growth in order to avoid an efficiency-equity trade-off. See Tables 6.1–6.3 for the country variation in various social expenditures in OECD.

Social expenditures in a broad definition make up the largest part of the public sector from a financial point of view. They are also the most difficult to handle politically, especially when the social costs have been allowed to run wild. To the social state belong the following costly items:

- education
- health care
- social care
- income protection.

These items, three allocative and one redistributive, tend to be the most costly ones in the budgets of governments at various levels of the state. And there is no strong theory identifying how demand and supply of these programmes are to be expressed and allowed to find an equilibrium. What is necessary (low expenditures) in a poor country is not acceptable in a rich country, but in both the First World and the Third World social policies are relevant state tasks and cannot be handed over to the market.

The allocative social policies have to struggle with two difficulties. First, there is the internal efficiency problem – productivity – meaning whether supply can be organised in such a manner that output is maximised at the same time as costs are minimised. Second, there is the question of *incentive compatibility*, or whether these allocative programmes can be structured so that they do not invite excessive utilisation or overuse. The income maintenance programmes have their own special difficulty, namely how they can be contained and stabilised in a long-run perspective, give the demographic trend. Changing demographics force countries around the world to re-examine their public pension systems. The EU nations are among those facing the greatest social, budgetary, and economic challenges as a result of their ageing populations, as they will be forced to rethink their public pension programmes and move away from traditional pay-as-you-go (PAYG) pension models to new systems based on savings and investment. The need for pension reform has engendered heated political debate in Europe, which mirrors the debate over social security reform in the United States.

Handing social policies entirely over to the market will not enhance economic growth or social justice. Public education is less problematic than public health care, because demand can be channelled much more easily in the former than in the latter. What is true of public health care also holds for social care, i.e. they are vital services for the population that cannot be handed over to the private sector.

Conclusion

Is government a mechanism for allocation, i.e. efficiency, or is its main task redistribution, i.e. social justice? This question has resumed its relevance today when the teachings of Chicago School economics offer less policy guidance. The world according to Chicago has been shattered by the severe economic recession in recent years, as well as the disclosures about fundamental problems of firm management in the market economy. In addition, deregulation and privatisation did not always result in the Stigler outcome, i.e. more quantity at lower prices. The call today from Friedman that government everywhere represents a threat against liberty and affluence in the world seems somehow misplaced, as what is needed is not less public policy but better public policies.

After decades of deregulation and privatisation the search is no longer for a minimalist state where most services have been turned over to the market and government reneges on its justice ambition to protect the vulnerable. The state is still a major player in the economy in various roles and there is little reason to expect that this will change in the twenty-first century. Governments in both rich and poor countries conduct several policies with differing ambitions:

- security, defence, law and order – rising commitments;
- infrastructure – lingering commitments;
- social policies – commitments in need of reform;
- regulatory policies – rising commitments.

The performance in many private enterprises has been such lately that citizens look for government for services, support and protection. In the poor countries of the world it is not less government that is at stake but better government, or government that is non-corrupt and delivers basic state functions, transparent governance. In rich countries the market economy needs a complement ranging from proper public services to social policies over income protection and the regulation of the private sector. This policy mix is more Cambridge than Chicago, especially in the emphasis on social policies and their contribution to economic development of the country. Social policies are necessary in any society, rich or poor. However, they can become too large and they pose principal–agent problems.

Note

1   The US billion is used throughout (1 US billion = 1000 million).

Appendix: Social spending in OECD countries

Table 6.1 Categories of social spending as percentage of gross domestic product (GDP) 1995 (countries sorted according to the relative size of private spending).

Country	Private	Public	Total
Netherlands	3.73	25.92	29.65
Sweden	2.76	33.03	35.79
Germany	2.38	26.70	29.08
Belgium	2.07	25.07	27.14
Korea	1.55	3.67	5.22
Italy	1.44	23.75	25.19
Iceland	1.25	18.63	19.88

(Continued)

Table 6.1 (Continued)

Country	Private	Public	Total
Denmark	1.15	32.41	33.56
Finland	1.08	31.24	32.32
Austria	1.08	27.88	28.96
Norway	0.94	27.62	28.56
Slovak Republic	0.87	13.53	14.40
United Kingdom	0.86	25.84	26.70
Portugal	0.82	17.51	18.33
France	0.65	28.98	29.63
United States	0.46	15.41	15.87
Australia	0.30	17.79	18.09
Japan	0.26	13.47	13.73
Spain	0.04	20.94	20.98
Switzerland	0.00	26.20	26.20
Poland	0.00	24.74	24.74
Luxembourg	0.00	23.30	23.30
Greece	0.00	21.15	21.15
Ireland	0.00	19.61	19.61
New Zealand	0.00	19.32	19.32
Canada	0.00	19.23	19.23
Czech Republic	0.00	18.64	18.64
Turkey	0.00	7.46	7.46
Mexico	0.00	7.44	7.44

Source: OECD (2003)

Note: The OECD Expenditure Database includes internationally comparable statistics on public and private social expenditure at programme level. The 13 social policy areas covered include: old age cash benefits, disability cash benefits, occupational injury and disease, sickness benefits, services for the elderly and disabled people, survivors, family cash benefits, family services, active labour market programmes, unemployment, health, housing benefits, other contingencies.

Table 6.2 Education expenditures as percentage of GDP 1995 (countries sorted according to the relative size of private spending)

Country	Private	Public	Total
United States	1.7	5.0	6.4
Germany	1.3	4.5	5.8
Japan	1.2	3.6	4.8
Australia	1.0	4.5	5.5
Mexico	1.0	4.6	5.6
Spain	1.0	4.6	5.5
Canada	0.7	6.2	6.9
Hungary	0.6	4.9	5.5
Czech Republic	0.5	4.9	5.4
Ireland	0.5	4.7	5.3
France	0.4	5.9	6.3
Austria	0.3	6.3	6.6
Denmark	0.3	6.4	6.7
Norway	0.2	7.0	7.2
United Kingdom	0.2	4.8	5.1
Italy	0.1	4.5	4.6
Netherlands	0.1	4.6	4.7
Sweden	0.1	6.3	6.4
Turkey	0.1	2.4	2.5
Belgium	0.0	5.0	5.0
Finland	0.0	6.3	6.3
Portugal	0.0	5.3	5.3
Poland	—	5.5	—
New Zealand	—	4.9	—
Greece	—	2.9	—

Source: OECD (2001a)

Table 6.3 Health care spending as percentage of GDP 1995 (countries sorted according to the relative size of private spending)

Country	Private	Public	Total
United States	7.2	6.0	13.2
Greece	4.1	4.8	8.9
Mexico	3.3	2.3	5.6
Korea	3.0	1.7	4.7
Canada	2.7	6.6	9.3
Australia	2.7	5.5	8.2
Switzerland	2.6	7.0	9.6
Belgium	2.6	6.1	8.7
Portugal	2.6	5.0	7.6
Netherlands	2.5	6.4	8.9
France	2.3	7.3	9.6
Austria	2.3	6.2	8.5
Germany	2.2	8.0	10.2
Italy	2.1	5.3	7.4
Ireland	2.0	5.3	7.3
Finland	1.8	5.7	7.5
New Zealand	1.7	5.6	7.3
Japan	1.6	5.6	7.2
Poland	1.6	4.4	6.0
Spain	1.5	5.5	7.0
Denmark	1.4	6.8	8.2
Iceland	1.3	6.9	8.2
Norway	1.3	6.7	8.0
Sweden	1.2	6.9	8.1
Hungary	1.2	6.3	7.5
United Kingdom	1.0	5.9	6.9
Turkey	1.0	2.4	3.4
Czech Republic	0.5	6.8	7.3
Luxembourg	0.5	5.8	6.3

Source: OECD (2001b)

7 Public teams are different from private teams

Introduction

The public, or the population of a country, expects the delivery of services from various groups of public employees that we will call 'teams', independently of how they are organised. The government has, basically, a contractual relationship with its various teams, from which follows the question of the *quid pro quo* of the interaction. Thus, we must ask: To whose advantage does the interaction between government and its teams result, the principal or the agent?

Team production in the private sector has been analysed in management theory as involving two kinds of decisions (Ouchi and Barney, 1987). First the top-level managers have to decide whether to set up their own teams (in-house production) or to buy services from outside teams (outsourcing). Second, the top-level managers have to monitor their own teams, selecting managers to run these teams efficiently. Team production involves the measurement of the productivity of the members of teams, which is more easily done for the group as a whole than for individual members of the group – the 'metering' question (Alchian and Coase, 1977; Cole, 2000; Bratton and Gold, 2003).

In this chapter the two central problems in team production – in-house versus out-of-house production and the monitoring of teams – will be examined in relation to the soft sector. The government business sector will be examined in Chapter 8. The key point made here is that the team problems are more difficult to solve in the public than in the private sector. The organisation and evaluation of teams is enormously facilitated by the existence of a clear and explicit profit function. When the objective function is not measurable or highly complex, team production is likely to become inefficient, as the necessary signals on effectiveness and productivity are lacking.

In the Weberian framework the key difference between public teams and private teams is derived from incentives. Public officials pursue a vocation – this is one of Weber's key ideas, whereas people in private teams maximise their selfish interests. We will try to derive the chief difference between public and private teams from institutions, not incentives. Public organisation is impossible without the use of institutions, especially if the rule of law is to be enforced. Let us begin by pinning down the key problems in public organisation.

Macro view of public organisation

Setting up and running organisations in the public sector can be analysed from two angles. First, there is the macro aspect of public organisation, dealing with the basic structure of public organisations involving the amount of decentralisation and the employment of various kinds of agencies, as well as the nature of the juridical bodies used to check government. Besides the federal model, one may distinguish between three ideal-types within the unitary framework, namely the British heterogeneous model versus the French homogenous model as well as the Swedish agency and Ombudsman model. Second, the micro aspect deals with the relationship between the managers and the employees in any public organisation and covers the problems of how to motivate and steer the crew towards a number of goals such as efficiency, job satisfaction and economy, given the legal restrictions within a rule of law framework – the 'crew' question.

Recent public sector reforms have included both aspects of public organisation, macro and micro. Thus, the macro reforms cover decentralisation, i.e. devolution as a macro objective figuring prominently within unitary states, and fiscal equalisation, attempted especially in federal systems. On the other hand, the micro zest for restructuring public organisations has targeted management and incentives in the running of any agency in the public sector.

The following macro aspects of public organisation have been much discussed during the last 20 years:

- *Overall structure: (a) Central government–regional government.* The division of tasks between the centre and the periphery is a contested matter in both federal and unitary systems. One may argue that federal systems have a bias for regional governments – states – whereas unitary systems display a bias for the central government. In reality, there are many combinations, such as centralised unitary, decentralised unitary, centralised federal and decentralised federal states. In theory, there is a strong preference for decentralisation, but in reality, centralisation is often the only response to public sector challenges, given the emphasis on equality that is typical of well-ordered societies.
  (b) Regional government–local government. The allocation of tasks between provinces or regions and communes is no less problematic. In some systems it is the regional level which has the upper hand, but in other systems the regional level tends to be hollow, as regions or provinces

are squeezed in between the central government and powerful communes.

- *Central government level: ministries – statutory agencies.* Central government can be organised according to the full ministerial responsibility model, placing the subunits under the leadership of large ministries as departments or executive agencies. Or the subunits can be organised as independent bodies outside the ministries – the statutory agency model, under which ministries tend to be small policy-making units, whereas the large agencies have major implementation responsibility. The legal status of the agencies or boards that make up the executive branch of government depends upon whether they can be changed with or without the approval of parliament. Statutory bodies and, even more so, constitutional bodies cannot be reorganised only by executive decision. Some constitutional or statutory bodies such as the Ombudsman or the auditing bureau are the agents of parliament and thus strictly speaking not part of the executive branch of government at all.

- *Judicial branch: administrative courts – tribunals and ordinary courts.* The judicial system in a well-ordered country comprises a wide variety of organisations. Two ideal-type models come to mind, although they are sometimes combined in a few countries. The civil law model favours a clear separation between two kinds of courts, administrative ones and ordinary courts. Only the former can handle complaints against the state, whereas the latter takes on private law matters. The common law model identifies the ordinary courts as competent for all kinds of legal issues, but it may complement the ordinary courts with a broad mix of tribunals, whose decisions may be tested in the ordinary courts. Although courts are public organisations, the difference between a civil law tradition and a common law tradition has political implications. Compare the French system with *Conseil d'etat* at the apex, together with the *Conseil constitutionnel* on the one hand, with the American Supreme Court on the other, where the Supreme Court really restrains the powers of the executive and the legislature.

- *Legislative branch.* Legislative organisation has been much discussed as one-chamber systems are evaluated against two-chamber systems. Here we will emphasise whether a country operates the special political and legal organisation of the Ombudsman. This office, whether in its Swedish or Danish version, has spread around the globe and constitutes one of the most effective mechanisms for accomplishing the rule of law.

Decentralisation has been a key macro objective in the public sector reforms during the last 20 years, argued on both efficiency and justice grounds. Thus, it is believed that services are better delivered by service providers close to the customer – flexibility, which would imply that provision should be placed with regional or local governments. The same conclusion is reached when participation is emphasised. Regional and local governments derive their legitimacy from their constituencies, which may express the demand for public services in a manner that reflects varying preferences. Yet, decentralisation is more a catchphrase than a real trend in many countries as it has its limits as a public sector reform strategy. The quest for equality sets clear limits on decentralisation or deconcentration. In federal systems, the income support from the federal government to the states has increased sharply in an effort to equalise service provision and taxation – fiscal equalisation. In unitary systems, the huge income support systems were always mainly national and have remained so despite all decentralisation.

The general analysis of public organisation is part of institutional research where one tries to isolate the outcomes of the operation of institutions. Besides the cross-sectional approach that is typical of general institutional analysis, one may look upon institutional evolution in terms of a longitudinal perspective on institutions. According to one approach to institutions, public organisations are heavily dependent upon legacies, or special administrative traditions – path dependency. I shall mention a few country-specific macro governance models.

Country-specific models of public organisation

Although there is great institutional variety in handling these macro aspects of public organisation, I employ a six-category classification for describing how countries differ in terms of macro organisation, not bringing up authoritarian systems but restricting myself to well-ordered societies. Thus, I have:

- *The Washington Model:* Three features stand out in this model, namely centralised federalism combined with pure presidentialism on the foundation of common law, which in its American version accepts strong legal review for all judges, finally Supreme Court.
- *The Bern Model:* Decentralised federalism is to be found in Switzerland *par preference.* In this country the regional level is the strongest one – the cantons, – in accordance with classical federal theory. The cantons, together with the communes, carry huge budgets and are responsible for many allocative and distributional programmes. Swiss dualistic federalism displays symmetrical features despite the immense size differences between the cantons. German federalism – *The Bonn-Berlin Model* – is different, as it is based upon the concepts of implementation, federalism and *Politikverflechtung* (Scharpf, 2004; Hesse and Ellwein, 2004).
- *The Whitehall Model:* One may discuss whether the classical British model of governance still exists after all the changes that have occurred since Mrs Thatcher started her neo-liberal revolution and Blair introduced far-reaching devolution. Yet, Whitehall still denotes the power of large

ministries in running a unitary state in accordance with the *ultra vires* concept of parliament sovereignty.

- *The Paris Model:* Perhaps one needs to go to France in order to have an example today of a centralised unitary model? In any case, Paris is the home of ministerial rule, meaning that the country is ruled by the great ministries in the central government through an emphasis on the principle of equal treatment under the law. It is enforced by the system of the *grands corps, grands écoles* and the *préfets*, although some devolution has taken place since 1980.
- *The Stockholm Model:* The Swedish model of governance includes two specific features, namely the large statutory agencies at arm's length from the ministries as well as the Ombudsman. The huge agencies were created early in the history of the Swedish state, as they date back to the reforms made by Chancellor Axel Oxenstierna in the mid-seventeenth century. The Ombudsman as an office of control of the executive branch and also of the judicial branch was introduced in 1809 in an effort by the *Riksdag* to promote the rule of law before the advent of democracy.
- *The New Zealand Model:* Structuring governance in accordance with market mechanisms became the central feature in the New Zealand extensive reforms that took place in the 1980s and 1990s. Thus the welfare state was scaled back dramatically and New Public Management was introduced in both the business sector and the soft sector. The new philosophy of contractualism for the public sector was carried to its extreme in the New Zealand model as various kinds of short-term contracts within a tendering/bidding regime replaced the long-term contracts typical of the bureaucracy.

It is conceivable that one may wish to introduce more country-specific models of public organisation. Perhaps one can claim that each country has its special style of framing its public sector – institutional path dependency? Much public sector research is devoted to the analysis of how the major country models change over time as a result of public sector reform and country traditions.

The main idea in macro reforms is decentralisation. It has been especially attractive in unitary systems, whereas federal systems continue their semi-nal track towards more of centralisation. As public sector reform has been very intense during the last 20 years, one may point out that they have been driven mainly by micro ideas about management, i.e. incentives and con-tracting. Let us attempt to pin down the key reforms of public organisation in relation to the problem of how to set up, instruct, steer, monitor and evaluate public teams of employees – *the team question*. It does not matter whether public organisation occurs at the central government level or at the regional and local government level. There occurs the same problem of setting up a mechanism for the execution and implementation of policy, whatever the level of government may be.

Public teams: people and rules

In principle, the people who take on the tasks of providing public services are in the same situation as the crew on an aeroplane. The pilots know how many they are and their work is managed in accordance with a plan comprising basically a division of labour as well as a hierarchy of command. Each person has a special job and each job has a work description. This formal organisation will never be true of the real situation, as strong elements of informal organisation always intrude upon the plan. For public teams it used to be true that informal organisation mattered much, as the civil service in various countries developed special codes of behaviour which expressed *inter alia* social status. The French *corps* exemplify this to an exaggerated extent, but in many countries the higher echelons of the civil service developed a special culture on the basis of prestige.

The civil service comprises the teams in the ministries and the central agencies. These teams attempt to uphold the image that they are special in relation to other public employees in order to receive higher prestige and better terms of contract. In some countries they are employed by a special agency in accordance with central recruitment criteria. In other countries each ministry recruits its own employees. The codes of civil service teams comprise formal and informal rules singling out these teams as special in various ways: employment, working hours, pension, health care, training, retrenchment, etc. Although these codes distinguish between the civil service proper and all other kinds of public employees, they have become more difficult to uphold when the public sector expands, bringing in new kinds of teams or when the philosophy of outsourcing is introduced in relation to ministries and central agencies.

The large teams of employees in the public sector are not to be found in the civil service, at least not in most countries. The huge groups of public sector employees are the teachers in primary and secondary education as well as the health and social care personnel. They are often organised as regional or local government teams. Higher education often has its own teams, the academic profession. Yet these distinctions became less relevant as the number of public employees grew tremendously during the twentieth century. Thus, regional and local government employees have often struggled successfully to receive the same employment security as the civil servants. And the civil service has not been spared when new methods of service delivery have been attempted, resulting in retrenchments.

Here we will underline the general problems when setting up public teams, whatever code of conduct they may cherish:

- *The nature of the team: insourcing versus outsourcing.* This question involving the choice between setting up a public team or relying upon a private team may be resolved by some combination, or a public–private partnership.

- *The size of the team: the metering problem.* This question involves determining the size of the public team, which depends upon how the contribution of each single participant can be measured.

These two questions concerning the nature and the size of the teams to be employed in the provision of services are central in any micro perspective on public organisation. They tend to be resolved by the employment of managerial theory. What, then, is public management?

The management of public organisations has become a major theme in the reform movement New Public Management (NPM), which delivers specific answers to the two team questions above. NPM is generally seen as a new version of an old doctrine, namely managerialism. It is argued in public sector reform that public organisation is in need of managerialism. Let us discuss the latter claim before we examine the two problems of team production.

Micro perspective on public organisation

There has been a strong dose of managerialism in all the public sector reforms whatever country-specific model one adheres to. Managerialism has a history in government which dates back to Taylorism in the early twentieth century, but the new managerialism concerntrates on contracting and outsourcing. Managerialism relaxes the ethical perspective on public teams. Ethics in traditional public service used to involve codes, ethics oversight agencies and transparency. For the new public service the central question is value for money. This question concerns how to achieve the public interest when implementation of policy is shared with organisations that have other interests. There is pressure in contracted-out programmes for the contractor's goals to affect the government's goals. When policy choices are handed over to contractors, the issue of accountability becomes acute.

Old managerialism

Managerialism emphasises the use of management tools and techniques. A simple definition of managerialism as it relates to the public sector would equate it with the importation of business management practices, designed specifically to increase economic efficiency. Managerialism is an ideology which may be encountered in any organisational setting, a technology which views analytical tools, developed to help managers make decisions, as ends in themselves. Thus, managerialism displays faith in the ability of managers for problem solving, especially the top echelons of management, the CEOs.

Concern with efficiency has proved significant throughout the history of public administration and the search for tools to improve the delivery of public services continues unabated. Recent trends ranging from total quality management (TQM) to reinventing government show that managerialist themes remain relevant. Managerialism targets economic efficiency, or the pursuit of maximum output with minimum inputs. The relevance of efficiency in public administration was established by Woodrow Wilson in the United States, Max Weber in Germany and Henri Fayol in France. The managerial ideology focuses on the tools and techniques of management science and the ability of managers to use those techniques to resolve problems.

Profit-seeking organisations used to harbour managerialist values. The Chester Barnard theory outlined how managers (agents of the owners) ensure the compliance of the work-force (as their agents) in the pursuit of the organisation's goals, although he largely bypassed the negative implications for the individual or the environment of the organisation (Barnard, 1972, 2003). According to Barnard, managers use a variety of means to inculcate appropriate values within their subordinates, enhancing cooperation in the achievement of organisational goals. Employees submit to managerial control and sacrifice large measures of their freedom because of the material rewards made possible by their cooperation. As long as these organisations continue to provide sufficient economic benefits, the employees submit to managerial control, enhancing the influence of large, complex organisations and their managers in modern society.

The search for efficiency in public service was stimulated by the progressive movement active in the United States in the late 1800s and through the early decades of the twentieth century. Taylor and his theory of 'scientific management' developed techniques such as time-and-motion studies and incentive pay systems. His work focused on increasing efficiency, as Taylor viewed it as a means of achieving satisfying outcomes for everyone. Thus, the application of his techniques would lead to more profits for owners and investors. Consumers would enjoy lower prices deriving from lower production costs. Employees would benefit from higher compensation, but workers would also benefit from the change in management his methods required. The US Congress passed the Pendleton Act in 1883, which established the federal civil service system, promising the elimination of politics from personnel decisions ('spoils system') as well as greater efficiency in government operations. The application of science to administration provided the method by which those goals could be realised. Scientific management employed the measurement and classification of work processes. It became embedded in civil service job classification rules, which required that jobs be classified and graded according to the amount of skill and training required for acceptable performance, the relative difficulty of a particular job, and the degree of responsibility associated with a position.

Luther Gulick bypassed the minutia of work processes in order to turn his attention to organisational structure, proposing that there were principles of administration upon which a science of management could be built. These principles addressed the proper span of control for effective coordination of work, unity of command, and the division of labour within an organisation. Adhering to the principles would promote unity of purpose among organisation members and thereby maximise technical efficiency. As a member of the Brownlow Commission, Gulick's ideas and recommendations were used by Roosevelt and the New Deal. Gulick saw the role of the bureaucracy in the United States as assisting the national government, working through its administrative apparatus. The new managerialism with NPM is more radical than old managerialism, as it calls for the employment of market decision-making mechanisms to a much higher extent.

New managerialism

Within NPM, there is an emphasis on management but also on competition. Thus, NPM favours the various mechanisms of tendering and bidding; it also endorses the implications of the use of these market tools for public management. NPM entails a reflection upon the following questions.

In- and/or outsourcing?

In classical public administration a radical separation was made between bureaucracy (in-house production) and public procurement (outsourcing). Core functions belonged under bureaucracy, whereas things such as equipment and materials could be supplied by means of public purchases. Public procurement would be short-term market-orientated activities, often centralised to one purchasing department covering several bureaux. Bureaucracy, on the other hand, would be the one and only mode of putting together a team of permanent staff on a long-term basis. This sharp distinction between procurement and bureaucracy is hardly valid any longer after decades of public sector reform.

The line separating in-house and out-of-house provision of services is all but sharp today, as tendering/bidding mechanisms have come to cover far more than merely equipment and materials. One consequence of the increasing use of market testing is that public teams have become less internal (Kaufman, 1976, 1989). Today, public teams may comprise both permanent staff and subcontracted personnel. It would be up to the managing board of the team to find the optimal combination of in-house and out-of-house production. One could analyse this problem as a choice between two modes of production under a given budget restriction (Figure 7.1).

Given two production lines combining in-house and out-of-house production (isocost curves), a team could maximise output and minimise costs by choosing EF or GH along two budget lines. The slopes of the lines express both the available resources and the current technology in using in-house and out-of-house provision. If out-of-house production becomes cheaper, then the use of it increases.

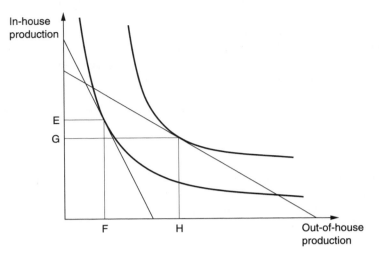

Figure 7.1 In-house and out-of-house production.

In private management theory the employment of outsourcing has recently been hailed as the most important change since the creation of scientific management with Taylor and Fayol, who favoured in-house production along a hierarchical model. The so-called 'Nike revolution' in management started an altogether different use of outsourcing, retaining only core functions within the firm. Downsizing became the key strategy in the private sector around 1990 and it has meant that giant firms have changed their structure altogether (e.g. French Alcatel), suggesting that it may sell most factories and then subcontract with them.

Now, the choice between in-house and out-of-house production can in private management be made according to some rational principle, e.g.:

- asset-specific knowledge (Williamson)
- transaction costs (Coase)
- monitoring capacity (Alchian).

Thus, according to economic organisation theory, one may view the firm as a nexus of contracts, where one set of contracts is long-term, establishing an employee relationship with power of the manager to direct work, and another set is short-term under which the firm buys services from individuals. The firm should find an optimal amount of long-run contracts and short-run contracts based on considerations of price as well as risk. In short, the firm would outsource standardised work but in – source work involving asset specific knowledge (Williamson, 1999; Williamson *et al.*, 1993; Williamson and Masten, 1999).

In the public sector, where public organisation prevails against a background of rule-of-law notions – such as predictability under the rules, rights and the possibility of complaint and redress – matters are not quite so easy. In-house production appears often the best form of public organisation when legality, predictability and security under the laws are to be fulfilled. The rule-of-law nature of public administration sets definitive limits on outsourcing, even when this would be cost efficient. In the soft sector, as well as in the social security sector, public administration focuses on the case or the dossier. It contains all the relevant information about the case administered. How could the handling of the dossier be outsourced without hurting the rule-of-law requirement?

Monitoring: how much?

In-house production presupposes monitoring, but what is the optimal amount of it? Alchian and Demsetz (1972, reprinted 1987) argued that organisation in the private sector runs into the difficulty of the so-called metering problem. When one has a crew of people, then one must first decide on who goes where and who does what. Then one must get information about whether this division of labour really works. In principle, like Alchian and Demsetz, one would like to know the marginal value of each member of the team – i.e. metering them on a continuous basis. But metering is not costless (Pugh, 1997; Pugh and Hickson, 1997). Thus, I arrive at the problem of monitoring (Figure 7.2).

Monitoring is an activity which displays decreasing marginal value but increasing marginal costs. Thus, when monitoring is introduced it may have great benefits, but the value tapers off as monitoring increases. Monitoring works best by anticipation, meaning that when a team cannot predict whether it will be evaluated or not, it will keep its productivity record

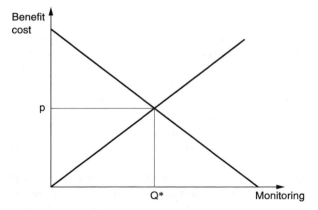

Figure 7.2 Monitoring: costs and value.

on track. If there is massive or continuous evaluation, then monitoring is trivialised.

One of the great risks in monitoring is collusion among agents. A monitoring team may tacitly cooperate with the team that is evaluated in order to protect it from the negative consequences of critique. Both teams are agents of the principal, but one is supposed to investigate the other. One way to solve the collusion problem is to divide government into several principals – executive, legislative and judicial – and let one of them be the principal of the service-providing teams (executive branch) and another be responsible for the monitoring team (legislative or judicial branch).

Monitoring may target either rule obedience or productivity or both. Or there may be different monitoring teams which target different aspects of team performance, such as legal, financial or efficiency aspects. One key question is whether monitoring really has consequences when performance is considered inadequate in an evaluation of some sort. When evaluation is made a regular and predictable phenomenon, then the teams concerned will develop strategies to neutralise the potentially disruptive impact of monitoring. Only if evaluation is done in an unpredictable manner with more-or-less severe budgetary consequences will monitoring work to the benefit of the principal.

Competition between agents

Principal–agent theory implies that agents will only lower their price if they have to compete with each other. Whenever an agent has a monopoly position, then he/she will capture economic rents some way or another. Competition, thus, has to be introduced into the public sector. The question is, however, whether this is really possible, or whether it is efficient in a broader sense. The introduction of competition into the public sector has called for not only the deregulation and incorporation of public enterprises (see Chapter 8), but also the creation of new governance mechanisms in the provision of classical public services such as compulsive competitive tendering, tournaments and auctions. Government has always employed competitive purchasing techniques within its procurement activities (Laffont and Tirole, 1993), but the new purchaser–provider model requires government to buy most of its services from the set of providers through competition. The purchaser–provider scheme has in some cases led to a complete reorganisation of local governments. The general lesson is that transaction costs or management costs go up, whereas the standard production costs go down when the purchaser–provider mechanism is employed.

Thus, competition among agents will only result in an efficiency gain if the gain in reduced production costs is not eaten up by the increase in transaction costs including management costs. Besides, there is the risk of collusion among purchaser and provider agents. Often government employs a regulatory agency to check the quality and price of its agents. However, government can never be sure that regulation works or that the regulatory agents do not collude with the agents they monitor. Regulation is never costless.

Tendering/bidding

The core of NPM is the purchaser–provider model, meaning that government should attempt to create an internal market for the provision of public services and choose between alternative service providers on the basis of the price or the value of their products. Government will promote efficiency in the public sector if it enlarges the scope of public procurement – this is the gist of NPM.

Government as rational purchaser makes sense in many connections. Government is a major player in the economy, buying lots of things through a massive set of public contracts. With a little bit of imagination, government may replace insourcing with outsourcing or auction out the use of its assets (Tirole, 1988). When government employs tournaments and auctions, then it gets better information about marginal value and marginal cost, thus counteracting the probability of Niskanen budgeting in bureaucracies. The central question is, though, how far tendering/bidding may be used in relation to the provision of public services. Setting up an internal market may prove difficult if few or no suppliers are forthcoming naturally.

Accrual budgeting

'Accrual budgeting' is the term for budgetary reforms which supplement input budgeting with output budgeting. The basic problem in accrual budgeting is the estimation of the value of the outputs connected with public services, as well as the recognition of all the costs incurred, now or in the future. When a strict NPM scheme is followed, all public services being tendered, the value of public services will be estimated. However, such a market valuation is only available for public services that can be tendered.

Public sector reform targeting the budgetary process has not been successful in accomplishing change, as emphasised by Wildavsky (1986a,b; Wildavsky and Swedlow, 2000; Wildavsky and Caiden, 2003). The budgetary process cannot be transformed into a planning procedure and its usefulness for governance is limited. The yearly budgetary process where requests fight with appropriations has a special logic. It tends to be cash-focused as well as incremental, meaning that the yearly budget has a fixed base in relation to which small yearly changes – plus or minus – are made. The yearly budgetary process also tends to focus on inputs despite the many reforms that underline outputs and outcomes.

Budgeting in the public sector tends to be heavily institutionalised, because public money is, after all, to be accounted for. What matters first and foremost for the legislative assembly when it formally approves the budget with all its appropriations is to be able to predict and control the cash flows involved. These cash sums must be covered somehow on the income side of the budget, through taxes, charges or borrowing, if printing money is not allowed. Budgeting still tends to focus on expenditures, despite all the efforts to introduce outputs or outcomes into budgeting. The main benefit of accrual budgeting is that it is easier to see whether the budget strategy is funded in a sustainable manner because accrual financial statements would reflect the full cost of service provision (including depreciation) and disclose all financial obligations incurred each year (such as superannuation and long service leave liabilities), even if the cash costs will rise in future years. Thus, accrual budgeting provides:

- *Longer term focus:* Shifting attention from year-by-year cash management to managing service delivery over the longer term.
- *Better resource decisions:* Showing the full cost of service delivery, including the effects of decisions made now that will result in increased cash outflows in the future.
- *Greater accountability:* Improving the transparency of government accounting, detecting, e.g. where funding levels will not provide for asset replacement.

The accrual budget shows the full cost of services, including non-cash expenses such as depreciation and liability for employee entitlements, while the statement of financial position shows where agencies are building up liabilities or running down cash reserves to deliver services. This will allow more sustainable provision of services by government providers. Accrual budgeting develops government's role as 'owner' of the public sector agencies providing services. Management of the 'equity' of these agencies relies on the information provided by the financial statements as part of the accrual budgeting cycle.

Limits of new managerialism

New Public Management has one narrow and one wide sense. Sometimes the term is used rather indiscriminately to refer to any and all public sector reforms during the last 20 years. But most often it refers to a specific subset of these reforms, namely the emphasis on management tools in the provision of public services, especially contracting. NPM is thus a new form of managerialism. Yet, managerialism, whether old or new, remains a contested philosophy for public organisation. The argument in favour of managerialism implies that public teams need strategic management to the same extent as private organisations or firms. I shall shortly indicate what the criticism of the new managerialism aims at, arguing that public teams are not merely any team of people to be instructed, motivated and monitored.

Red tape

NPM has aimed at removing rules and regulations for state agencies, allowing for more discretion and degrees of freedom for bureaucrats. Civil servants and professions need discretion to use their expertise without obsolete regulations and pointless paperwork. Yet the rules are there in order to enhance due process and fairness. Due process requires time, e.g. when protecting against arbitrary dismissal and promoting fairness in hiring, promotion and assignments. There is a trade-off between reducing due process regulations and the substance of individual rights and enhancing governmental fairness: Can government procedures be streamlined without harm to fairness?

Agencies protect people through regulations and their enforcement. Much public policy aims at the regulation of the economy and the private sector, which has to be done through the issuing of rules to be enforced through institutionalism by means of state sanctions for failure to obey. Red tape informs about rights to many forms of human associations, parents and children, students and teachers, labour and management, borrowers and lenders, brokers and investors, management and individual workers, researchers and their human subjects, husbands and wives. How could racism and sexual harassment, as well as child and spouse abuse, be counteracted without government regulation (Frederickson and Smith, 2003)?

Accountability

When contracts replace hierarchy, the logic of governance changes. Instead of coordination and staffing, as well as systems of oversight, the focus is on formulation of requests for proposals or competitive bids, the description and measurement of deliverables and the development of incentives and sanctions. When governmental activities are carried out by non-governmental organisations, hierarchies are replaced by contracts between governments and contractors and the chain of authority from policy to implementation is replaced by a process of negotiation that separates policy-making from output delivery. Top officials cannot give orders to contractors, because they can only shape the contractual incentives which the contractors pursue. The many transactions between governments, contractors and subcontractors may be conducive to corruption. The increased propensity for corruption associated with contracting out can only be counteracted by greater transparency in public affairs.

The competition argument claims that many governmental functions, such as state-run schools, would be more effective if they were conducted as businesses. The capacity of market competition to increase efficiency is no doubt correct, as market competition assumes an open and even playing field where actors buy the best product at the lowest price. The main ethical issue associated with markets is not kickbacks and bribery, but fairness.

Fairness is not a concept that fits well into the logic of markets. But fairness, both procedurally as in due process and in outcomes as with equality, is often the core issue in government. The private market is designed to be efficient but democratic government is designed to be fair. Government is more than a smart buyer, as emphasised especially by George Frederickson in many publications.

Downsizing

It has become fashionable to cut the number of employees in the civil service or state agencies merely to re-employ them under private law contracts. This is then called 'cutting government' but in reality, there is no real downsizing, only a transfer of the employees from public to private law employment. It is true that the support for cutting government begins to evaporate as soon as cutting government means entitlements. When asked which federal programmes 'should be cut back in order to reduce the federal budget deficit', a majority of Americans said 'no' to cuts in unemployment insurance (64 per cent), environmental spending (67 per cent), Medicaid (73 per cent), Social Security (86 per cent), and Medicare (88 per cent), while 65 per cent of Americans favoured cutting government and reducing the deficit a majority would wish to prevent cuts in federal programmes that aid farmers (52 per cent), provide loans to college students (65 per cent), put more police on the streets (68 per cent), and fund school lunches (77 per cent) (Kettl and DiIulio, 1995). Downsizing the bureaucracy appears to be much easier and cuts can be made across the bureaucracy, leaving programmes in place but with fewer staff. Downsizing only means reducing the number of those who work for government. For every one federal civil servant there are almost five others in the hidden bureaucracy, working for government but not as a part of government. The hidden bureaucrats are in the defence contract companies, the space contract companies, the beltway bandits, and in the non-profit and non-governmental organisations with governmental contracts (Marquand, 2004; Etzioni, 2001; Suleiman, 2005). In the rhetoric of reinventing government, a way was found to save the bureaucracy by hiding it. The federal bureaucracy provides more and better services for less, supporting the reinvention slogan of 'a government that works better and costs less', because those who once worked directly for government are under contract in the shadow bureaucracy. The US Federal Government has shrunk the formal bureaucracy but at the same time it provides the same services.

Public organisation and public teams

Public employees work in teams with government as their principal, whether it is a federal, regional or local government. The civil service is one type of public team, having often special conditions of employment with the national government. The general trend in the development of public employment has, however, been to reduce the differences in pay and favours between the alternative public teams. However, a public team is not merely any team of people. There are certain pertinent differences between public and private teams, which need to be pinned down. I shall emphasise the following characteristics.

Relevance of administrative law

In public organisation a set of specific norms has to be satisfied, especially in the soft sector and the social security sector. These norms have emerged from the past as the implications of the enforcement of the rule of law in the public sector. These norms vary somewhat from one country to another, depending upon which legal family the country belongs to: common law, civil law or Scandinavian law. They include *inter alia* the following norms:

- impartiality
- openness and publicity
- written documentation
- predictability
- compensation
- complaint
- redress.

To enhance these basic principles of justice, public administration employs the dossier mechanism, i.e. the collection of all relevant information about a case in one single file. This dossier should in principle be open to the persons involved, and constitutes the basis for any decision or action.

The dossier mechanism is not known in the private sector, where the fundamental unit is the transaction, which needs to be recorded correctly, however. Public organisation without the dossier mechanism would easily fall prey to arbitrariness and appropriation. By collecting all the relevant information in one place one enhances openness and counteracts arbitrariness as well as appropriation. The dossier may be circulated among those concerned and multiplied if necessary. However, managing the dossier takes time and consumes resources. It restricts the employment of mere efficiency criteria in public management, as other criteria like equality, probity, accountability and due process also need to be taken into account. Whereas institutional development in the private sector may be analysed as transaction cost minimising, the guarantee of the rule of law in the public sector requires more.

Expertise and monopoly

Quality in the private sector is mainly derived from competition, whereas in the public sector, quality is mainly a function of expertise. Public organisations use time to improve their operations by acquiring better and more useful knowledge. Private organisations target profitability and use information in order to be competitive. The standard image of a governmental agency is that of Kaufman's immortal organisation that develops a singular expertise, which takes time to emerge (Kaufman, 1976). This is the basic reason that there is most often only one bureau active within one area.

Expertise is linked with costs. The principal–agent framework predicts that any advantage in terms of knowledge will be used for strategic purposes. Expertise tends to be transformed into asset-specific knowledge, whose price will be bid up. Expertise and uniqueness go together. Public teams will develop expertise but at the same time underline their uniqueness. Expertise is the foundation of monopoly in the public sector, but it is also a guarantee of quality in service provision.

As government's reliance on contracting out has increased, there is a clear danger of its disinvestment of its own intelligence capacity – 'hollowing out'. Government has often employed world-class experts on virtually every issue: mapmakers, chemists, engineers, attorneys, housing economists, librarians, agricultural analysts, food safety specialists. Surrendering ever more expertise and influence to contractors is a transfer of knowledge from government to private interests, undermining the accountability of government. The basic logic of hollowing out is: Voters elect officials to make policy, and elected officials delegate power to administrators. These administrators delegate the delivery of goods and services to private partners. And those private partners have an advantage in expertise over government officials with which they effect public policy (Pierre and Peters, 2000).

Conclusion

Public organisation involves the setting up of public teams, which requires the resolution of two questions in the crew problem, namely whether to rely upon a crew of one's own as well as deciding upon the correct size of the crew. These questions – insourcing versus outsourcing, as well as the metering problem – call for the use of management theory. However, public management is different from private management, as not only are the rules of the game different but they also play a larger role in public than in private management.

The *differentia specifica* of public organisation include: (1) non-profit purposes; (2) accountability; (3) political involvement. The key question then becomes how these properties of public organisation are to be married with the *genus proximum* of public organisations, which is the performance of teams in order to achieve objectives through management. The problem of managing a team is a micro problem involving incentives. In a micro perspective on public organisation one needs to decide whether to have in-house or out-of-house production, as well as how the marginal contribution of each member of the teams is to be measured. The specific properties of public organisation derived from the rule of law constitute restrictions on the management problem and they contribute to making public teams different from private ones.

In the macro perspective on public organisation it is not the management perspective which is at the centre. Instead the question of decentralisation looms large, as with the theory of fiscal federalism (Ter-Minassian, 1997). In setting up a public sector, a society must decide about the vision of tasks between various levels of government, as public organisation at the macro level includes the relationships between the three basic political powers, the executive, the legislature and the judiciary. In addition, macro public organisation includes the positioning of the central civil service, to be located either in ministries (executive agencies) or in separate statutory bodies. There is institutional path-dependency in macro public organisation, as different countries have varying administrative traditions. In the micro perspective on public organisation, the problems of principal–agent interaction surface whether it is a matter of public administration or public management.

8 Public firms

Introduction

Public enterprises constitute a significant portion of the economy in both well-ordered societies and in Third World countries. But their governance regime has not been identified with success. It seems almost as if it is the case that whatever regime one puts in place for these firms, one ends up facing unresolved problems. There are a few contradictions in the concept of a public enterprise which remain whatever governance regime one chooses – see *Bureaucrats in Business* (World Bank, 1995).

One may distinguish between two ideal-type regimes for the public enterprise. On the one hand, there is the *traditional regime*, which places the public enterprise in between a bureau and a firm: the trading department model. The trading department is basically a public monopoly protected by public regulation and controlled legally by the finance ministry. On the other hand, there is the *neo-liberal regime*, or the private sector model of a joint-stock company, which operates in a deregulated environment and where the role of government is strictly limited to that of owner of equity. The neo-liberal regime appears superior on the basis of efficiency, but there are a few major problems, which may be stated in terms of the principal–agent model, e.g. that the CEOs tend to choose the strategy of looting. The underlying game is called adverse selection.

The relevance of the neo-liberal philosophy in relation to the public sector has been displayed most forcefully in its business sector, where the new governance regime of the public enterprise has been implemented in several countries. This involves a move from the traditional model of the public enterprise to the joint-stock model, a development which Thynne designated early as 'incorporation' (Thynne, 1994). Together with deregulation and partial privatisation, the policy of incorporation has meant that little remains of the traditional public enterprise. The purpose of this chapter is to discuss pros and cons of this major transformation, as well as analyse the new strategies of the public joint-stock company. When the government monopolies have been deregulated and perhaps partly privatised as joint-stock companies, which strategies do these often giant firms pursue when faced with fierce competition? Besides the impact of country tradition, the choice of a governance regime for the public enterprise is the result of deliberations about the principal–agent problems involved in setting up and directing a firm.

The contradictions inherent in the public enterprise

The traditional public enterprises in Europe or the public utilities in the United States always faced conflicting demands upon them from various groups in society. Thus, they had to struggle with trade-off between conflicting goals. These contradictions result from the following goals, which cannot be satisfied simultaneously:

- *Profit:* Should public enterprises really make profit? On whom? Can they instead make a loss because it results from a Pareto-optimal allocation?
- *Ownership:* Who owns the public enterprises? The state or the population? Or shareholders, or perhaps their stakeholders?
- *Competition:* Should there be complete deregulation of public enterprises or public utilities? For instance, when all forms of competition are allowed, even those that may bring down a public enterprise, then what can be done if a public enterprise goes bankrupt?

To handle these goal tensions and ambiguities in one way or another, two set of rules have been institutionalised. Thus, we have:

- *The old regime:* Monopoly, trading department, cost prices.
- *The new regime:* Competition, joint-stock company, profitability.

Whichever regime government chooses to put in place, tensions are bound to arise between various goals for the public enterprises. Thus, we have the following contradictions:

- *Competition versus public necessity:* If there is competition, then one must accept creative destruction. But can public enterprises really be allowed to go down?
- *Profitability for owners versus public service:* It is true that enterprises exist for making profits, but why would public enterprises maximise profits when they are supposed to provide vital services to the public? If allowed to make profits, then what is the proper profit level in a public utility, given their market dominance? Who will pocket the gain?

There is a risk that the different roles of government become confused when a regime for public enterprises is put in place by the state, as there is hardly available a philosophy of how to trade the various objectives above against each other. In the economy, government typically plays various roles which are not easily combined. Thus, we have government as (1) owner; (2) regulator; (3) umpire. It is not difficult to imagine tensions between these roles. We need to consider the following questions: If public enterprises, owned by the state, are placed under a competitive regime, then can they also be left when they face bankruptcy – does creative destruction apply? If public enterprises are to be run as profitable companies, then what is the sense of profit here? Could it also include windfall profits from market power guaranteed by government? If government is to be a just umpire (impartiality, neutrality, objectivity), then how can it be the owner of some of the players in a competitive economy?

Resolving the key questions about management and ownership of a public enterprise takes us into the main theories of public regulation and industrial organisation (Spulber, 1989; Tirole, 1988; Laffont and Tirole, 1993). Here I will emphasise the principal–agent perspective on the management and ownership questions in relation to public firms (Laffont and Martimort, 2001).

Public enterprises and the economy

In the advanced economies of Western Europe, public enterprises have always been very important players. They have been strongly present in infrastructure, where the European solution to the problem of market failure was different from the American one. Thus, in Western Europe firms operating in infrastructure – including telecommunications, railways, air transportation, water, sewage and energy in its various forms – were socialised or nationalised and owned directly either by the national government or by regional and local governments – the European public enterprise model. The contrasting American solution included privately owned utility companies under a public regulatory regime setting both quantities and prices – the American public utility model.

Public firms remain today of utmost importance in the economies of Western Europe, but their status and behaviour have been radically changed during the last 20 years. They were always special due to their mission of serving their ultimate principal, the public. At the same time, as other enterprises they had to follow the logic of business. The tension between public mission and business is still there, despite all the institutional changes, including the creation of the internal market in the EU in 1987. But the trade-off is now struck differently, as the economics of public firms now weigh much more heavily than do the politics of these firms.

Massive deregulation has changed the US public utilities and the parastatals in the Third World have been restructured in many countries.

Both institutional change and the choice of new strategies drive the transformation of public enterprises. It is difficult to tell which is the most important change factor. Both institutions and strategies matter. The key problem is that of consistency. When one sector of the economy changes so quickly and profoundly from one regime to another, there are considerable risks for contradictions between rules, behaviour and mission. There are some striking differences between the old system of traditional public enterprises and the new competitive system. The basic interpretation of the new situation is that public firms develop specific strategies as a response to the competition regime under which they have had to operate since deregulation started. The aim of these strategies is to present the firms with market stability, but at the same time they cannot engage in traditional tactics to enhance monopoly power. The outcome is a situation where a few giant public firms compete, while also engaging in strategies to enhance market power.

The internal changes made during the 1980s and 1990s have focused on the legal transformation of public enterprises into joint-stock companies. The external changes transforming the environment of public enterprises have involved replacing regulation and legal monopolies with deregulation and competition. The latter change in particular has been driven by the evolution of a common market in Western Europe, regulated by one competition regime, covering the production not only of private goods and services but also of public infrastructure.

New institutions for the firm, as well as for a sector of the economy, trigger new behaviour strategies. What needs to be discussed is whether these responses to institutional change promote or counteract the basic mission of the enterprises concerned. Here the term 'public enterprise' will be used to refer to the traditional enterprises before large-scale deregulation set in, and 'public firm' for enterprises after the move to deregulate infrastructure. Deregulation has led to the choice of a different governance mechanism, namely the incorporated company or limited liability firm in which government is a key owner of equity (Thynne, 1994).

In a deregulated market with large firms, whether public or private, there will be a search for strategies that make all of them equal players in a level playing field: 'like to like'. Since private firms seek to maximise profit, public firms will do the same. There are various strategies that enhance profit maximisation, and all players will use them: 'like to like'. Thus public firms in Western Europe engage in strategies that increase their market power and they use their capital as the key instrument in the oligopoly games that result from incorporation and deregulation. When firms make a huge profit, then the CEOs will try to pocket some of it – whether the firm is private or public: 'like to like'.

The recent institutional changes in both firm nature and firm environment create a similar business climate in all the countries despite historical legacies. The internal market of the EU has been enlarged by means of new directives, which concern infrastructure and require that all public and private firms operate on a level playing field. Thus, the changes have brought about a convergence in both legal form and behaviour.

The old regime

In a market economy the state is not an owner of many firms; it is more preoccupied with being the umpire of the market. But all advanced countries have known exceptions, with some favouring public enterprises as part of economic nationalism and others accepting them only when absolutely necessary. Infrastructure is one area where state involvement in one form or another has been defendable from an economic point of view. Another area is the war economy, requiring the production of materials for defence: mining, steel, aeroplanes, tanks, and so on. In addition, governments have sometimes wished to set standards in firm management through the establishment of 'excellent firms'. In other cases, they have been forced to become the owner of large enterprises which would otherwise have gone into bankruptcy; but their aim with such 'accidental ownership' has usually been to find quite quickly a new viable ownership structure in the private sector.

Some countries have adhered to an economic regime that deviates from the decentralised market economy. The command economy will not be examined here, but the interesting and often neglected point is that economic nationalism emphasised the virtues of state ownership. According to the model of state-led economic development formulated by German economists in the nineteenth century, the state should own or support key industries. Traces of this model are found in the large numbers of public enterprises in countries like Austria, France and Italy, but also in South East Asia, as with Singapore. The French model is particularly interesting, as state-owned firms have long been considered to be the apex of the economy, setting the example for others to pursue. These enterprises have employed huge numbers of people. Things have been different in countries which have adhered to the decentralised market model most consistently. Thus, employment in public enterprises has been very low in the United States. Somewhere in between the two extremes of the US and France are the other European countries that have employed public enterprises mainly for the provision of infrastructure.

Traditionally, the public enterprises used for infrastructural purposes operated as trading entities within the public sector under the control of a responsible ministry and with close links to the Ministry of Finance or Ministry of Trade and Commerce. They financed their operations by user fees in part, but governments regulated both quantities and price, as well as financed their often occurring deficits. Their capital was part of the consolidated state budget.

There were various country-specific arrangements for identifying particular enterprises and defining their conditions of operation, such that they ranged from having the status of a bureau to being bodies with some degree of autonomy. While a few were organised as joint-stock companies (as private law entities), the rest had some form of public law recognition. In some cases, they were bodies established under special legislation and thus were examples of what is often called 'statutory corporatisation'.

Basically, those operating in infrastructure domains were monopolies which were given their monopoly position under a scheme of regulation and were motivated with reference to the perceived needs of natural monopolies (Sherman 1989; Spulber, 1989; Baldwin and Cave, 1999). Thus, in Germany, for example, the 'kommunale Daseinsfürsorge' was the base of local economic activities and had constitutional recognition (Grundgesetz, Art. 28). This emphasis on the creation and maintenance of monopolies often led to economic activities in energy, water, transport, sewage, and so on all being brought under the one enterprise structure. Often the public enterprise combined different tasks such as production, transportation, distribution and oversight.

The new regime

With the creation of the EU internal market and its competition requirements, as well as the increasing globalisation of markets and capital, there was a perceived need in Western Europe to transform existing public enterprises into modern public firms. The transformation had two key components: one involved their internal reconstitution as joint-stock companies; the other saw a change in the rules of the market through a process of deregulation. The combination of the two components has had major implications for public enterprise structures and behaviour. The incorporated basic public firm model today is that of a joint-stock company. This legal form is now considered the natural choice for the management of government-in-business activities. Thus most public enterprises have been transformed into joint-stock companies in which government ownership may vary from a strong minority position to the possession of the total equity.

Incorporated public firms behave differently from the traditional public enterprises, as the institutions are different enough to allow for the elaboration of new strategies. It is in the interest of the key players to change their behaviour when a public enterprise is transformed from the public law form to the private law form of a joint-stock company. The incentives of the owners, managers, employees and other stakeholders lead them to revise their strategies quite considerably. The choice of the joint-stock company form is based on a number of considerations that are often played out in a confusing way. The key reasons are:

- *The reduction of losses.* Joint-stock companies have an obligation to maintain their capital, which is checked on a yearly basis by some form of publicly recognised auditing. The owners of a joint-stock company can always choose not to cover losses or inject new capital, which would have the consequence that a loss-making firm would go into bankruptcy.

When a government is the equity owner it has the right to refuse to cover any such losses.

- *An increase in managerial discretion.* Top managers used to complain much in traditional public enterprises that they were under the strict control of the finance minister or a minister of trade and commerce. It is assumed that top managers want to exercise considerable discretion when they run a company – this is true of private as well as public firms. Often these managers drive the transformation of a public enterprise into a public joint-stock company as a means of securing better salaries, more prestige and more managerial autonomy.
- *An emphasis on business.* A joint-stock company has one clear mission, namely to make money. The problematic nature of the real function or purpose of the traditional enterprise is clarified, as public firms must not only cover their costs but also return a profit to their owner. This raises the questions: Why, then, state ownership? To whom does a profit in a publicly owned firm belong?
- *Economic flexibility.* From a strictly legal point of view the joint-stock company is a more dynamic form for business activity than the traditional public enterprise. It can take decisions more quickly, can enter into alliances more easily, and can initiate new activities with less inertia. Since its basic control mechanism – its equity – is highly divisible and fungible, a joint-stock company is highly instrumental in both ownership operations and market strategies.
- *Adaptation to globalisation.* Economic life that increasingly involves cross-border activity requires a minimum of common institutions. Since the joint-stock company is a universal form of economic management, its global use significantly reduces transaction costs. It is recognised similarly in the two major legal systems of the world, English law (common law) and Continental European law (civil law), which involve two different models of control. The first comprises an underlying set of regulations, and the second is through direct financial intervention.

The transformation of government business from the traditional public enterprise format to the joint-stock company has occurred in all West European countries. It has been done with different timing and resulted in different institutional mixtures, with the most radical reforms being in the United Kingdom, where deregulation and privatisation started before the introduction of the internal market. Overall, the traditional public enterprise has almost been phased out. The new public firms are now in place and are operating in a transformed market structure.

The creation of the internal market all over Western Europe concerned primarily the private sector (or the market sector) where most of the players are private entrepreneurs and privately owned joint-stock companies. Logically, however, deregulation of the national economies of Western

Europe could not be halted at the border with the public sector and public enterprises. In so far as competition makes sense, there was no valid reason why the public sector would not be included in the EU competition regime. Perhaps the core public sector or the entire soft sector could be exempted from the competition regime because of its strong political nature. But the business sector of government had surely to be subsumed under the EU competition regime as part of the internal market. In this regard, it is important that the European Court of Justice ruled that public services such as electricity, gas and water are to be considered as commodities. This stimulated the European Commission to create directives enhancing competition in the production and provision of these commodities. Thus, when governments engage in business they are considered to be bound by the rules of the internal market.

The inclusion of public procurement in the EU competition regime was rather easy as most governments already had competitive systems in place for government purchases of inputs to their production processes, especially where these purchases concerned standard technical equipment and material. But stretching the competition regime to cover the whole business sector has involved a considerable amount of new legislation out of Brussels, particularly concerning the infrastructure sector.

The EU has had to resolve some problems in relation to so-called natural monopolies. In order to enhance contestation in respect of essential infrastructural goods and services, it has been necessary first to get an understanding and acceptance of basic principles and rules of contestability including open entry, no hindrances to trade, mutual recognition, free movement of labour, capital, services and goods, no subsidies, full-scale tendering in all EU member states, third-party access, and level playing fields. It has then been necessary to get member states to implement a competition regime that covers their own large public enterprises, which often acted to protect their vested interests.

Contestability in the classical sector of public enterprises – infrastructure – is not achieved merely by implementing the four freedoms: the free movement of labour, capital, goods and services. The Commission has put in place a number of special *directives* that handle the separate areas constituting infrastructure, such as the gas, electricity, telecommunications directives, etc. In these directives, it has attempted to undo the problem of natural monopoly that once offered the rationale for traditional public regulation and public enterprise.

The EU favours competitive mechanisms such as tendering/bidding in all forms of public procurement. However, the offering of smaller public contracts to various private suppliers is one thing; the arrival of competition in giant systems involving water supply, sewage and energy is quite different. The net poses a real difficulty for arranging a tournament or auction to ensure contestability. In much of infrastructure there is only one net and its possession carries market power. In the various directives the Commission tries to come to grips with how contestability is to be institutionalised, even when there is a natural monopoly.

This is a slow process. Full contestability requires the solution of many technical and economic problems in relation to access and use of common carriers. National monopolies tend to demand a long period of slow adjustment to contestability in the form of required changes in national rules and licences. Take the case of French Gas, which has a 10-year period in order to make the transition from no entry to open entry.

It is no exaggeration to state that the EU competition regime has met with various country responses, and France, with its many public enterprises, has been the slowest to implement the basic principles. The process of putting in place a common competition regime for the entire EU economy over the whole of infrastructure is far from finished, but the basic rules have been defined. But, while the rules about contestation between public enterprises are not yet fully in place, the firms concerned have already begun to adapt to the new requirements. It is thus pertinent to consider their responses.

Behavioural consequences of the new system

The new regime of joint-stock companies, deregulation and the internal market is based on the idea of competition on a level playing field. The old system emphasised public control, whereas the new system stresses fair competition. When public firms operate at arm's length from government with the aim of profit maximising in a competitive environment, which strategies do they pursue?

Strategies

In answering this question, one may be tempted to focus on stunning stories about public firms engaging in naked strategies to increase market power and profits. However, there are restrictions on such strategies, some of which stem from other government activities, most notably government as regulator and government as umpire (through the judiciary). How, especially, could a government accept its own firms engaging in monopoly practices when it has made the move from the old system to the new system in order to ensure contestability? Also, the internal market of the EU sets definitive limits on the feasibility of collusive behaviour. What then are the theoretical possibilities, and what is the available evidence, given that the making of cartels from collusion is hardly feasible because of the strong anti-trust regime of the EU?

Assume that what public firms want to do is to stabilise their situation in a market. Since they tend to be very large, it is likely that the environment is not the classical competitive situation involving huge numbers of sellers and buyers. Such competitive markets are hardly of any interest to huge public firms, as they offer few profit-maximising opportunities.

The large public firms tend to be located in an environment characterised by oligopoly, which presents possibilities for profit maximisation through market power. Public firms could set their prices and the quantity of goods produced so that they increase their profits. Firms can increase their profits either by cutting costs, by increasing prices, or by producing more outputs. Where public firms are very large, cost-cutting measures improve profits only up to a certain limit. Once inefficiencies have been removed, the best idea is to engage in strategies that result in market power. Figure 8.1 outlines the various possible outcomes of the institutional changes (Carlton and Perloff, 2004; Cabral, 2000).

The basic situation facing a public firm after deregulation can be modelled by showing a market sector, be it gas, electricity or telecommunications. Suppose that demand for the good or services is captured by a normal demand curve *D*, and assume that the cost of production is constant in the short run. Then the allocative outcomes in Figure 8.1, covering all possible outcomes (from one firm monopoly to perfect competition) depend on the choice of strategies.

The optimal quantity in the market outlined in Figure 8.1 is where price equals cost, which gives the competitive market equilibrium at 72 units in this example. This outcome is the Pareto-optimal outcome, but it implies zero profits for the producer and a maximum consumer surplus. The public firm will not locate at *Q* if it can avoid it. It can only raise profits by reducing

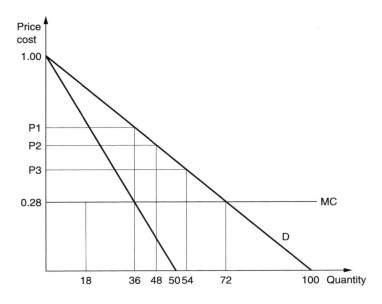

Figure 8.1 Public firms: strategies and outcomes.

output, which will raise prices. The ideal point for the public firm is total market power, meaning that it is the sole producer and can set output at the monopoly point. If it is in such a position, it will maximise its revenues by first calculating its marginal revenues. Then it will set marginal revenues equal to marginal cost, like any monopolist. It will reduce output to 36 units, or half the amount of the Pareto-optimal output. Profits will skyrocket, such that the consumer surplus will be much reduced, resulting also in a dead-weight loss.

In a contestable world, this outcome is not sustainable as profits are so high that they will attract new entrants into the market. However, given the size of the operations it is likely that only one or two intruders will challenge the public firm. What, then, is the outcome? The public firm cannot deter another firm from entering the market. It will try to collude with the newcomer, which may well be another public firm. If they collude successfully, they may split the monopoly profits between them. Output will still be half of that which is best for the consumer. However, such an agreement is not in the best self-interest of the two colluding firms. They will be tempted to defect from the collusion and to try and increase their profits by expanding output through acting unilaterally.

When two public firms collude, each may produce 18 units and share the profits of a monopoly equally. However, each could do better by unilaterally expanding output. Figure 8.1 shows the outcome – known as the Cournot outcome – when the two firms act unilaterally to maximise profit but take into consideration the consequences for the price of the output of the other firm. When one firm brings forward more output than the monopoly solution, then the price will fall somewhat. Thus, firm one will set its output such that it will produce nothing when the other firm supplies the whole market, and it will only supply the monopoly quantity when the other firm supplies nothing. This means that they will arrive at the Cournot point of producing 24 units each. The profits will now be down, but it will still be rational for each firm to act unilaterally and expand output if they believe collusion is not going to work, or if they act myopically. Figure 8.1 also shows another oligopolistic strategy that public firms will be very interested in when they face a challenger, which again could be another public firm. One of the two firms could do better than its Cournot point by unilaterally proceeding before the other firm can act. Thus, it will decide to produce the monopoly quantity of 36 units itself and leave it to second firm to take the rest of the market – this is called the Stackelberg leader solution to oligopoly. Here the total output will be 54 units instead of 48 under the Cournot solution. Profits will fall, but the Stackelberg leader will do better than in the Cournot solution, selling 36 units, while the Stackelberg follower only sells 18 units.

The Stackelberg strategy seems to be plausible for giant public firms in a deregulated world. Because of sunk costs there will be few potential entrants into the market where the public firm used to be a legal monopoly. However, the huge profits involved in market power is likely to attract at least one newcomer, often another public firm from within the same country or from outside. If they can collude, they can divide the huge monopoly profits. If for some reason cooperation does not work, then the dominant firm may try the Stackelberg strategy option of leading the market. If the two firms are equally strong, then the Cournot solution is the more likely outcome.

The two firms are not likely to start a price war – the so-called Bertrand solution. There is only one outcome from such a price war, namely zero profits. In Figure 8.1, a price war would lead to the Pareto-optimal outcome, which is good for the consumer but bad for the public firm. If the deregulation reforms really work and strong contestability is introduced, then more newcomers will enter. This will make collusion even more difficult, because more players mean higher transaction costs. Coordination will become more difficult and each firm will decide itself what to do given the response functions of the others – the Cournot strategy. Thus, output will increase and profits will fall the more newcomers enter. Such a Stigler process of free entry could end in a Cournot reaction, with a large number of firms operating at the competitive Pareto-optimal solution of 72 units but with no profits, or with two firms engaged in reckless competition.

Oligopolistic tendences

The evidence from various countries in Western Europe indicates that deregulation has not stimulated a large number of new entrants into infrastructure. At most, there are between two and five major players in areas such as telecommunications, electricity, postal services, and water supplies. Thus, there is a small set of players moving around with strategies that give them market power. The outcome is that the markets in which public firms dominate are neither monopolies nor fully competitive.

Straightforward collusion is practically impossible to achieve, partly for legal reasons and partly for strategic reasons. Collusion is a crime which antitrust authorities police in each country, and the EU Commission engages in far-reaching surveys of market structure. When the EU frames its competition policies, it enacts regulations that open entry and outlaw collusion. However, there are not many newcomers in markets where huge investments are required on entry. Besides, collusion is difficult to accomplish when there is much myopia. If public firms act with a limited time perspective, they will avoid collusion, which requires mutual credibility to be built up over time. In economic life there is, as a rule, heavy discounting, meaning that a safe profit today is worth more than huge profits in the future. However, one dominant firm may attempt to become the market leader. The behavioural responses to the institutional changes will take some time to work themselves out and will be affected as EU directives are applied across more and more sectors. The consequences of institutional transformation include a new set of strategies on the part of the public joint-stock companies. They now behave as any private firm of the same size and importance in the economy. They tend, from one country to another, to adopt the following set of strategies, and it is predicted that they will increasingly do so in the years ahead.

Cross-border alliances

Public firms have become very keen on marriages, and these complete or partial marriages tend more and more to involve public firms operating in different countries. Thus, in a deregulated economy the national scene has become too small for these often very large public firms. What makes partial marriages so easy to accomplish is of course their incorporation as joint-stock companies. The 'I buy you and you buy me' strategy can be negotiated and implemented over the weekend when it is a matter of 5–10 per cent equity.

Petty mergers are different from full-scale mergers where two giants become one. This is not easily accomplished between public firms, because politics and nationalism are just around the corner. A good example is the planned merger between two Nordic telecommunication operators, Swedish Telia and Norwegian TeleNord, which failed after long negotiations.

Horizontal integration

Take-overs have become common between public firms. Thus, one public firm in one country expands its activities in another country by transforming a public enterprise or firm into one of its subsidiaries. The key idea is that there is a magic size that promotes efficiency and it requires expansion into similar activities in another country. Electricity companies in Germany and Sweden, for example, have begun quite extensive horizontal integration, penetrating from their home country into neighbouring countries in the first instance.

Horizontal integration appears to be much more in line with business strategies today than vertical integration. Look at the electricity sector in Northern Europe. There the transformation of the electricity market may be seen as an ideal example of how the new system works itself out. In the old system, each public enterprise operated in a regulated market based on licences and faced weak market competition from its opponent firms, whether they were public or private. The focus of the enterprise was narrow, being preoccupied with serving one segment of the market, often based on geographical criteria. A few giant enterprises exercised considerable market power due to heavy vertical integration, closely linking production, transmission and distribution in one organisation. Thus, for example, in Sweden the electricity market was dominated by state-owned Vattenfall and local-government-owned Sydkraft, where the first dominated in the northern parts of the country and the second in the southern parts, although there were other players too. Vattenfall prevailed in the market due to its control over the high-voltage transmission system.

In the new system that has emerged since deregulation, the market for electricity has changed radically. There is now a *bourse* for the buying and selling of electric power linking all the Nordic countries instantaneously. The transmission net has been separated from the production system, and the principle of third-party access has been introduced in the distribution nets. There is in principle free entry. The firms have been totally changed as a result of the new strategies linked with 'like to like'. Thus, Vattenfall has expanded into Germany, Poland and Norway, becoming a major distributor of electricity in Northern Europe by means of a take-over strategy or through asset swaps. Sydkraft is no longer controlled by the local governments in southern Sweden, as it now has German (E On Energie) and Norwegian (Statkraft) owners. EOnE's take over of Sydkraft makes it one of the largest electricity producers in Europe besides Italian Enel. Another German producer, RWE, also has enormous capacity. The largest producer is, however, French Electricité de France (EdF), followed by Enel, RWE and EOnE.

PreussenElektra, a German firm, invaded Sweden via a deal with Sydkraft, which owned shares in VEBA, PreussenElektra's mother company. Several attempts by American and other foreign energy companies to gain a foothold in Germany since the beginning of the 1990s failed. The German 'family' successfully defended its closed shop until 1997, thanks to independent power producer (IPP) activities and the stock holdings of the large German utilities. The situation changed when the Swedish power company Sydkraft AB (already a minor shareholder in VEBA), together with PreussenElektra, bought a share of Hamburgische Electricitäts-Werke (HEW). RWE had also expressed an interest in the package, but lost out in the bidding. Then, when the Berlin Government sold its majority holding in Bewag in May 1997, the deal was closed by a consortium of PreussenElektra, VIAG, and the US company Southern Energy. In 1999, Vattenfall bought more shares in HEW. Also, EdF took over the state of Baden-Württemberg's 25 per cent stake in EnBW. These changes in the ownership structure of the German electro-scientific industry (ESI) are the result of changing framework conditions, the liberalisation of the electricity market, and the privatisation of ESI firms. The new stockholders will certainly influence the corporate strategies of the firms in the future. In the case of Bewag, Southern Energy not only chairs the supervisory board, but is also represented on the board of directors. But after the EonE merger, the HEW shares had to be sold, and the State of Hamburg started to sell more of its shares in HEW. This was the chance for Vattenfall to get a majority stake in HEW.

Germany has the largest energy market in Western Europe, as its population is over 80 million and it has an annual electricity consumption of nearly 564 TWh. Vattenfall began competing for a market share in Germany when the foundation for further expansion was laid through the acquisition of a majority holding in HEW. Vattenfall started its operations in early 1997, gaining substantial experience in the German electricity market leading up to the markets being deregulated in April 1998. The operations of Vattenfall in Germany are carried out through HEW. In October 2000, Vattenfall signed a contract with HEW's other shareholders, EonE and Syd-kraft, concerning the take-over of their shares. By the beginning of 2001, Vattenfall owned over 70 per cent of the shares in HEW and thereby became the first international player with a majority interest in a leading German power company. HEW signed agreements to take over a majority holding in Berlin's utility Bewag, and in December 2000 acquired the East German power producer, VEAG. Vattenfall, together with HEW, has the ambition to become one of the top four in Germany's power business, at the same time as EonE seeks to become the second largest player in the Nordic market.

Vertical integration goes against the competition philosophy of EU, whereas horizontal integration appears to be acceptable because the size of the market has become global. No firm is so gigantic that it could domi-nate the whole world by itself. Firms that are based on vertical integration are often required to separate the various elements from each other within the company so that they become independent joint-stock companies, merely owned by the mother company as a holding company.

International expansion

The mergers and acquisitions as well as the horizontal integration that occur after deregulation take on a global scale. Public firms now consider that they must position themselves in the global marketplace. It is not merely walking across the border to your neighbour; it may actually involve being present in a different continent (Wettenhall 1993), as in the case of French giant EdF.

This global drive is sometimes expressed in rather peculiar ways. Thus, the railway enterprise of Switzerland – Schweizerische Bundesbahn (SBB) – declared it needed to begin operations in the UK, although it has had to struggle for a long time with losses on its operations in its home country where it is the main provider of these services. Some people fail to see the link between railway services in the UK and Switzerland. Another rather drastic initiative is the move by China Telecom (through one of its mobile subsidiaries) to acquire a stake in West European telecommunications firms.

Monopolistic competition

Public firms not only position themselves geographically; they also increas-ingly develop brands and engage in advertising in order to attract certain customers and to create an image that their products are special. Many have invested heavily in creating a distinctive firm image, finding a so-called

logo that identifies them. The public relations of these firms are emphasised more and more as they search for a niche in a giant market. Whereas
traditional public enterprises used to identify with their rather dull mission of providing a standardised product like power or water, the new firms
have now positioned themselves as distinctive enterprises, allocating a good
or service to a special brand. Such a brand may fail to identify a unique
product, but it could in the best case indicate other things that come with
the product, such as service reliability.

Asset swaps

The new public firms feature in daily newspapers as they often engage in
rather dramatic moves that involve immense capital expenditures. They can
use their stock as instruments in alliances, as stock is very fungible, highly
divisible and very effective in terms of power. So-called asset swaps can be
used to forge alliances where a company sells some stock just to get enough
capital to acquire stock in another company. This kind of asset exchange
is very attractive because it presents a minimum of transaction costs, and
power is after all closely linked with capital. An asset swap strategy is very
different from a takeover strategy, as the goal is to create a friendly alliance
and not to swallow the other company. Asset swaps are far less costly than
takeovers, especially if the latter have to be unfriendly ones. An asset swap
strategy can be seen as the same as collusion in order to create a cartel, but
it may also be adopted by firms that compete in one market.

An example is the electricity sector in Southern Europe. Endesa SA, which
is the largest power company in Spain, is challenging the 54-year reign of
the French government-owned utility Electricité de France (EdF) over the
French market, the first such initiative by a non-French company. Endesa has
agreed to buy a small French power company, Société Nationale d'Électricité
et de Thermique (SNET). SNET hopes to challenge EdF, which has come
under fire from the EU for dawdling on opening the domestic electricity
market. EdF, Europe's biggest power producer, controls more than
90 per cent of the French market.

Asset swaps have gained popularity among European utilities as a means
of expanding into neighbouring markets without the complications of
buying an entire company. However, they may become so large that they
require not only national government approval but also acceptance by
the EU. The Spanish government's approval of the creation of one of
the world's largest power utilities through the merger of Endesa and Iber-
drola resulted in conditions for maintaining competition that were so severe
that the deal was inhibited. Had the fusion and the attending asset swaps
taken place, some 50 per cent of the electricity generation and distribution assets that make up the Spanish power market would have changed
hands. The deals would have realised more than 20bn euros and could
have brought two new power players from abroad into Spain. The two

power groups account for 80 per cent of Spain's electricity supplies and were called on to shed about half their combined assets. If the tie-up had gone ahead, the Endesa-Iberdrola group, which already has a large franchise in Latin America, would have used gains from its sales in Spain to finance an aggressive acquisition strategy in Europe.

Overall assessment of 'like to like'

The outcome of internal institutional changes and the creation of the EU competition regime is that public firms in Western Europe now have become full-scale players in the market economy, first and foremost in the European economy and second in the global economy. They engage in a set of strategies that are likely to be witnessed more and more in the years ahead. They are more 'firms' than they are 'public', although their 'publicness' remains significant. The emphasis is on their economic enterprise targets and not on political goals or public missions. Their prime objective is that of any firm, namely profit maximisation, which requires the acquisition of some degree of market power. But straightforward collusion is not allowed by the EU.

Instead of servicing the ordinary citizen, the public firms target certain categories of consumers and develop images that signal to the consumer such things as high quality, safety and reliability. They tend no longer to be enterprises of the people. They orientate themselves as self-searching firms looking for their best niches, whether they produce one commodity or several. All of these strategies are employed to a varying extent and with different success. Some firms may use all of them, whereas others concentrate on one of them. It depends on the sector of the economy, as well as on the business culture of the country – a historical legacy. The common denominator of all of the strategies is the oligopoly behaviour.

Public firms are no longer the sole producers in their market sector. Competition has increased, although more in some areas than in others. In air transportation the European market is now fully competitive, with both public and private firms active in the market. Several firms are publicly owned, but they engage in global strategies with private firms, playing 'like to like'. In stark contrast are the railways, which comprise one giant state enterprise in each country, facing very weak competitive pressures. In between these two poles are the markets where one public firm has a dominant position but faces obvious competition from a few other firms, public or private. This is true of energy and telecommunications, and increasingly also of water and sewage, other than where local government enterprises or bureaux continue to provide these services.

'Like to like' becomes the game as soon as the public firms face an oligopolistic market where they can attain market power by strategies that reduce output and raise prices. Since public firms cannot really form cartels or engage in collusion when their government owners have explicitly committed themselves to a competition regime, the best response to the institutional reforms of the last two decades is to use the Cournot or Stackelberg approaches or try monopolistic competition. This is all about profit maximisation. But how about the public mission?

A public enterprise has always been a mixture of two different worlds, government and the private sector. Since these two worlds have their own institutional logic, it is small wonder that public enterprises always had to operate with in-built contradictions. Government is not business, but public enterprises were firms. Have the recent institutional changes – incorporation as joint-stock companies and deregulation – been able to reduce the inherent tensions?

The trade-off in the old public enterprise regime was definitely that politics dominated over economics. This implied that the public interest in low user fees and large quantities of goods prevailed over the self-interests of enterprises in high profitability and efficient operations. The new regime has swung the balance in favour of economics to such an extent that it is pertinent to consider what remains of the politics of public enterprises.

When public firms today behave like any private firms, engaging in strategies and tactics that all have the single goal of increasing market power, what is the gain to society or to the public? When public firms succeed in arriving at market power, they will reduce allocated quantities and raise prices just as any private firm would do. What the public gets is higher prices but more efficient firms. There is actually a trade-off involved here, although higher prices and lower quantities are always a burden to the consumer. The public will not have to pay for the losses of public enterprises – this is their short-term gain. Many of the public enterprises used to run up quite substantial losses that had to be covered by taxes in the ordinary yearly state budget. Often these losses were due to X-inefficiency, which the public at large does not benefit from. The new public firms cannot run up losses as governments are not allowed to subsidise them. Another gain for the public is the separation between efficiency and redistribution. This is a long-term positive outcome. When public firms serve social ends like providing jobs, developing a region or offering low-priced services, then the costs will be covered by the public whether or not they benefit from the goods and services being produced or provided. This is often an inefficient way of implementing social policies, because the desired social ends could be better served by direct income support and not indirectly through pumping tax money into X-inefficient firms.

There is possibly also the long-term gain on the part of the public in becoming the owner of large and well-managed firms, although this ownership role is a tenuous one because the public often owns no stock directly in a personal capacity. But what precisely is the nature of state ownership of equity in joint-stock companies? Who is the state? If the state is a legal entity only, a juridical corporation, then it holds its assets in trust for its principal, the body politic. But this indirect ownership of huge equity assets may not matter much to the public.

The trade-off from the perspective of the public is that they may have to pay higher user fees for the services provided by these new public firms, but they will stop paying for loss-making inefficient enterprises. In some but far from all sectors, the charges have come down so substantially that the consumers have actually gained directly. What, then, remains of the public mission of public firms if they focus on profit maximisation? Why cannot these firms be fully privatised?

Government is no longer the basic governor of its public enterprises. In the new system the national government must combine two roles, namely that of umpire in a deregulated economy with a competition regime and that of the owner of the equity of the public firms, wholly or partially. The regional and local governments too are confined to the role of owners of equity in their public firms within infrastructure, which obey in principle the same rules as other firms. In order to avoid conflicts between the umpire role and the ownership role, governments allocate these roles to different bodies. Thus, the role that aims at safeguarding a level playing field is handled by courts or special regulatory agencies, whereas the ownership role normally rests with a ministry. One outcome of the new system is that governments frequently look on their ownership of assets rather passively, leaving it to managers to engage in asset swaps and similar manoeuvres, resting content with receiving dividends and other income from its assets.

The transformation of public enterprises has entailed the movement from a regulated system to a competitive one. Key questions include: In which sector of the economy has this movement been on the whole successful, and in which sector have the outcomes not matched the hopes? In response, it is appropriate to concentrate the analysis sector by sector. Two sectors which provide a possible comparison between different sets of outcomes are telecommunications and postal services.

In the telecommunications sector, the competitive regime has been implemented in all West European countries and the outcomes must be regarded as positive. Prices have come down and there is contestability between different players, both public and private. The public enterprises working as operators have all been reconstituted as joint-stock companies and partially or fully privatised. The competition regime works because the problems concerning the net have been successfully resolved by means of the principles of common carrier and third-party access. In addition, alternative nets have been established through technological innovations.

Matters are somewhat different in the postal services. Postal services used to be huge public enterprises with many employees active around the country in the receipt and delivery of mail. These enterprises basically used a cost-pricing method under public regulation to cover their costs. Can such an enterprise be transformed into a firm working under a competitive regime? Take the example of Deutsche Post. It has not only been incorporated as a joint-stock company, but has also been listed on the Frankfurt Stock Exchange. With the floating of 29 per cent of its stock, the new firm has radically transformed itself to the meet the demands of a competitive regime. It has changed its name to Deutsche Post World Net, shed much of its labour force (from 394,000 to 244,000), and gone on a buying spree internationally, acquiring shares in DHL, Danzas and Ducros Services Rapides. Postal services now constitute only one third of the company's activities, compared with 45 per cent before the transformation. There is competition from other private companies, but Deutsche Post still maintains its monopoly for carrying mail that is less than 200 grams in weight. Interestingly, the European Commission has become interested in the new firm on the suspicion of anti-competition tactics. After the change to a competitive regime, Deutsche Post has developed into a major player with some 30 new acquisitions. However, *qui bono?* – for whom is this a good thing?

The road ahead for the incorporated public firms in Western Europe, and perhaps also in Eastern Europe when the enlargement of the EU proceeds in accordance with the Nice plan, is to adapt to the two major institutional changes that condition their behaviour, namely incorporation as joint-stock companies and deregulation. These firms will continue to engage in cross-European strategies to strengthen their market power and increase market stability. Governments will be torn by the trouble of playing two roles: owner and umpire. I predict that the latter role will prevail over the former, thus further opening up opportunities for various ownership mixes between the public and private sectors. However, complete privatisation is hardly in sight, as there is still something public about these firms within infrastructure. Perhaps it is their mission that will ensure that their public element remains significant, as these firms must keep delivering services and simply cannot be allowed to become bankrupt. Public services are necessary.

Conclusion

Public enterprises constituted as joint-stock companies have become very much like other firms, engaging in strategies to increase their control of markets. Public firms are now public in the thin sense only of governments holding all or part of their equity. In all other respects they are simply firms. Yet, sometimes their public mission surfaces, even though their basic motivation in the deregulated environment is profit maximisation. Thus, when they engage in questionable activities in the grey zone between what is or is not lawful, they are often called to order by governments reminding them of their public nature. Relevant here is the long debate about the behaviour of French oil producers Elf and Total or French power giant EdF.

Government faces a contradictory situation when it instructs their public firms to play 'like to like' because it is both judge and player. When a government deregulates and puts a competitive regime in place, it must apply the rules to its own firms. But can a government be both a neutral umpire and a profit-maximising player? Perhaps it would be best for society if most public firms were fully privatised. But many would reply that it cannot be done. Why? Because these firms are not just another firm. They often fulfil vital functions in the economy which must be forthcoming even when no private firm is able or willing to do so. Maybe that is exactly what their *public mission* is, namely to be present even when markets sink and private firms fail. Which society could survive today without a safe supply of energy and water, sewage disposal, and telecommunications? The most recent recession has shown how the population reacts to the loss of public services when deregulated and privatised public enterprises no longer deliver.

Public firms are today run by their managers. Their discretion will hardly be reduced in the future, as these managers engage in asset swaps and the like, increasing collaboration between firms. And they tend to engage in regional or global strategies to stabilise the market situation of their firms. Two questions may be raised in relation to this transformation of the public enterprise into a transnational player participating in oligopoly or monopolistic competition games: (1) Degree of competition: Is the competition created by anti-trust mechanisms such as the EU strong enough to prevent the evolution of giant cartels? (2) Public necessity: How is the delivery of vital services to be protected when the firms placed under the regime of the two Cs – choice and competition – go under according to the logic of creative destruction, typical of the market economy?

Running a public firm is an inherently principal–agent problem. From the macro point of view (umpire), government as the principal must clarify the rules of the game, considering its overall policy towards firm competition. On the other hand, the micro perspective (owner) calls for a clarification of how government relates to its own companies. Since the micro directives of the government towards one firm may not be in agreement with the macro

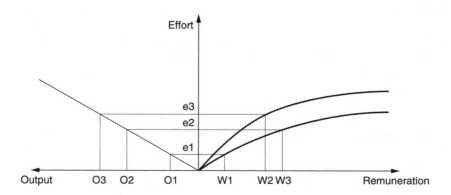

Figure 8.2 Looting in a principal–agent perspective.

directives concerning the entire economy, there is a risk for contradictions in the state policy towards its own enterprises.

One principal difficulty of the neo-liberal regime is the probability of the looting strategy by the agent, the powerful CEOs. When the traditional public enterprise is transformed into a joint-stock company, the combination of asymmetric knowledge and the split between owners and managers works to the advantage of the CEOs. They can be either low-effort or high-effort agents, but how can the government tell *ex ante* when they make a contract for several years where outcomes *ex post* may deviate considerably from intentions *ex ante* (see Figure 8.2)?

The principal is of course happy to sign an *ex ante* contract with the agent, promising a reformed public enterprise with larger output, fewer production costs but much higher remuneration of the CEO, i.e. at ($W2$, $e3$). But the danger is that the agent delivers an *ex post* contract at ($W3$, $e2$), considering all the benefits handed over to the CEO covering salary, bonuses, fringe benefits, assistants, etc. However, this solution could actually be worse for the principal than the traditional enterprise solution at ($W1$, $e1$). There is no given solution to the looting problem in the interaction between owners and managers of huge firms and public enterprises that have been incorporated into joint-stock companies (Kreps, 1990b).

9   Public insurance

Introduction

When Adolf Wagner suggested his law of increasing public expenditures out of GDP in the second half of the nineteenth century, he thought of not only the future need for public services but also the growing relevance of public insurance. Wagner saw the coming industrial society as harbouring incredible richness which could partly be used to secure a certain standard of living for the working classes when adversity strikes. The labour movement would, he clearly saw, demand compensation for the risks that industrialisation brought with it (Buchanan and Musgrave, 1999).

Since Wagner, social security has only kept going up in both size and coverage. At the turn of the twenty-first century public insurance costs more than the provision of services in many welfare states. And public insurance schemes are considerable in welfare societies, albeit their preference for the private sector. Social security has become a major headache for politicians as they search to fund these programmes where the clientele increases year after year. It will no doubt be a most explosive issue in tomorrow's politics due to the ageing of the population, meaning that fewer people in production have to support more people outside production. In addition, there is the growing problem of social exclusion, which costs considerably in terms of cash payments (Brooks and Razin, 2005; Modigliani and Muralidhar, 2004).

The purpose of this chapter is not to analyse each and every aspect of the complexity of social insurance, but merely to state the main problems of social insurance in terms of the principal–agent (P–A) framework. The P–A framework was developed for private insurance but it could equally well be applied to public insurance. Under insurance schemes the insurer is the principal and the insured is the agent, which would reverse the principal–agent interaction that we have analysed elsewhere in this book. The key question, then, becomes that of incentive compatibility: Can the state devise insurance schemes that solicit truthful behaviour on the part of the citizens? But one may also look upon the population as the principal and the politicians as the agents in the redistribution branch of government. Then one asks the question of reneging: Can government really deliver on its pension promises? (See also Esping-Andersen, 2002; Bartholomew, 2004; Pierson, 2001.)

The elements of pension systems

Pension programmes have become highly complex systems of rules, which is also true of other kinds of government cash payments. Pensions in well-ordered societies include:

- social security (pillar I)
- sponsored pension plans (pillar II)
- individual retirement accounts (pillar III).

The structure and management of pension fund investment involve the state and the banks and insurance companies, as they have consequences for the financial markets of the country. Unresolved issues of pension systems include the problem of low coverage rates of poor groups of people, the appropriate degree of paternalism, and the proper allocation of risk between individuals and the state. The relationships between pillars I, II and III vary from one country to another. There are, for instance clear differences between the Anglo-American world and much of continental Europe in the structure of the three pillars of retirement income (Bonoli, 2000; Holzmann and Stiglitz, 2001).

There are significant country differences with respect to the current funding of future pension liabilities. While the Anglo-American countries do not all fully fund social security entitlements they do rely upon the full funding of pension fund (pillar II) obligations, whereas continental European countries tend to rely upon unfunded social security (pillars I and II). In some countries much of the entitlements are paid through a system of existing funds, whereas in others the pay-as-you-go (PAYG) system predominates. Sometimes there is one great fund for all clients, but in other countries numerous funds may administered in a decentralised manner. Pension funds often place some of their money on the stock market, which may lead to financial disasters either for government or for the pensioners. Thus, few countries fully fund all expected social security pension obligations, as most contributions are less than expected benefits, and progressive redistribution towards low-income earners is a common policy. Governments carry the ultimate liability for social security pensions, often operating them on the PAYG basis. There is considerable debate about the future of social security in relation to private forms of pension and retirement income. There have been proposals in the US and elsewhere to partially convert social security to funded individual retirement accounts.

This crisis in most pension systems around the world results from the coming retirement of the baby-boom generation with projected longer average life expectancies as well as from lower fertility rates with much higher dependent to working age population ratios. For France, Germany and Italy the demographic trend is more significant than for Ireland and the UK, the US and Canada. Reinforcing the demographic crisis, France, Germany and Italy rely upon underfunded or unfunded social security systems for the provision of future retirement income. German employer-sponsored pension plans are often underfunded. In the Anglo-Saxon countries the majority of workers have funded supplementary pensions as a significant portion of their retirement income. The Anglo-American financial services industry provides a reason to shift retirement income obligations from the state sector to private pension plan sponsors. The growth of pension fund assets over the past 30 years in the Anglo-American economies explains part of the vitality of Anglo-American financial markets. Venture capital and the liquidity of Anglo-American securities markets constitute the power of pension funds and institutional investors. However, when large companies go bankrupt, like Enron and WorldCom, or face severe difficulties, like Marconi, Eriksson and ABB, then public pensions appear to be safer than private ones. The electorate in many advanced countries favours a public system of pensions. At the end of the day, it is the government that guarantees the entire pension system, however it is constructed. Government cannot let public pension funds that have been speculated on the stock market go down hill. Nor can government permit private insurance companies to falter – the state is the lender of last resort. Now, how do principal–agent problems surface?

The organisation of public insurance

The many changes of the public insurance schemes recently, driven first and foremost by the lack of money on the part of the state, imply that the population cannot really trust the politicians to fulfil their promises about future payments. The possibility of reneging on insurance promises is at its core a principal–agent problem, where the population is the principal and the politicians the agents. At the same time, government wants to reduce cheating in the social security system in general. Thus, public insurance may be looked at from both angles from within the P–A framework:

1   *The government perspective:* How can we enhance honesty in public insurance and make the programmes incentive compatible?
2   *The population perspective:* How can we make sure that the insurance promises of the past are fulfilled in the future?

In (1) it is the government that is the principal and the insured population is the agent, whereas in (2) it is the population that is the principal and the government is the agent. One may expect both these angles on social security to grow in relevance in the future as the resources that may be employed for public insurance become more and more scarce. The government as principal would like to minimise the occurrence of moral hazard in social security. In addition, there is also the possibility of adverse selection, meaning that people do not truthfully declare their nature, for instance whether a person is really in need of a lifelong disability pension already at the age of 40, besides the possibility of simple cheating with birth dates, etc. The population as principal would prefer the rules of social security to be stable and predictable. When politicians or central bankers signal that changes are needed in order to make social security sustainable in the future, social unrest often results. Even if the changes proposed only concern future generations, people still start fearing about the promises already made in social security.

Public insurance may be organised in different ways. One should debate whether some forms of organisation of insurance programmes are better suited to handle the principal–agent problems involved. The organisation of insurance includes a choice between two fundamental models or ideal-types:

- *PAYG system:* Payments are made from current incoming obligatory contributions without much saving in funds. If a person dies before reaching pension age, then some of the money accredited the person is not paid out to his/her family members.
- *Actuarial system:* Payments are made from a fund where the contributions have been accumulated over the years. All the money accumulated is paid out to the insured person or his family.

PAYG systems are to be found mainly in continental Western Europe and they are all operated through the national government. Actuarial systems, on the other hand, may be public or private and they are to be found mainly in Anglo-Saxon countries. Much has been written about the pros and cons of the two systems. In reality there are many mixtures between the two systems. Public and private insurance schemes are also combined in various complex forms. Switzerland combines all systems. All well-ordered countries provide a basic and egalitarian pension to all citizens (pillar I) which tends to be funded through a PAYG system. It is the construction of the additional pension system which differs much from one country to another, i.e. the second or third pillar. Countries may also differ in terms of how the pension system is constructed for public versus private employees.

Many countries are engaged in reviews of their pension systems, struggling with a range of issues concerning the adequacy, coverage and sustainability of their pension system. The first layer in the pension system is generally supported entirely by governments (pillar I). It is composed primarily of a programme (old age security) paid to all citizens or to low- and middle-income seniors at the age of 65 and over, who may in some countries qualify for an additional benefit if they have low incomes. A spouse's allowance may be paid to low-income persons between the ages of 60 and 64 who are widows or are married to the recipients of a guaranteed income supplement. The second tier of the pension system often consists of a publicly administered or regulated pension plan, which is an earnings-based programme covering all paid workers and providing benefits to their dependants (pillar II). Workers and employers make financial contributions to the programme. Workers draw benefits upon retirement. The second tier tends to include all workers, covering also part-time workers, and is sometimes indexed to inflation. The second tier may have drop-out provisions that accommodate women's child-rearing work. Sometimes it provides for the division of credits upon divorce and it pays benefits to surviving spouses upon death of the contributor. A disability benefit could be paid to workers who have contributed for a designated period but must leave work because of a severe and prolonged disability. The second tier is a defined benefit pension programme which contributes a predictable source of income to all pensioners. The third tier, on the other hand, tends to consist of tax-assisted employer-sponsored private pension plans as an individual retirement savings plan. Such occupational pension plans do not cover the entire workforce, because the private tier of a pension system is largely the preserve of those with above-average earnings (pillar III).

Pension programmes change in several countries, as governments have announced substantial amendments to both the first and second tiers of the pension system. All the programmes in the first tier may be combined into one senior's benefit, as a family income-tested benefit that will simplify the current system, make it more transparent and direct more assistance to low- and modest-income seniors. A significant shift in the second tier is that from PAYG to partial funding, which will help build up more funds from which future benefits will be paid. In order to achieve this, contributions must be raised more rapidly than under the PAYG system. Thus, young workers, their children and their grandchildren will have to pay substantially more for the same benefits than their parents and grandparents, which may cause intergenerational conflict.

Social security has two fundamental objectives: to guarantee all seniors a basic income and to ensure an adequate standard of living in retirement. These two objectives – the anti-poverty objective and the earnings replacement objective – comprise the core purposes of the pension system, where the key question for the government as principal is: What constitutes adequate retirement income and how large is a basic income? The state must avoid two fallacies:

I   Only government secures a high level of income security, which leads to systems that are too expensive.
II A very low level of income maintenance in social security does not lead to social exclusion and income disparities.

But how can government steer between falsely accepting overprotection (I) and wrongly rejecting the effects of underprotection (II), corresponding to Type I and Type II errors in policy?

Challenges: adequacy, coverage and sustainability

The pathways to retirement have become more diverse; some workers move into retirement quite comfortably. Some workers are being 'pulled into' early retirement through attractive monetary incentives, but many workers are being pushed into retirement against their will through lay-off, lack of work and health factors. The various programmes within the pension system operate as though there is a single age of retirement, though retirement is no longer equated with a single age (i.e., 65 and older) as it was in the past. Retirement is more a phase or a 15-year span from the early-to-mid fifties to the mid-to-late sixties.

The polarisation of the labour market and the increase in part-time employment and low-wage job opportunities, even for some highly educated young people, has profound implications for pension protection. Many workers are unable to make adequate private provision for their retirement. Those who earn below-average wages can be excluded from employer-sponsored pension programmes (pillar II). High unemployment poses serious problems. Lack of work reduces the number of pensionable years for individuals and weakens the contributory tax base of public programmes. The labour market problems experienced by young people today undermine their support for the pension system. The publicly supported components of the pension system are sensitive to changes when the labour market cannot provide the protections it once did. Over the past two decades, there has been a dramatic increase in women's participation in the paid labour market. Retirement is often discussed as though the retired population is a homogeneous group. However, dramatic differences between the levels and sources of retirement income of men and women exist. Calls for greater privatisation of the pension system come at time when the labour market is increasingly insecure. While many men in their fifties are beginning their retirement, many women are still actively engaged in the labour market at that age. Private pension coverage has improved for women, but fewer women than men remain covered by occupational pension plans. Most women cannot afford to contribute to the third tier. Pension reform must take into account the differences in male and female labour force participation. Women are disadvantaged in retirement relative to men because their lifetime average earnings are lower and their workforce attachment is more sporadic due to care-giving responsibilities.

In the next two decades, pension costs are expected to rise dramatically, with an ageing population in several countries. Close to 25 per cent of the population will be over age 65 by 2030. Seniors are generally more healthy and more educated than in the past. But the incidence of disability rises directly with age and population ageing creates associated pressures on the health care and social service systems. Health care costs could grow in real terms by about 70 per cent between now and 2025 because of population ageing to be considered relative to a country's ability to pay. In the European Union, for every 100 persons aged between 20 and 64, there are currently 28 persons who are 65 or over. This figure will double by 2050 and the proportion of those aged over 80 will increase sharply. In France, for instance, social expenditures have been allowed to expand over the maximum that is in agreement with economic growth and long-run solvability of the programmes themselves. At issue in France in the early twenty-first century is the generous state-funded pension scheme put in place at the height of the post-war baby boom. As the French population is declining, there would be financial disaster without a major overhaul of the rules of the system. Several countries face the same difficulty, which is simply that the number of working people contributing to the PAYG pension system is falling, while the number of beneficiaries is rising. Four workers financed each pensioner in 1960 and two in 2000. By 2020 the ratio could well be one-to-one. Modest reforms suggested in 2003 wanted state-sector employees to work an extra 2.5 years – up to 40 years – to qualify for a full pension, a move that would bring them in line with the private sector. Workers lack financial incentives to stay on the job longer but should face disincentives to retire early. The average French worker retires at 58.7 years old, earlier than workers in any of the other large European Union countries. One-quarter of the French workforce is employed by the government, which means the state-sector unions can block any reform. Drawn-out strikes in 1995 brought down the government of Juppé, who wanted to overhaul pensions too. Western Europe could consider the path of Chile or some Eastern European countries where the PAYG system has been abolished and instead private pension funds created, letting current generations fund their own retirement.

Data from many countries show that the yield on market assets has been sufficient to provide adequate retirement income. Whether such income is likely to be higher than income through PAYG systems is a debated issue. A market-based system would reduce the redistribution that several European welfare states consider important. Moving to a market-based pension system promotes labour market flexibility by more closely linking contributions and benefits and eliminates incentives for older workers to leave labour markets prematurely. There would have to be transition financing (with much protest probably), but it is cheaper to move to market-based systems than to continue current PAYG systems.

Yet, this market conclusion must be related to our hyperbola over social expenditures in Figure 6.1. There has to be a basic income floor put in by government. It is when pensions go beyond such a basic coverage and move to schemes of supplementary pensions that the problems begin. PAYG works well as long as a certain level of expenditures is not bypassed, when the system cracks due to the unfavourable ratio between people who pay in and people who take out pensions. The PAYG schemes allow for egalitarian solutions and cover the least fortunate part of the population. Market-based insurance schemes should target people who want to save in this form instead of investing their money in the stock market or build up assets in banks. Beyond the basic national coverage, pensions should be voluntary or private. Thus, there is a rationale for public insurance which when used with prudence stabilises not only the economy but also national solidarity.

What clearly speaks in favour of a public insurance scheme of some sort at a reasonable level of compensation is the instability of the private insurance markets. The state remains always the lender of last resort, meaning that it guarantees the private insurance companies in so far as their management of the money of the insured is concerned. A country cannot afford to let insurance companies go bankrupt, with the enormous negative impact this would have upon the financial market of a country. No matter how much regulation is introduced by government, the private insurance companies are never safe from shocks and financial disasters. To rely only upon private solutions could lead many people to the brink of private ruin, as happened in the Enron case, where large numbers of employees held shares in the company as their future pensions. This should be outlawed.

Adherents of the pure market solution for the income maintenance programmes tend to forget that no such system really exists, not even in the US. Government keeps a vigilant watch over the pension funds of the private companies, which are very vulnerable to the volatility in the stock market. This is the 'Marconi syndrome', meaning that firms do not pay sufficient money into their pension funds when business goes well, only to discover that they cannot fulfil promises made when business faces adverse times. It has been estimated that the total pension fund deficit for the top 500 US companies could have exceeded almost 300bn dollars in 2003. Underfunding is the typical story of private-firm pension funds, even with the healthy companies. The private pension funds are no safer than the PAYG schemes. In 2002, some 200 companies reported pension assets on the balance sheet when they actually had deficits in their pension plans. A further 60 firms claimed pension income as a boost to earnings when they really had deficits. An economic downturn worsens the pension schemes of the private firms in two ways. First, it reduces the value of capital held in pension funds in the form of stock. Second, it reduces the return on the capital held in these pension funds. The combined effect can be so dramatic that a company like General Motors was forced to shore up its pension funds with 20bn dollars in 2003. What happens when giant firms face such adversity that they must renege on their pension promises? Or when they simply cheat on them?

It should be pointed out that public systems of insurance need not be in deficit. Take the example of Norway where a PAYG scheme is basically sound, backed by the immense dollar assets generated by the Norwegian oil industry. Or one may refer to Switzerland, where the system was basically sound until the many separate public and private pension funds placed too much money into a sharply declining stock market. It may be added that Sweden managed to reform its PAYG system without too dramatic consequences.

In any case, a basic pension to all citizens is a fundamental obligation on the part of the state. It can be financed through different means: (1) centralised–decentralised scheme; (2) PAYG–actuarial scheme. It is only when the state takes on expensive supplementary pension schemes that it runs into major difficulties due to principal–agent problems.

The economic dependency ratio

Demographic ageing leads to the ageing of the labour force. In the year 2000, for every 100 persons in employment, 86 people over the age of 20 were without work in the European Union. Over half of them were *below* the age of 65 and most of them received social benefits. Demographic ageing could be compensated for by the increased economic activity of women and men between the age 20 and 64. Due to the reduction in the number of young people entering the labour market, in a number of European countries the average age of persons in employment is over 40. On the other hand, those aged over 45–50 experience career difficulties in many companies and are regarded as being too old to be promoted or to benefit from having training invested in them. Those over the age of 55 represent a surplus number of workers for which early retirement seems, in many cases, the only possible way out (Nyce and Schieber, 2005).

Important issues relate to the ensuring of a positive social impact of pensions. The second pillar should not replace the first pillar, which is the fundamental guarantee that everyone has access to a decent pension. In the private sector, the first pillar pensions often offer an income on retirement that is considerably lower than the salary granted just before retiring, since they are calculated on the basis of *average* salaries over the pensioner's whole career. Second pillar pensions, whether voluntary or obligatory, significantly contribute to reducing that loss in income as such. They answer the aspirations of increasing numbers of people when it comes to retirement. Pension reform should be backed up by measures to increase the employment rate in general, and the employment rate of older workers in particular. Just as an economically active society is a necessary condition to honour the pension debt of the first pillar, it is necessary for government to guarantee the rights created in the second pillar without undue strains on intergenerational income distribution.

How to fight poverty among pensioners more effectively; how to safeguard the existing pension systems, with their in-built solidarity; how to develop supplementary pensions as a complementary social protection for the many; how to increase employment opportunities for older workers – these are the key questions. The fundamental objective of pension schemes to provide people with a securely financed, adequate income after retirement and an income to replace earnings or derived income during working life has to be achieved while maintaining a sense of fairness and solidarity. What is at stake is social justice. In analysing objectives for pension systems one can start from the 10 'principles and objectives', subsequently endorsed by the Social Protection Committee in its progress report to the Nice Summit. These can be stated in the following optimistic mood:

1 *Maintain the adequacy of pensions:* The three pillars of pension systems, operating in combinations decided by the Member States, should enable people to remain financially autonomous in old age and, within reasonable limits, to maintain the living standard achieved during their working life.
2 *Ensure intergenerational fairness:* The efforts needed to cope with demographic ageing should be shared in an equitable way between the active, be they employees or entrepreneurs, and the retired generations.
3 *Strengthen solidarity in pension systems:* No-one should be excluded from pension systems because of low income or an unfavourable risk profile. Pension systems should have a redistributive element in favour of people with poor labour market opportunities or who had to provide care to children, disabled or frail elderly people.
4 *Maintain a balance between rights and obligations:* Benefits should reflect an individual's contributions to a pension system. In particular, postponing one's retirement should result in higher benefits.
5 *Ensure that pension systems support the equality between men and women:* In particular, adjustments are needed to strengthen the incentives for women to enter, re-enter and improve their position in the labour market.
6 *Ensure transparency and predictability:* It should be clear to pension scheme members what they can expect in terms of benefits under various circumstances.
7 *Make pension systems more flexible in the face of societal change:* Pension systems should be able to adjust to foreseeable changes in their economic and demographic environment.
8 *Facilitate labour market adaptability:* Pension systems should accommodate professional and geographic mobility and allow a degree of individual choice, for instance regarding the retirement age and the organisation of learning, working and leisure phases.
9 *Ensure consistency of pension schemes within the overall pension system:* Pension pillars should be mutually supportive and well coordinated.
10 *Ensure sound and sustainable public finances:* Reforms must ensure that the tax burden arising from public pensions is set at an appropriate level and that other essential public expenditures are not crowded out.

The fundamental objective of pension schemes is to provide people with a securely financed, adequate income after retirement, i.e. an income to replace earnings or derived income during working life. In addition, the pension scheme should cover those who have not participated in working life. The redistributive element is essential to pension systems, if they underpin social cohesion. Fairness and solidarity apply both *within* generations and *between* generations. Intergenerational fairness means *inter alia* that the efforts needed to cope with demographic ageing should be shared in an equitable way between the active generation of today – i.e. the retired generations of tomorrow – and the active generation of tomorrow. Intergenerational solidarity also requires that the older generation should not be excluded from the benefits of rising productivity in society, a principle which is of utmost importance to avoid the future marginalisation of the very old. Intragenerational fairness means that pension systems must maintain an equitable balance between rights and obligations as benefits should reflect an individual's contribution to the pension system. Intragenerational solidarity, however, requires that discrepancies in earnings between individuals during their working life should not lead to proportionate inequalities during retirement, and that, *a fortiori*, no-one should be excluded from pension systems because of low income or poor labour market opportunities. All this has to be achieved within a framework of fairness and solidarity – not easy.

Pension systems must meet three macro objectives, which are interrelated: social justice; economic sustainability and responsiveness to societal change. Pension systems will not be financially sustainable, if the burden sharing between current and future active generations is perceived as unfair from the point of view of future generations, because essential future public expenditure is crowded out, or if such expenditures are only sustainable with unacceptable levels of taxation. Pension pillars should be mutually supportive and well coordinated with a view to the overall objectives of the pension system they constitute. Good quality employment and social protection go hand in hand. The distinctive European social model is a prosperous society that does not tolerate poverty, a creative society that also offers security and confidence in the future. Yet, social security includes more than pensions. A key element is unemployment support, where again incentive compatibility must be respected.

Reasonable requirements of social security are that it be constructed so that it can identify the groups who really need social assistance, as well as that its rules do not entice behaviour that corrupts the rules. Workfare programmes attempt exactly this (Solow, 1998). Thus, it would be extremely helpful if governments could identify the people who misuse the system. Equally valid would be that governments could target the groups who really need social help. However, this is not easily done. There is a risk for both types of errors: Type I and Type II. Social policy would commit the Type I error when it accepts the wrong hypothesis that all forms of social assistance are vital or necessary for survival. Several forms of social security insure citizens at a high level of coverage, which is extremely costly to the state. Social policy would make the Type II error when it rejects the true hypothesis that a drastic reduction of support levels in social security would hurt the vulnerable badly and increase social exclusion.

The future: avoiding deficits or reneging?

Several governments know their system is not workable. Thus, they change the rules: Is this reneging on a large scale? Social policy-making faces the dilemma of steering between Scylla and Charybdis: it must neither overdo social assistance nor underperform in social security. Only if government knows much about the target groups is this feasible. However, governments may decide that they must change their programmes, because they are no longer viable, whatever the behaviour of the clients may be.

When governments today decide that social security is in need of an overhaul, they are looking for ways of diminishing the financial burden upon the state. The only option available is to introduce new schemes under which the recipient pays more or receives less. It is not possible to change the schemes for the citizens already insured, but the future generations will have to pay more or receive less. Often governments require full payment or they reduce the coverage to 50 per cent of the salary. Sometimes governments engage in partial privatisation, leaving it up to the insured to add private coverage to the public one. Thus, a large hiatus will be created in social security, as some past generations got a much better ride than future generations will get.

Governments are hesitant about raising the taxes or charges in order to make social security viable. Increases in taxes or charges have an indirect impact upon the economy, resulting in dead-weight losses from so-called tax wedges. It is considered better to partially privatise social security, meaning that citizens would have to find their own individual solutions in the market. However, changing social security is very sensitive from a political point of view. People expect to receive these benefits as entitlements constituting parts of citizenship. When governments change social security, they are considered as reneging on long-time established promises. One could counter-argue that these changes concern only future clients in the system and thus do not renege on existing rights. However, these changes are interpreted as the giving up of the universal and comprehensive welfare state, as conceived by Marshall and Titmuss (Alcock *et al.*, 2001).

From welfare to workfare: the moral hazard perspective

Behind the conception of a workfare state there is a P–A framework that looks upon government as the principal and the population as the agent.

This P–A approach is in accordance with the original P–A model in private insurance from which the whole idea of P–A interaction came. To put the case bluntly, the workfare state is the welfare state reformed in accordance with the economics of information, as it tries to eliminate opportunistic behaviour both *ex ante* and *ex post*. Basically, the workfare programmes target opportunistic behaviour in relation to public insurance. First, the workfare state limits the possibility of enjoying a free ride from the beginning by limiting in time the public support in relation to unemployment and sickness. After a certain period, a person receiving income support within unemployment or sickness schemes is automatically excluded from these programmes and placed within social assistance. Second, the support within social assistance is conditioned upon displaying effort. Thus, a person receiving income support within social assistance can also be cut off if he/she does not follow an agreed-upon activation plan (Solow, 1998; Handler, 2004).

In the workfare state, moral hazard is counteracted through monitoring and the threat of sunset rules. Workfare programmes have been introduced in a consistent manner in a few countries, such as Denmark and the United States, where the outcomes constitute a mixed blessing (Peck, 2001). One principal difficulty with workfare state programmes is that they are not easily made compatible with the conception of public insurance as entitlements, i.e. rights which cannot be renegotiated from time to time. The practical difficulty with the workfare programmes is whether the client ever leaves the workfare state: Perhaps he/she is merely pushed around on various workfare assignments?

In general, the risk of moral hazard in public insurance is counteracted by recognising incentives and using it to the advantage of the principal. Thus, the principal employs two general techniques to reform the welfare state in order to make it incentive compatible:

- *Same compensation in all insurance schemes:* In order to avoid that individuals are enticed to move from one programme to another in order to maximise utility, all insurance programmes would offer the same level of protection.
- *Negative incentives in insurance:* It must never pay to become a client in public insurance. The simple way of making sure that work is better than welfare is to limit the possible support in welfare to some 60 per cent of the normal salary. Usually this is done by also taxing the insurance payments.

Creating incentive compatibility in insurance implies paying less to the clients, which may be exactly what politicians today want to do for another reason, namely the fiscal crisis of the public insurance system. However, improving the fiscal balance of the enormous insurance system runs the risk of another kind of P–A interaction, namely reneging on the part of the state. The workfare state handles the moral hazard problem by monitoring the recipient of welfare and conditioning help upon effort. But how can citizens force politicians to fulfil pension promises?

Social security and social policy

Despite all the country variation in terms of social policy and social security, deriving from the immense variation in rules and regulations, one may identify a few constant features:

- *Social policy:* Allocative programmes – transfer payments. Social policy includes both the provision of services gratis and the paying out of cheques in order to provide for income maintenance. In some countries the allocative social policies dominate, whereas in other countries the transfer payments are more costly than the allocative social policy due to the extensiveness and the ambition of the income maintenance programmes.
- *Social security:* Poverty relief – public pension schemes. Social policy may comprise a limited transfer payments section where only people in dire need are covered. Or social policy may cover all kinds of situations where normal income is lacking: old age pensions, sickness pay, unemployment benefits, long-term disability pensions, maternity leave, child allowances, etc.
- *Pension schemes:* One-, two- or three-pillar systems. Public pensions may offer basic support to all citizens independently of their income and wealth – the first pillar. Or public pensions may have the ambition to cover most of the income earned yearly during the time of employment – the second pillar. Sometimes the state also endorses a third pillar, which, although always private, may be supported through taxation exemptions.
- *Financing I:* General taxation – social security charges. A country may finance its social policies through the general system of taxation or it may introduce a separate financing system besides ordinary taxation, which though remains obligatory. A system of social security charges does not cover all kinds of social policy costs, as it is orientated towards covering costs for social policies that go beyond the guarantee of minimum standard of living.
- *Financing II:* Pay-as-you-go against actuarial systems. The costs of social security may be financed by means of current income from taxation or social security charges. Or they may be covered from the build up of funds where individuals own the capital that they have saved. These funds may be public or private, although the obligation to pay into them is sanctioned by public law regulations.

In general, social policies may be described as either means tested or as universalist, as well as either redistributive or insurance based. The trend in social policy reforms is today the opposite of the trend in the 1990s when Esping-Andersen wrote his well-known analysis of welfare capitalism regimes (Esping-Andersen, 1996; Blakemore, 2003; Percy-Smith, 2000). Now governments introduce more means-tested criteria and relax universalist principles. They also play down the redistributive ambition and emphasise the insurance principle.

The simple truth is that no country can afford a social policy that is comprehensive, universalist and redistributive. The difficulties concern both the macro and the micro aspects of social security. From the macro perspective on the entire economy, a full-scale welfare state model of social security runs into the problem of taxation that is too high – creating tax wedges – reducing investments and the entrepreneurial initiative. Looking at such a welfare state from the micro perspective the key question is that of incentives. On the other hand, governments seem very reluctant to engage in the option of complete privatisation of social security or the complete means-tested option. As a matter of fact, almost all governments that can afford it run a basic programme of income support which is universal and paid from general taxes – this is the first pillar. The differences arise when it comes to the second pillar, its existence and construction. All governments attempt to insert qualifying criteria relating to situation of the person in question as well as financing devices which connect the transfer payments with individual contributions.

Conclusion

Insurance is a classical theme in the P–A literature, the difficulties deriving from both adverse selection and moral hazard. It is the insurance company that is seen as the principal and the insured person is considered as the agent. Moral hazard arises when the insured person starts behaving differently due to the insurance offered by the principal. This possibility could, however, be avoided if the principal knows in advance the agent's type, or how the agent has a tendency to pretend. This is the adverse selection problem of knowing which agent one contracts with, the careful one or the careless one. If one applies the P–A perspective on public insurance, then the P–A framework helps in understanding the most recent reforms of the public insurance schemes, including the so-called workfare state programmes. Moral hazard in public insurance is best counteracted by inserting incentive compatibility schemes into the rules.

Public insurance harbours a decision-making problem that is not easily resolved and that keeps surfacing in the politics of social welfare. First there is the risk of a Type I error, or wrongly rejecting the true hypothesis that public insurance matters very much for the ordinary voter. He/she will not want to rely solely on the market. Second, there is the danger of a Type II error, or wrongly accepting the false hypothesis that only complete coverage is good enough in public insurance schemes. Committing the Type I error leads to social unrest and the reinforcement of social exclusion. Committing the Type II error, on the other hand, is conducive to the fiscal crisis of the state, as well as economic stagnation.

The problems in social security analysed above are related to the crisis of the welfare state. Publicly provided welfare is no longer seen as a means to remedy the flaws of the market economy; rather, it constitutes part of the very problem it was designed to solve. The systemic deficiencies of existing welfare systems – lack of incentive compatibility and welfare dependency – have become apparent, even to the adherents of the welfare state. From Sweden to New Zealand, in Germany and England and throughout Europe, a fundamental transformation in the welfare state has occurred: from broad-based entitlements and automatic benefits to an enabling approach through policies focusing on selective support based on income and behaviour. These new systems – workfare, incentive compatibility etc. – favour work and responsibility over protection, but they rely much upon civil society while reducing the role of government. Welfare supporters on the Left have implemented reforms associated with the policy agenda of the Right. However, social policy cannot be reduced to such a low level that it neglects those left behind (Castles, 2004; Taylor-Gooby, 2004; Lewis and Surender, 2004).

10 What is public management policy?

Introduction

With the emergence of New Public Management in the 1990s, one has started to talk about public management policy. This may at first sound awkward, as if one could combine public policy and public management. They are simply two different concepts for analysing the public sector. Yet the recognition of the place of management in public organisations calls for a discussion about the ends and means of public management, i.e. about how public organisations are to be operated. Public policy consists of the decisions of government in relation to its organisations, focusing on the ends and means of the teams it sets up. Public management, on the other hand, is basically running the public organisations. By 'public management policy' one refers to the recent reforms in OECD countries of how public organisations are to be run as well as the outcomes of these efforts.

The making of public management policy entails a reflection as to how public organisations are to be managed. Gone is the time when there was only one answer to this question, namely formal organisation or bureaucracy. NPM is one example of public management policy, referring to the public sector reforms where governments try to insert market mechanisms into their public organisations. Governments have conducted various public management policies for the purpose of reinventing government in general.

If public management policy is the re-engineering of government, then one may ask what the basic principles of public organisation may be. Probing this question may offer a new perspective on the state, which is linked up with the growing literature on the economics of organisation and information. The purpose of this chapter is twofold. First, I will look briefly at some examples of public management policies in the OECD countries. Second, I will discuss the new idea of public management and its core concepts that replace public administration, although the rule of law framework must be retained.

NPM: country-specific models or experiments

In Chapter 1 two meanings of 'NPM' were distinguished, one broad sense and another narrow sense. In the broad sense NPM stands for the emphasis on outputs and outcomes, as well as the employment of the strategies of decentralisation, networking and benchmarking. In the narrow sense NPM is a new and distinct model for conducting government, employing market mechanisms such as tendering/bidding and internal markets, for instance government buying in a competitive market the services it wants to provide. Let us look at little bit closer at what was involved in the various country models of public sector reform that emerged in the 1980s and 1990s.

I will make the abstract discussion of NPM in Chapter 1 more concrete by listing some of the major reforms in OECD who recently countries restructured their public sector. Each country brings its own experience into play when reforming government, meaning that one may speak of country-specific models building on country traditions and institutions, which is conducive to 'path dependency'. Reforms of the public sector may be done in a centralised manner or within a fragmented structure comprising more than one level of government. Below I list some of the main features of public sector reform in a few OECD countries, starting with the three so-called NPM countries (Pollitt and Bouckaert, 1999).

New Zealand (centralised decision-making)

Public sector reform in New Zealand was theoretically conceived of with a mixture of ideas from the Public Choice School, economic organisation theory and Chicago School economics. The key principles were:

- private sector organisation for commercial purposes;
- non-departmental organisations instead of ministerial departments;
- small organisations instead of large organisations;
- single-purpose instead of multipurpose organisations;
- separate policy from operations and implementation;
- separate operations from regulation;
- separate provision from review and audit;
- flat organisations instead of long hierarchies;
- straight-line accountability.

The reforms and the application of the principles above led to a sharp reduction in the size of the public sector, in the number of public enterprises and in people employed in the public service. The New Zealand model was the most coherent NPM model introduced in the OECD countries.

Australia (mixed decision-making)

Public sector reform had a practical orientation, focusing on enhancing the new field of public management, including:

- total quality management (TQM)
- benchmarking
- results-based budgeting, accrual budgeting
- entrepreneurial public service leadership (Centerlink).

There was also a strong ambition to cut back on the public sector. Thus, we also find:

- downsizing
- outsourcing (Commonwealth Employment Service)
- privatisations (Telstra)
- user-charging.

A noticeable change in the civil service occurred: less tenure, more external policy advice and less unionisation, plus a reduction in size. In the state of Victoria, NPM was put in place in a most consistent manner during the 1990s (Tangas, 2003).

United Kingdom (centralised decision-making)

Public sector reform in the UK was initiated by Thatcher, inspired by Hayek's philosophy of the market as a rational spontaneous order, and it was conducted in such a comprehensive way that one no longer speaks of the British public sector but of *plural government*. Thus, we find:

- massive privatisations
- 140 executive agencies (Raynerism)
- internal markets (health care)
- non-elected bodies.

The public sector was reduced but there was also the new phenomenon of reregulation, i.e. the setting up of lots of new regulatory agencies to overlook the deregulated and/or privatised providers. Whitehall was reduced considerably in size due to outsourcing and downsizing.

Canada (fragmented decision-making)

Actually none of the Canadian governments can be said to have used the concept of NPM in full, although the Canadian Federal Government came close to this model, starting from the time when Kim Campbell became Prime Minister in 1993. Cautious federal government reforms and sometimes radical provincial government reforms are to be found:

- downsizing
- decentralisation
- privatisation
- Ontario government ('Commonsense Revolution').

USA *(fragmented decision-making)*

Before the Clinton presidency, public management policy focused on managerialism in the form of adoption of business leaders at the top in a search for the advice of management gurus, e.g. the Grace commission. There were frequent piecemeal recommendations for:

- contracting out
- user fees
- privatisation.

The reinventing government policy of Clinton and Gore (National Performance Review – NPR) was more comprehensive, aiming at both reducing waste and empowering officials and raising morale. The NPR, together with its successor, strategic management or performance management (Government Performance and Results Act – GPRA) resulted in a downsizing of about 10 per cent of the 3 million federal employees in Washington.

When it comes to the countries outside the NPM sphere, the story is different. There occurred several public sector reforms, but the emphasis and strong reliance upon market mechanisms is lacking.

Germany *(fragmented decision-making)*

The countries adhering to the *Rechtstaat* tradition have hardly adopted much of the NPM philosophy. However, there is ongoing public sector reform including:

- local government innovation with the so-called New Steering Model;
- result-oriented budgeting;
- commercial book-keeping;
- decentralised resource accountability;
- indicators for quality standards;
- customer orientation;
- outsourcing.

France (centralised, incremental decision-making)

The modernisation of the French state has been a goal since the 1980s and 1990s, but the reforms do not follow the NPM concept and there is no hollowing out. Instead one finds:

- decentralisation to regions
- deconcentration from Paris.

Finland (centralised decision-making)

In Scandinavia there have been ambitious attempts at public sector reforms since the 1980s, some of which adhere to the NPM philosophy. Thus, Finland has tried:

- TQM, accrual budgeting;
- block budgeting, framework budgeting, strategic budgeting;
- flatter hierarchies, managerial governance;
- incorporation on a large scale;
- performance-related pay.

Sweden (fragmented decision-making)

Similarly, in Sweden both general modernisation and specifically NPM-inspired reforms have been implemented:

- decentralisation: free local government project;
- performance emphasis, budgetary steering;
- internal markets in health care with regional councils.

NPM was put in practice by several of the huge regional governments allocating health care, including the Stockholm country council and *Region Syd.*

The Netherlands (incremental decision-making)

There has been ongoing public sector reform with some NPM-inspired proposals:

- cutback management;
- privatisation and incorporation;
- executive agencies, ZBOs (zero-based budgeting, which requires that a programme be justified from the ground up each fiscal year) or autonomous administrative bodies;
- human resource management (HRM);
- decentralisation.

The Dutch public sector reforms have used the network model, underlining the relevance of public–private partnerships.

The OECD itself, through its PUMA programme, has advocated efficiency-enhancing reforms for a long time. Since the OECD headquarters in Paris has the best available information system on the member states, it comes as no surprise that the OECD has been influential in framing the debate on public sector reform. The PUMA project has been criticised for being too influenced by the NPM philosophy and insufficiently respectful of the public administration emphasis upon the rule of law and justice.

As underlined several times in this book, public management is the delivery of public services under the constraint of the rule of law, at least within the OECD countries, that all practice constitutional democracy and the market economy, called 'capitalist democracies'. Thus, 'public management policy' could be defined as the search for the most efficient institutions for public organisations to deliver their goods and services, given the restrictions emanating from the rule-of-law requirements.

Speaking generally, public sector reform has been reasonably close to the NPM philosophy for more than a decade. In Chapter 1 a distinction was made between a broad and a narrow definition of 'NPM'. It is the narrow definition which may be used to classify countries more or less as 'NPM countries'. Thus, the crucial mechanisms that the public sector reforms aim at inserting into public organisation are market similar devices such as tendering/bidding, tournaments, auctions and contracting out, as well as user fees. On the other hand, decentralisation, deconcentration or state modernisation in general hardly amount to NPM, but these reforms have none the less been important in the public management policy in many OECD countries. Each country develops its public management policy on the basis of its institutional legacy – 'path dependency'. However, one may speak of a few guiding principles in the making of a public management policy, such as the search for a post-Weberian organisational model.

Guiding principles of public management policy

In the public sector reforms of OECD countries, whether inspired by the NPM philosophy in its narrow sense of imitating market mechanisms or merely by the ambition at state modernisation, one finds a set of key ideas about how to manage public organisations. The following principles may be underlined:

- *Value for money:* The public services have a specific value, although they are not sold on a market. Public organisations should have the overriding goal of delivering services with the highest possible value. Public management reform should not only be based upon outputs but also take outcomes into account with a view to extracting value in society from the provision of services in the public sector.

- *Policy versus delivery organisations:* The management of public organisations should identify their output objectives as well as assess performance using output indicators or benchmarking. Policy-making is mainly a political task which should be separated from delivery management.
- *Towards more quantity and quality:* Public management should maximise the efficiency of public organisations, which involves either internal efficiency (productivity) or external efficiency (effectiveness). Public management involves organising service delivery within public organisations or within public–private partnerships so that there are more and better outputs.
- *Constrained maximisation:* Public management is the implementation of public policy under the restrictions stemming from the rule of law. This means that efficiency is not the sole consideration in public management, as the requirements of justice have to be fulfilled.

The means and ends of public management policies vary from one country to another. The so-called NPM countries adhere to the narrow definition of NPM, using market mechanisms on a large scale. The so-called *Rechtstaat* countries adhere to the broad definition of NPM, calling for the modernisation of the state. In the Netherlands there is strong emphasis upon governance through public–private partnerships or networks. In the making of public management policy it is an open question whether it is the structure or the culture of the organisation that is targeted. And the implementation of public management policy depends upon both legacy or history and strategy or incentives. The narrow NPM strategy has been the most contested of public sector reforms. The NPM strategy involves the introduction of market mechanisms into the public sector, including:

- incorporation
- partial privatisation
- tendering/bidding
- internal markets
- outsourcing
- user fees
- deregulation
- purchaser–provider split.

It has been argued that the NPM strategy entails too radical an application of public procurement together with a private organisation model such as the joint-stock company, as well as with user fees. There could well be a clear risk for NPM excesses such as massive incorporation, outsourcing and agentisation – the *hollowing out* of the state (Pierre and Peters, 2000). In a less pessimistic interpretation of recent public sector reform one may speak of the coming of a new model for public organisation: the post-Weberian type of public organisation.

Towards a post-modern public organisation

When each and every public sector reform is added up, public organisation has fundamentally changed its traditional face. Table 10.1 presents in a succinct form the main characteristics of the traditional public sector organisation – the bureaucracy – in comparison with the reinvented or re-engineered public sector organisation – the post-bureaucratic organisation (see the analysis in Kernaghan *et al.*, 2000).

The post-Weberian structure results from both kinds of NPM reforms: the narrow and the broad conceptions. The making and implementation of public management policy is driven by both principals and agents: politicians, bureaucrats, consultants and stakeholders, as well as the general public. It is generally believed that a government must conduct some form of public sector reform. What, then, drives government to conduct public management policy?

Public management reform: what is the drive?

Since public management policy is on the political agenda in most OECD countries, one may wish to reflect a little upon the driving mechanisms behind the making and implementation of reforms of public organisations. I will focus on incentives here in order to map the variety of interests that may be displayed in reform processes.

An interesting interpretation of public sector change is launched in *The Federal Civil Service System and the Problem of Bureaucracy* (Johnson and Libecap, 1994). The authors enquire into the changes of the federal bureaucracy, especially the change from patronage to meritocracy in the United States during the last 100 years and the reinventing government policy. The argument amounts to a combination of public choice theory and neo-institutionalist economic theory, suggesting that bureaucratic reforms will be driven by both the selfish interests of the players involved and the general interests of society, here called 'efficiency gains' or 'transaction costs', where society may hope that the first are maximised and the latter are minimised. But who is 'society'?

This novel analysis has a paradoxical conclusion, namely that bureaucratic reform today, such as reinventing government, is not very likely to be successful. How, then, could the entire American spoils system be changed, starting with the Pendleton Act of 1884? I will discuss the variety of incentives involved in the making and implementation of public management policy.

Selfish motives

Bureaucratic reform may be driven by the parties involved such as politicians, national or local, as well as the civil servants themselves. It may also be driven by external groups, such as interest organisations or different

Table 10.1 The bureaucratic and post-bureaucratic organisation

Bureaucracy	Post-bureaucratic organisation
Organisation centred:	Citizen centred:
Emphasis on needs of the organisation itself	Quality service to citizens (and clients/stakeholders)
Position power:	Participative leadership:
Control, command and compliance	Shared values and participative decision-making
Rule centred:	People centred:
Rules, procedures and constraints	An empowering and caring milieu for employees
Independent action:	Collective action:
Little consultation, cooperation coordination	Consultation, cooperation and or coordination
Status-quo oriented:	Change oriented
Avoiding risks and mistakes	Innovation, risk-taking and continuous improvement
Process oriented:	Results oriented:
Accountability for process	Accountability for results
Centralized:	Decentralized:
Hierarchy and central control	Decentralization of authority and control
Departmental form:	Non-departmental form:
Most programmes delivered by operating departments	Programmes delivered by wide variety of mechanisms
Budget-driven:	Revenue-driven:
Programmes financed largely from appropriations	Programmes financed as far as possible on cost-recovery basis
Monopolistic:	Competitive:
Government has monopoly on program delivery	Competition with private-sector program delivery

Source: Kernaghan *et al.* (2000: 3)

citizen groups. One may wish to differentiate between executive and legislative politicians, as well as between various kinds of organised interests. Of course, bureaucratic reform may be demanded or rejected, meaning that there are interests linked with reform and interests counteracting reform. The analysis of reform processes often targets the relative strength of the two sides of the status quo, i.e. the push for change and the resistance to change.

In the major reforms of the federal bureaucracy initiated by the Pendleton Act in 1884, selfish interests no doubt played a major role, following Johnson and Libecap's analysis. Thus, patronage benefited local politicians more than federal politicians. However, its benefits for the bureaucrats did not match the utility derived from secure position and tenure. The growth of the federal government after the Civil War led to organised interests among the employees, to whom secure employment outweighed the short-term gains from patronage. But there were also general interests in society that favoured the reduction of patronage.

General interests: efficiency gains and transaction cost reduction

Various citizen groups in civil society were increasingly dissatisfied with patronage and poor public services, calling for reforms that would diminish corruption. They could make a coalition with national politicians, to whom patronage posed transaction costs that were too high. The use of one central admission system typical of both the 1854 Northcote–Trevelyan reforms in the UK and the 1884 Pendleton Act in the US was meant to both enhance efficiency in service delivery and reduce transaction costs in allocating jobs in the growing bureaucracy.

The theory of Johnson and Libecap, focusing on transaction costs, may be contrasted with the analysis of Hennessy (2001) in *Whitehall*, where the massive changes in the central government bureaucracy in the UK by Thatcher are enquired into. If central admissions were so crucial to enhancing efficiency and reducing transaction costs, eagerly sought after by national politicians in coalition with citizens, then what explains the recent changes in bureaucracy inspired by the NPM philosophy, preferring decentralised recruitment? Evidently, Thatcher managed to undo some of the monolithic bureaucracy of Whitehall, acting on the basis of her preference for executive agencies under strong control from the Prime Minister's office. Interestingly, several OECD countries have moved away from the central admission system typical of the Northcote–Trevelyan and Pendleton reforms. Can we conclude that it is again a matter of either increasing efficiency or reducing transaction costs? Reforming the bureaucracy is a game where special interests of politicians and bureaucrats blend with the general interests of citizens. What is at stake is how to marry merit with political accountability (see Ingraham's enquiry in *The Foundation of Merit*, 1995). Country solutions to public management policy issues – blending merit and accountability – will, besides incentives, depend upon the managerial technology available, which changes over time.

The IT revolution and transaction costs

Providing public services relies upon production functions where the use of manpower is heavy. However, technological change is a highly relevant factor in public sector reform, as the use of the internet and the new information technology (IT) may revolutionise government in more than one way. Thus, the IT revolution increases productivity in government and also enhances the delivery of new products. The new IT changes the flow of information within government and between citizens and government, altering the interactions within government and between citizens and government.

IT is transaction cost saving, but this fact is not enough for it to be introduced all over government and its organisations. It must also be in the interest of the key players to seize upon the benefits from a reduction in transaction costs. One should not postulate that the various players are driven by the altruistic motive of reducing transaction costs in general. It is when a reduction in transaction costs coincides with the maximisation of self-interests among the stakeholders – politicians, bureaucrats, professionals, interest groups and citizens – that public sector reform will be transaction cost saving.

The IT revolution has consequences for transaction costs which in turn impact upon the self-interests of the stakeholders. It is when IT changes the relative costs of alternative organisational forms that it becomes interesting to the various players and stakeholders to start changing organisational structure. Changes in the technologies of public management bring about a fundamental change in the structure of public administration. The IT revolution has made new public service delivery mechanisms possible and also opened up more variety in the production of public services. New products have become feasible. The new public organisation (Kernaghan *et al.*, 2000) has to some extent been made possible by IT. However, its relevance also depends upon whether it is in the interest of many of the stakeholders to support the new structure.

'E-government' holds an enormous potential for restructuring the interaction within public organisations and between government and the citizens. E-government refers to the use by government agencies of IT (such as wide-area networks, the internet and mobile computing) that have the ability to transform relations with citizens, businesses, and other arms of government. These technologies can serve a variety of different ends: better delivery of government services to citizens, improved interactions with business and industry, citizen empowerment through access to information, or more efficient government management. The resulting benefits can be less corruption, increased transparency, greater convenience, revenue growth, and/or cost reductions. Traditionally, the interaction between a citizen or business and a government agency took place in a government office. With emerging information and communication technologies it is possible to locate service centres closer to the clients. Such centres may consist of an unattended kiosk in the government agency, a service kiosk located close to the client, or the use of a personal computer in the home or office.

Analogous to e-commerce, which allows businesses to transact with each other more efficiently and brings customers closer to businesses, e-government aims to make the interaction between government and citizens, government and business enterprises, and interagency relation-ships more flexible, friendly, convenient, transparent, and inexpensive. E-commerce has evolved already through four stages: (1) publishing, (2) interactivity, (3) completing transactions, and (4) delivery. To date, most e-government activity has centred on publishing. There are vast differ-ences among countries in the maturity of their e-government effort. Perhaps one may claim that even the most mature countries have tapped less than 20 per cent of the potential. E-government may range from e-voting to direct citizen communication about individual rights.

The public management function

I shall quote from a few telling passages from the new literature on public management where one makes an analysis of the public manage-ment function. Interestingly, one finds both the position that politics and administration are completely fused and that they interact somehow. Thus we have:

> How much of the performance delivered by important public programs can be attributed to the efforts of public managers, those who organise people and resources to get the job done? (Brudney *et al.*, 2000b: 1.)

It is not obvious who the 'public managers' are in this quotation. But it seems likely that we can interpret 'those who organise people' as the CEOs of bureaux. The authors continue with the following statement:

> What has all the fuss about "reinvention" and "reform" in public man-agement and governance amounted to? In a world in which devolution, contracting, privatization, and other such instruments increasingly occupy center stage, what is the role of public management in "mak-ing a mesh of things," to borrow Paul Appleby's classic aphorism? (2000b: 1.)

Here it seems that the 'public managerial task' is pitted against public sector reform strategies such as devolution, contracting and privatisation.

Perhaps it is adequate to speak about the making and implementation of public management policy, which would comprise both traditional bureaucracy and the mechanisms of NPM?

> Public managers, therefore, are necessarily involved in an array of tasks extending far beyond the narrow notions of management often discussed. Public managers, even if simply interested in accomplishing management tasks, typically become active in collective choice (O'Toole, 2000: 19).

If 'collective choice' means the decisions of parliament or the legislative assembly, then we have here a broad definition of public managers as both politicians and bureaucrats. However, this is by no means the only interpretation of this quotation. Bureaucrats also engage in collective choice, especially if there is a collegial mechanism for governing the bureau.

It is true that 'top executives', meaning the higher echelon of the civil service, are in constant interaction with politicians and that their efforts in implementing policy have political implications. Establishing and accepting this fundamental fact about public management does not entail, however, that one needs to reject the 'politics–administration dichotomy'. One must distinguish between three propositions:

1   Politics is always (can always be) separate from administration.
2   Administration always involves politics.
3   Politicians and bureaucrats interact in the making and implementation of policy.

It seems to me that only proposition (3) is defensible, as both (1) and (2) are untenable. Proposition (3) should be developed by means of the principal–agent framework into a theory of public management, i.e. contracting as getting the job done, e.g. 'making a mesh of things' (Appleby) or 'muddling through' (Lindblom). To what extent can top-level appointed political executives make significant policy choices? Participants in the debate over this question within the field of public management have taken a variety of positions.

At one extreme, public managers are said to be so constrained by large-scale political and institutional forces that they have little room for significant choice. The organisational process model of Allison and Zelikow (1999) is representative of this view: the choices of top-level executives are limited to the menu of routines supplied by their subordinate organisations. Wilson (1991) argues that it is the mid- and lower-level managers, as well as the professional and organisational constraints under which these managers work that determine organisational effectiveness.

It is clear that the top-level managers may include politicians, or more specifically the politicians who hold executive positions. A key question in public management is how executive managers may interact with middle-level managers to impact upon 'organisational effectiveness' – a matter for principal–agent contracting.

External constituencies impose equally important constraints on the ability of political executives to choose their own course of action. Public agencies operate in an 'embedded hierarchy' of other agencies, interest groups, and branches of government that limit the autonomy of agency executives. Legislatures also impose administrative constraints on public agencies; while intended to maintain accountability, they also contribute to the growth of bureaucratic rules and 'red tape'. The consequence, Kaufman (1981) asserts, is that political executives generally have relatively little impact on policies and programmes: 'They certainly do calculate and negotiate to accomplish all they can. But they make their mark in inches, not miles, and only as others allow' (Hammond and Knott, 2000: 49–50). At the other extreme are accounts of political executives who were able to forge great changes in public policies less constrained by political and institutional forces.

> These political executives successfully altered the relationships between their organisations and their political environments and shaped the activities of their mid- and lower-level managers (Hammond and Knott, 2000: 50).

In these quotations, the set of political executives is narrowed down even further to the leaders of public agencies. They may of course be ministers, politically appointed bureaucrats or merely bureaucrats. The principal–agent game concerns (1) how these 'political executives' are accountable to government, either the cabinet or president or parliament, and (2) how they conduct the business of their organisations by contracting with teams, their own or others. There are conditions under which a political executive has some political autonomy of which he/she can take advantage, but there are also conditions under which he/she will have little or no autonomy at all. The analysis also reinforces the argument that political executives need to 'find the correct managerial space for action'.

> In our terms, the effective executive needs to identify the relevant policy space so that he can take advantage of what autonomy is available (Hammond and Knott, 2000: 71).

There is a clear risk that public management theory develops according to the evolution of private management thinking, i.e. it results in truisms or general statements that are highly probable if not trivial. Of course, a political executive (who is that?) may have either much or little autonomy; of course he/she should find the correct action space, etc. I shall try another look at public management which does not amount to merely the accumulation of proverbs. If bureaucrats are the political executives or work for them, then how do they behave? The literature on bureaucracy assumes that bureaucrats are risk-averse, i.e. risk-avoiding and conservative. At the same time the literature, or the reinventing government movement, requires bureaucrats to be entrepreneurs, individuals who take major risks in an effort to achieve major performance breakthroughs.

> Although diametrically opposed in terms of objectives (scholarship versus practical advice), both stress a concern with individuals and agencies that deviate from the norm (i.e., those that fail and those that succeed beyond expectations) (Meier *et al.*, 2000: 77).

The answer to the question posed in this quotation – agents as risk-averse or risk-neutral – depends on the contract signed with the principal. In public organisations, such as bureaucracy, agents tend to be risk-averse, but under various schemes of NPM, such as tendering/bidding, agents could well be both risk-neutral and risk-prone.

How to identify the set of executives or managers in public management is a troublesome question, as one may cast the net broadly or narrowly. There are both top-level managers and bottom-level managers:

> Public management research and theory are preoccupied with top-level managers. This exclusive attention on top management limits our understanding of governance because leadership and policymaking also occur at other levels, including the street level (Maynard-Moody and Leland, 2000: 109).

Police officers, teachers, caseworkers, rehabilitation counsellors – the entire range of street-level workers – make discretionary decisions about the amount and character of services provided to citizens. Their choices and oversights alter the distribution of government services and, for better or worse, the way government programmes are delivered to and perceived by citizens. If the set of managers is perhaps so large that it includes both top level, middle level and bottom level, then how can one impose some structure upon this set? One way to do so is to look at the contractual relations between the persons in this set. Public management is a large nexus of contracts. How managers behave, however, depends first and foremost on the strategies they develop in relation to their contracts:

> In sum, public managers have three alternatives to the warrior position. What might be termed "missionary" strategies attempt to expand the customer base of a public agency without redefining the needs of the consumer. "Visionary" strategies, by contrast, seek to meet a richer set of needs of which recipients are only dimly aware. Third, "inventors" attempt to combine both expansion and enrichment strategies by

creating values that do not presently exist for a customer base that not yet exist because a felt and articulated need has not yet been defi (McGregor, 2000: 137–138).

Of whatever type public managers are – warriors, visionaries or inventors – they are a new and growing group of people. They come from both the public and the private sectors. Often they have different titles from those traditionally used in the civil service. Are they bureaucrats or not? One may argue that recent public reforms, whether NPM inspired or not, have increased the domain of discretion for executive decision-making, i.e. 'managerial autonomy'.

First, public managers can limit their frame of reference and assume there is one best way and apply it to whatever context or situation they confront. Second, they can develop a contingency approach to management and match strategy, structure, tasks, or processes to fit particular situations. Third, public managers can take the holistic stance that only a certain number of organisational configurations are possible. It is not difficult to mention a few management functions, but how can one make a comprehensive and exhaustive list? There is no lack of attempts to come up with a typology of the basic functions in public management:

> This perspective undoubtedly emerged from the work of Weber (1946) and Taylor (1911) and most prominently from Gulick's classic POSDCORB typology (1937) but also reflects more contemporary thought. For example, Rosenbloom (1989), in his discussion of the practice of public administration, devotes significant attention to the core functions of budgeting and human resources management. Cohen and Eimicke (1995) additionally include gathering, organising, and using information as a key managerial tool in the public sector (Ingraham and Kneedler, 2000: 244).

Yet, which are these 'core functions' in government, when looked upon from the output side? I shall attempt to list as many of these as possible.

Core public mangement functions

Ingraham and Kneedler classify public management into four typical functions. Given the recent interest in public management I will look in detail at these below.

Financial management

Government financial management systems distribute money for public purposes through procurement, accounting, cash management, and reporting. Key components include the ability to engage in accurate revenue and expenditure forecasting, a long-term focus, the practice of planning for contingencies, awareness of the linkage between cost and performance, and appropriate flexibility.

But is financial management really a 'core function' in government? Of course, taxation and budgeting are tremendously important in politics, but in public management it is perhaps the achievement of specific objectives or the respect for established rules and rights in administrative and constitutional law which constitutes the so-called core. What, then, about personnel management?

Human resources management

Personnel systems are concerned with recruiting, retaining, motivating, training and terminating public employees. Key components include: the use of coherent rules and procedures, efforts at workforce planning, timely hiring, sufficient professional development programmes, and meaningful reward structures and disciplinary actions.

It is not clear how one can make a distinction between financial management and human resources management. People cost money immediately they start working for government. They need premises and materials. Thus, budgeting and financial management cannot be separated from personnel management. Recent efforts to work the recognition of incentives into the salaries of bureaucrats and professionals in government translate at once into new routines for financial management. Thus, the distinction breaks down. But what about the management of non-labour assets, such as capital and land? Government is a major owner of both these assets.

Capital management

Capital management involves planning for, maintaining, and disposing of long-lived resources. Key elements include: active engagement in long-range planning and prioritisation of projects, adequate budgetary resources for infrastructure maintenance and repair, and attention to the relationship between capital and operating budgets.

How to separate capital management from financial management only a Kantian scholar with the highest capacity for abstraction could tell. Again, one is not convinced that capital management is a core function, as capital may be employed for many different purposes in relation to the specific objectives of public management: health, education, etc. Thus, it is the objective, like education, health care or communication which is core, not the management of the capital invested in these functions itself.

Information technology management

Managing information technology includes the development, maintenance, and use of technological systems to collect, analyse, and communicate data.

Especially in public institutions responsible for executing complicated pro-grammes and interfacing with large, diverse constituencies, information technology performs both primary and integrative functions. Key compo-nents include: the timeliness, accuracy, reliability, usefulness, and cost-effectiveness of data and the ability of all personnel to use the information systems (Ingraham and Kneedler, 2000: 245–246).

The IT revolution has most certainly contributed considerably to the emphasis put upon information technology management. But it is one thing to underline all the potential uses of information technology, and quite another matter to identify how information technology is employed in core functions such as voting, taxation, social security, health care, edu-cation, etc. Government does not build up huge capacity in information technology for its own sake. It is the uses that are of core importance.

Does public management matter?

Finally, I shall discuss the hypothesis that public management matters. One finds it with several authors in the new literature, for instance:

> From the front lines to the top political executives, a variety of actors – including, in some instances, many not formally part of the apparatus of government – are involved in significant ways with the challenges of public management. When considered in conjunction with the first-mentioned theme above – does public management matter? – one is struck by the expansive, almost daunting, terrain on which the subject must be considered (Brudney *et al.*, 2000c: 258–259).

It is all too easy to reply 'yes' to this hypothesis about the importance of public management, but it is far more difficult to specify how and for what public management matters. The authors go on directly to state the following:

> Public management issues and research questions appear from the bot-tom to the top of government and from the managerial issues within line public agencies, to the challenges of managing public programs in complicated multi-actor settings, to the politico-managerial agen-das of governance. This heterogeneity, in turn, is both energizing and potentially stultifying: there remains much to learn, and in many venues (2000c: 258–259).

If public management occurs everywhere in government, then maybe is it everything, meaning nothing, according to the famous Wildavsky criti-cism of the old idea that governance is planning (Caiden and Wildavsky, 1980; Wildavsky, 2002). I suggest that public management becomes more accessible if it is analysed as a series of principal–agent games.

Although the principal–agent model was developed for private sector interaction, it seems eminently suitable for the analysis of the interaction

Table 10.2 Public management: the black box

Inputs	Public management	Outputs
Appropriations	Principal–agent contracting	Programmes
Capital, labour, knowledge, materials, premises, etc.	At various levels of government between politicians and employees, as well as between employees	Performance outcomes

between politicians and bureaucrats in democratic policy-making and policy implementation. If public management is the governance of public programmes, often in public–private partnerships, then unpacking the black box between inputs and outputs in Table 10.2 must entail an understanding of how politicians and bureaucrats interact to get the job done through the making and monitoring of contracts.

Now, indiscriminately calling all decision-makers in public management 'managers' makes one neglect the politics/administration separation. Public management involves politicians contracting with the managers, who contract with teams in turn, about how to get programmes running and how to deliver services in order to achieve results. This interaction is the central focus of both public administration, emphasising rules and justice, as well as public management, underlining efficiency.

Understanding how these contracts are made and how they can be improved upon in repeated interaction is a central task in public management theory. One may analyse public management as a long series of contracts between principals and agents, making deals about what to do and how to be remunerated. Schematically speaking, the politicians decide to set up an organisation to implement a programme or deliver a service. They contract with a CEO in order to provide him/her with the resources necessary for running the bureau. This entails that he/she contracts with a team of employees. Thus, we arrive at the nexus of contracts forming the *core* of public management. These contracts are not merely managerial ones, as they are made by government in the context of the legal entity that we call the 'state'. Public management is principal–agent contracting within a setting of the rule of law in well-ordered societies. It involves as inherent questions: *Quid pro quo? Cui bono?*

These critical questions about public management may be stated in terms of the principal–agent framework:

- Is the bureaucracy reasonably well paid in order to avoid corruption? Can the principal trust the agent?
- Does the bureaucracy deliver services of an acceptable quality? Can the principal expect to get what he/she contracts for?

- Is the bureaucracy productive? Can the principal write contracts that elicit performance from the bureaucrats?
- Is the bureaucracy efficient? Can the principal write contracts that somehow involve the monitoring of the bureaucracy towards results that have value for society?
- How can the public managers solve the team question, i.e. finding and paying their employees according to their marginal product value? Under what contractual arrangements will the contracts between the CEO and his/her employees be efficient?

What happens in the black box of public management when inputs are transformed into outputs is the making and enforcement of a long series of principal–agent contracts, from the contract between the politicians and the CEO to the contracts between lower-level managers and the employees directly responsible for service delivery.

In a democracy the elected politicians play a key role in policy-making when channelling the demand of the electorates for political action. They may be seen as the agents of the population as the principal, or they can be looked upon as the principal who contracts with the civil service as the agent in order to get the job of government done. In both interpretations of the politicians, they are not merely public managers. Instead they contract with public managers in order to get the job done. Thus, under a principal–agent framework we arrive at a tenable politics/administration separation. One may pinpoint the problem in a succinct manner by posing the question 'Who are the public managers?' in relation to the core of the state, the civil service. In a well-ordered society the civil service is insulated from the political process through a variety of institutional mechanisms, including tenure, neutrality, loyalty to any government, whether Left or Right, professional recruitment and advancement, clear lines of subordination, defined tasks, protection against arbitrary disciplinary measures and firing, etc. Thus, some kind of separation between politics and administration is always done, although the exact solution varies from one country to another, reflecting historical traditions or institutional legacies.

In all civil servant systems there is a point of transmission between the politicians and the bureaucrats, as some positions at the top of the civil service are reserved for political appointees. These bureaucrats will only serve one master and they are expected to resign when the government changes. It is the size of this transmission mechanism that varies from one country to another. Thus, in the UK, for instance it is very small, whereas in the US this section is very large due to the remnants of the so-called spoils system.

The separation between politics and administration is institutionalised in not only the central or federal government but also in regional or provincial governments, as well as in local governments. Here one finds the typical

separation between the elected council on the one hand and the permanent bureaucracy on the other. Again the exact demarcation between the
politicians and the bureaucracy will be different, depending upon whether
the government of the province or community adheres to the premier or
president type of executive.

When major public administration scholars attacked the poli-
tics/administration separation, they did not deny the institutionalisation
of a demarcation line between politicians and bureaucrats in the modern
state. That would not only be untrue from an empirical point of view but
also a rejection of a basic element in democracy theory. One finds in both
the model of participatory democracy and in the model of representative
democracy an emphasis upon a separation between politics and administration. Thus, Rousseau for instance underlines that the executors of the
popular will, established through a referendum, must only put in effect what
the sovereign people have decided (Rousseau, 1997). And Weber focusing
on parliament and its key role in a modern democracy makes the key point
that even charismatic politicians cannot rule effectively without a neutral
and competent bureaucracy (Weber, 1994).

The criticism or rejection of the politics/administration separation with
Waldo or Appelby amounts to the argument that bureaucrats often have a
major political influence upon the making of policy, as well as that bureaucrats when implementing policy do not engage in merely the neutral and
effective implementation of government actions and decisions. This point
is no doubt correct and this insight forces us to rethink this separation
and model it in a more appropriate way than did, for instance Rousseau in
participative theory and Weber in representative democracy theory.

Conclusion

Several OECD countries have embarked upon the making and implementation of public management policy. It involves the transformation of public
organisations, the bureaucracy and the public enterprises in response to
the search for greater efficiency. Economic organisation theory implies that
institutions are usually modified slowly and in response to changes in the
benefits and costs of the groups directly affected by them. Although it is
always possible to imagine institutional alternatives whereby all parties could
be made better off, in practice such outcomes are impossible in a world of
high information and transaction costs. Given the presence of transaction
costs that are particularly apparent in the political arena, institutions that
inhibit the public interest and reduce efficiency can and will persist.

Yet, public management policy in several OECD countries has accomplished major change in both the governance of public enterprises and
the bureaucracy. Chapter 8 examined the far-reaching transformation
of the traditional public enterprise into a modern joint-stock company
– the incorporation strategy. Here we have underlined the tension in

bureaucracy reform between merit and political accountability. The NPM philosophy is an attempt to increase both technical competence and political accountability at the same time though the use of, for example, executive agencies replacing parts of the bureaucracy or tendering/bidding mechanisms.

E-government will most probably be the next major reform movement in public organisations. The goals:

- better service delivery to citizens
- improved services for business
- transparency and anti-corruption
- empowerment through information
- efficient government purchasing

are relevant for both First World and Third World governments. E-government would be feasible for three reasons: (1) Storage capacity – government agencies keep enormous amounts of information and data. The IT revolution makes information gathering and storing much easier. However, there is the risk against personal integrity. (2) Dissemination capacity– government agencies need to spread lots of information to citizens about their rights as well as about changes in programmes. Again there is the question of personal integrity when agencies share information. (3) Inter-action capacity – citizens can speak to government directly from home. This enhances government rationality as well as legitimacy.

Conclusion: contracting in the public sector

Introduction

When one speaks about the public sector, then the key word is 'public'. It makes the crucial distinction between the public and the private. When analysing the public sector, the relevant theories are classified as 'public' policy, 'public' management and 'public' administration. It is believed in the well-ordered societies that there exists a 'public' domain where there occurs a 'public' discourse which is separate or different from the 'private' domain with its 'private' discourse. To clarify this distinction one often employs the concepts of state and market, although some scholars may wish to add a third concept, namely, the family.

Something is thus called 'public' when it is somehow part of the state. Public policies are the programmes or commitments of the central, regional or local governments. Public management is the steering and monitoring of teams of employees in the state, the regional or local governments, in order to accomplish efficiency. Finally, public administration is the institutionalisation of the government in all its aspects with a view towards achieving the rule of law.

In political science the public is identified with the obligations for a collective of individuals. Thus, the public sector emerges from statute law taking the forms of constitutional law or administrative law, which are both always binding upon all citizens. The state entails authority, i.e. there is a high probability that obedience is forthcoming towards a command. In economics the private sector or the markets are analysed as contracting between separate persons. The logic of markets is the making of deals: bargaining, agreement and the enforcement of deals. Consequently, private law results from the mutual regulation of rights and duties between individuals.

Yet, paradoxically the theme of this book is that the public sector is also basically contracting. Government results from the contracting difficulties among citizens, and the state is structured in terms of contracting between principals and agents. To understand why contracting is basic for understanding the public sector, one needs to recognise the implications of transaction costs for public organisation. The aim of this final chapter is to theorise how transaction costs permeate public organisation, as the implications of transaction costs for private organisation have been analysed already.

Transaction cost theories are employed within so-called 'new institutional economics' or neo-institutionalism, which is a new branch of economics attempting to endogenise rules, meaning explain them as resulting from choice, given either full information or bounded rationality. 'New Institutionalism' refers to the variety of schools that seek to explain political, historical, economic and social institutions such as government, legal orders, markets, firms, social conventions, the family, etc. in terms of economic decision theory.

I will distinguish here between transaction costs *ex ante* and transaction costs *ex post* the contract.

- *Bargaining costs:* the time and effort put in *ex ante*.
- *Enforcement costs:* the time and effort put in *ex post*.

The state and transaction costs

Government was never absent in Manchester liberal economics, which launched the concept of the minimalist state. It is often underlined that Adam Smith devoted much space to underlining the importance of government to the proper functioning of markets. Thus, the state comes first and markets second. One may derive this approach from Hobbes and his theory of the natural condition, which tends towards anarchy if government is not introduced through the great covenant, i.e. a kind of gigantic PD game.

The point here is that this traditional perspective in political economy makes the market a function of one exogenous entity – government in the Anglo-Saxon tradition, the state in the Continental tradition. However, it leaves the question of the origins of or reasons for government unanswered. As in the Manchester liberal theory, markets are endogenous and the state is exogenous; what is lacking is a theory of the logic of public organisation in the first place.

The night-watchman theory of government focuses on the market as the optimal mechanism for human interaction, but it admits that markets can only flourish if supported by government. After society has erected a state it may proceed to employ markets to provide itself with the goods and services it needs. The role of government is to provide society with the presuppositions of markets, which include:

- guarantee of contracts agreed upon;
- punishment of contract violations;

- removal of contract violators from society;
- awarding of compensation for contract violations;
- guarantee of money with which to contract;
- protection of the country against foreign intruders.

The night-watchman government would provide these services to the market, after which markets could take on any allocative task. The idea is that the market cannot provide its own presuppositions. This is Hobbes' theory of the state, and it certainly still seems valid. Behind it, one finds the need to minimise transaction costs.

Contractual validation requires uniformity and efficiency in the application of rules. Citizens would support one enforcer, as the existence of many enforcers would endanger the presuppositions of the market, i.e. it would result in anarchy, as in stateless societies in the Third World. Citizens would be prepared to negotiate about the creation of a state by, e.g. establishing a constitution and a fiscal regime, but such bargaining could not go on endlessly. Thus, minimising transaction costs would be the ultimate rationale for government. However, the relevance of transaction costs does not end here.

The classical market failure framework has suggested a number of concepts with which to analyse state intervention in the economy. Thus, public policies would target the following chief market failures:

- externalities in allocation;
- economies of scale in production;
- asymmetric information in transactions;
- inequalities in distribution.

We have discussed the market failure theory in Chapter 6, where two views on this approach were contrasted, the Chicago and Cambridge positions, respectively. Suffice it here to underline that market failure is in reality nothing but transaction costs, *ex ante* or *ex post*.

Transaction costs and political organisation have the same source, namely the collectivities that human beings set up and maintain, from local governments to nations, federations and international organisations. When groups may decide to provide themselves with goods and services, then transaction costs arise immediately. Whether the group provides itself with public or private goods, it must decide upon quantities and qualities in the service programmes, thus incurring decision costs, of which transaction costs constitute one part. In addition, there are the enforcement costs in relation to the implementation of the public programmes. Groups in well-ordered societies minimise transaction costs in decision-making by employing the democratic procedure of simple majority voting. And they minimise transaction costs in enforcement by resorting to an elaborated mechanisms for public administration and management.

Government must resolve the principal–agent difficulties which arise when the state establishes a political organisation for a group, i.e. a government or state. Here, we find again a contractual approach helpful when analysing the typical principal–agent difficulties in public organisation, namely the occurrence of hidden actions and hidden knowledge. Bureaucracy is beset by the first difficulty, whereas public enterprises struggle with the second, especially under the new regime of incorporation and partial privatisation. NPM suggests that government should contract more frequently in order to handle moral hazard, but this raises the question of how government can come to grips with hidden knowledge when it outsources the provision of services or market-tests its CEOs or teams.

Suppose we start from the Hegelian separation of society into the public sector and the private sector, recognising at the same time that there are more and more public–private partnerships. The private sector seems to be more coherent than the public sector, which is actually the opposite of what Hegel argued in his admiration for the state. Private sector coherence appears both in theory and in practice.

Different public sector approaches – is there a common core?

The analysis of the private sector offered by modern economics is truly impressive. There are now so many economic specialties – agricultural, industrial, macro and micro economics for instance – that one gets the impression that each and every part of the private sector is covered, also the family and crime. In addition to an almost complete coverage there is the coherence that is derived from the employment of one single model of human behaviour, the neoclassical decision-making model with its further elaborations into modern game theory.

When one looks at the variety of approaches to the public sector, then the overall impression is the opposite one, meaning heterogeneity, conflict and diversity. Thus, public administration does not go down well with public management or strategic management. Public policy and policy implementation look upon the world in a way that is entirely different from public administration. Finally, there is post-modern public administration suggesting a new interpretation of identity and borders with the public sector. There is little coherence between the alternative frameworks, let alone a cumulative growth of knowledge. Where could one find a unifying framework which could encompass these different approaches?

Different forms of public sector organisation – is there some commonality?

In real life the private sector also appears more coherent than the public sector. There is a clear distinction between markets and firms with the exception of the case of monopoly. Several markets appear to operate according to the competitive model of Walras and the Chicago school, especially in a glob-alised economy. The organisation of the firm has been analysed recently, meaning that the players in the market economy can be easily identified: consumers, entrepreneurs, employees, managers, shareholders, etc.

This simplicity and clarity has no correspondence within the public sec-tor, where organisational heterogeneity has come to dominate, especially lately. With so-called *plural government* it is suggested that we do not speak of government any more but use the word 'governance' instead. There are now so many different forms of public organisation that one searches almost in vain for some commonality. Thus, government uses insourcing as well as outsourcing, in-house production as well as out-of-house production. Sometimes it relies upon the traditional bureaucracy. Sometime it prefers the incorporated enterprise. There are elected bodies and non-elected bodies. There are quangos, executive agencies and independent entities, public–private partnerships, etc. How could one reduce such complexity and organisational variety to a common denominator?

The advantages of the principal–agent approach

The central idea behind this book is that the principal–agent model may be applied to the public sector. As it is a highly abstract and general model it can accommodate various frameworks and it may be applied to many different forms of organisation. By extending the principal–agent model from its use in the private sector to the public sector one may shed light upon several topics in public administration and public management. The advantages of the principal–agent (P–A) framework for the analysis of the public sector may be briefly summarised as follows:

The P–A framework accommodates democratic theory. The public sector is the interaction between citizens, government and its agents. One may wish to speak of the latter two as the agents of the fundamental principal, the citizens. Or one could speak of two principal–agent relationships:

> between the population and the politicians: the electoral contract;
> between the government and its agents: the post-electoral contract.

One cannot simply transfer the principal–agent model from the private sector to the public sector. One must clarify who the players are and how the rules of the game restrain the incentives of the players. From the point of view of democratic theory the population and the electorate are the prin-cipal of the public sector. Since the electoral contract is so ambiguous and vague, one typically regards the government as the principal and the civil servants as the agents.

The P–A framework harbours different contractual mechanisms: long-term and short-term contracts. Government needs agents to get its job done. It may hire them on a long-term basis, as with the bureaucracy mechanism, or it may buy the services of agents on a short-term basis, as with the internal market mechanism. What the outcomes are under alternative institutional arrangements between the principal and the agents depends upon how the incentives of the two parties play out under alternative rules. Whatever the rules are, strategic behaviour on the part of the agent is always a possibility, given that the agent knows more about the activity than the principal.

The P–A framework targets value and its division between the players in interaction, the population, the government and its agent. The principal needs the agent to deliver public policies. Government derives much of its legitimacy from offering public services to its population. The value of these services can be called 'social value', as one would have to add together the utility of various citizens of public goods and services to arrive at their total value. The central question is whether there is a social profit, meaning that citizens derive more value from the public policies than they have to pay on the cost side. The *quid pro quo* for public services is taxes and user fees. Hopefully they cover the costs of the operations of government, but it is also essential that social value is larger than total cost, meaning there is a surplus for the basic principal, the population. Government will pay its agents from its revenues with the hope that there is again a surplus to be shared among the government members.

The P–A framework emphasises the relevance of asymmetric information for principal–agent interaction in the public sector, as it is, the agent who has the professional skills for delivering the public services. The agent will require a remuneration, the size of which depends upon the interaction between the principal and the agent. The agent will demand at least his/her reservation price plus compensation for trying hard in incentive compatible contracts. But there is nothing that prevents the agent from demanding a high share in the social value of the services he/she delivers. Thus, the outcomes of principal–agent gaming depend upon strategy in the evolution of interaction in games with asymmetric information.

The P–A framework explains the special nature of public management by underlining the features which set it off against private management, namely government as the principal and the rule-of-law framework restraining the entire interaction. I would suggest the following definition: Public management is the accomplishment of the policies of government through the implementation of agents within the restrictions that derive from the rule of law.

The P–A framework explains the constant search for new institutions in the public sector with the lack of stable equilibria in the gaming between the principal and the agent. The principal may choose either long-term or short-term contracts with the agent, where bureaucracy represents the first governance type and public procurement the second. There are many intermediary forms such as tournaments, auctions, internal markets, leasing, franchising, executive agencies, etc. Principal–agent outcomes will depend upon the availability of agents and the amount of competition between them. The institutional set-up will have a major impact upon the outcomes of principal–agent interaction.

Institutions which increase competition among agents favour the principal. Institutions which decrease the costs of monitoring agents favour the principal. Institutions that work the other way around favour the agent. One consideration when choosing between alternative governance forms is transaction costs, *ex ante* or *ex post.* The principal and the agent would have a mutual interest in not allowing excessive transaction costs to dissipate the gains from the interaction. However, transaction costs depend upon the institutions arrived at, as well as the strategies of the players involved and the technologies employed. Major governance changes often reflect transaction cost saving innovations, such the IT revolution today.

The P–A framework highlights the implications of risk in public sector management. In traditional public administration the principal assumes all the risk in providing public services, as the bureau as agent is virtually completely protected against almost all implications of failure except embezzlement and corruption. Public management policy should be devised so that the risks are borne by both players. A number of institutions have been recommended by NPM to make the agent share the risks involved in public services provision. The P–A framework encompasses both bureaucracy and NPM. It may be employed in the making of a public management policy. I shall pin down some of the lessons from public sector reforms in OECD countries following a P–A framework.

Reasonable and unreasonable reform attempts

Governments all over the world have engaged in many NPM reforms. Here, I wish to underline the following major reforms:

- privatisation
- deregulation
- downsizing
- outsourcing
- user fees.

What, then, is next? The two logics of public sector reform in the twenty-first century include:

- Increasing needs from modernisation. Thus, people want the following:

  - social security
  - social welfare
  - education
  - health care

- transportation
- environmental services: water and sewage, etc.

This means that there is a limit to the philosophy of privatisation and market-isation, meaning that the needs for public services will not be decreasing in the future. However, at the same time we have:

- Decreasing resources from post-modernisation:

    - ageing population
    - new family pattern
    - large immigration
    - tax fatigue
    - financial globalisation.

The capacity of government to meet these needs will not increase dramatically. Thus, government must be prudent: I would argue that the reasonable government strategies include the following:

- principal–agent awareness
- risk sharing
- post-modern organisation.

But I wish to warn against government arrogance in reforms. Thus, I claim that the following are unreasonable government strategies:

- complete incorporation
- complete privatisation
- quick deregulation
- arbitrary tax limits
- complete outsourcing
- massive executive agencies
- massive reregulation.

The public sector in a well-ordered society would comprise at least the following programmes:

- public services – user fees and public–private partnerships;
- social policy – basic altruistic commitments;
- regulatory agencies – recognising the market.

One could if one so wishes call such a public sector a neo-Wagnerian model, but the important point here is that there is a crystal clear limit to the reduction possibilities of the public sector, using the Chicago School or Public Choice School approaches. Government is necessary in a post-modern society, but it may choose among alternative modes of public organisation, including outsourcing.

Looking at the extensive literature on public management reform, one finds one universal outcome, namely the inverse relationship between production costs and transaction costs. When the former goes down, the latter goes up, and vice versa. Traditional public administration was production cost heavy, using lots of employees and few top managers. Public management changes this ratio, decreasing the number of staff and increasing top-level management with the entailed risk of becoming management costly. The gain in cost reduction may be dissipated in increasing managerial costs. The public management revolution has led to higher salaries for top-level managers. It is an open question whether the efficiency gains of reducing staff match the increasing managerial costs. The public management revolution also leads to higher costs for tendering/bidding, as well as for outsourcing. Often these costs can be recovered by reduction in in-house costs, but not always.

Conclusion

The principal–agent (P–A) approach models the interaction between two sets of people, the principal on the one hand and the agent on the other (Ricketts, 2002). The interaction is supposed to take some time, involving multiple moves and frequent interplay. Thus, it is a game with many moves which can take a considerable time to be played. To analyse such a complicated game and derive strategic solutions the P–A model assumes that the agent works for the principal in exchange for remuneration to be paid by means of the value of the output that the agent produces.

The agent is assumed to maximise his/her utility, which depends upon the remuneration and the disutility of his/her effort in connection with the production of the output that the principal wants the agent to provide. The principal is maximising his/her utility in relation to the value of the output minus the remuneration of the agent. The agent is risk-averse, whereas the principal is risk-neutral. These assumptions set up a game of long duration under which there is both cooperation and conflict. Thus, both the principal and the agent want an output that has value marketwise or otherwise, as they both get utility from it. What is conflictual concerns the split of the gain from the output where the principal and the agent have opposing interests. The key question is whether the two actors can coordinate on Pareto-optimal outcomes, or whether there is a loss of output due to the strategies of the two players.

The P–A model would not have received so much attention in economics if it had not added one critical assumption to the framework, namely asymmetric information. Given full information the game has the standard solutions in economic theory, which depend upon the type of the market, i.e. the availability of agents, resulting in perfect competition or monopoly.

With asymmetric information the determinate solutions are more difficult to come by and the game has several interesting applications, as analysed in the economics of information. Asymmetric information games cover insurance, sharecropping, CEOs and stockbrokers (Ricketts, 2002). Can the P–A model also be applied to plural government?

I suggest not only that the P–A framework is applicable to public organisation but also that it is highly suitable for analysing relations involving accountability. The two main phenomena in principal–agent interaction – hidden action and hidden knowledge – may be identified in public organisation. In addition, one may speak of transaction costs which the principal incurs when he/she attempts to handle asymmetric information. I shall show what is involved using a few diagrams.

The employees in the public sector, constituting about 20–30 per cent of the workforce in a well-ordered society, may be seen as a collection of teams, headed by a chief or two or more chiefs. Government employs these teams to fulfil their electoral promises concerning the public sector and its services or money contributions. The problem in public organisation is to choose the mechanism of structuring these teams so that they operate both efficiently and in an accountable manner. All the experiments in public sector reform show that there is no standard solution to the problem of organising public teams so that they achieve policy objectives. I shall pin down where the difficulties lie with the help of the principal–agent model.

The problem of hiring and instructing the agent to provide an output of services in the public sector would be trivial if the principal fully knows the technology to be used and can hire agents known to be either low-effort or high-effort agents. Figure C.1 shows the two contracts that the principal will offer these two sets of agents, including the wages $W1$ and $W2$, corresponding to the effort levels $e1$ and $e2$ which result in different outputs, $O1$ and $O2$. The solutions are Pareto optimal and both players maximise their utility.

Figure C.1 offers a naïve solution to the problem of implementing public policies. Since government has set the objectives and knows the technology, it hires the agents it needs, offering $W1$ to an agent who delivers low effort and $W2$ to an agent delivering high effort. Both contracts maximise the gain for the principal and they are Nash equilibria. Matters become entirely different when the assumption about perfect information is replaced by the asymmetric knowledge assumption (Rasmusen, 1994). The solutions will vary depending upon the number of agents competing for the contracts. The agent may capture the entire gain, either by shirking or by claiming an excessive remuneration. The principal–agent framework was developed for modelling the long-term interaction between two persons, where one party knows more than the other. Such interaction was not easily put into the categories of classical game theory. Principal–agent relationships were identified in the private sector, especially where risk was to be allocated between the parties in a joint venture.

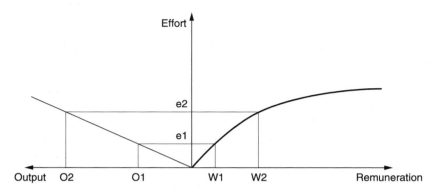

Figure C.1 Principal–agent interaction I (principal's convex preferences deleted).

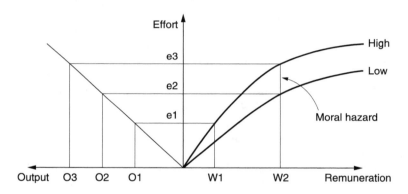

Figure C.2 Principal–agent interaction II (principal's convex preferences deleted).

In the principal–agent framework, the principal cannot observe the effort put in by the agent. He/she can only verify output in the court. But since output depends upon both effort and the situation including randomness, it is impossible for the principal to control post-contractual opportunism on the part of the agent. Thus, it is probable that the agent will shirk, meaning take one wage according to an agreement about effort but put in another and lower level of effort. Figure C.2 shows this.

Shirking may be so costly to the principal that he/she loses all the gain from interaction. The agent increases utility by moving to lower indifference curves in Figure C.2 according to the trade-off between salary and effort. However, a lower effort translates into a lower output, which hurts the principal.

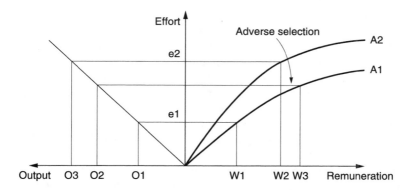

Figure C.3 Principal–agent interaction III (principal's convex preferences deleted).

Bureaucracy is the institution which is most vulnerable to shirking. Using long-term contracts with bureaucrats in order to enable them to develop policy expertise, government opens itself up to post-contractual opportunism. As a response, government prefers the solution *W1* and *O1*, which is a Nash equilibrium that is not Pareto optimal.

The principal wants to offer a low-effort agent one wage and the high-effort agent another wage. What happens if he/she cannot separate the two kinds of agents when contracting with the agent? The problem is not moral hazard as in Figure C.2, but adverse selection. The agent will pretend. Its logic appears from Figure C.3.

The principal would like to offer *W1* to the low-effort agent and *W2* to the high-effort agent. Both contracts may fulfil the agent's reservation utility, but they are not incentive compatible. The high-effort agent will pretend he/she is a low-effort agent, which forces the principal to offer this agent contract *W3*, where there is again a loss of output. Pretending leads to informational rents. If the principal offers *W1* to both *A1* and *A2*, then *A2* may mimic *A1* and also deliver only *O1*. Alternatively, *A2* may demand a huge salary difference (*W2*) in order to accept a contract for the input of high effort, earning a rent from the contractual difficulties.

When government employs short-term contracting to buy services from various teams, then it opens itself up to the risk of pre-contractual opportunism. It cannot separate the agents into low- and high-effort agents when arranging for tournaments or auctions. Thus, contract *W2* and *O2*, which is Pareto optimal, is not enforceable.

Transaction costs are difficult to identify fully and measure. They do not play the same dominating role in public organisation as within private organisation though. Public organisation has one principal – the government or the state – which is under an accountability norm in relation to its principal, the body politic, the nation or the population, as it were. Public organisations cannot minimise transactions no matter what, since they must maximise accountability, given certain restrictions such as efficiency.

If the principal knows how to produce an output and he/she is risk-neutral, then he/she can just employ an agent and instruct him/her what to do. However, if the agent knows more about the output and the agent is risk-averse, then the principal may contract with the agent about some risk-sharing arrangement under which both benefit. There are no determinate solutions to the ensuing game, where the principal and the agent fight about the split of the mutual gain. Given hidden knowledge or hidden action, the solutions may not be Pareto optimal.

This kind if thinking is applicable to the public sector, especially the provision of services. Bureaucracy poses the problem of hidden action, whereas New Public Management entails the difficulty of hidden knowledge. Principal–agent theory derives its widespread acceptance in the social sciences from the following attractive scientific properties:

- simplicity
- measurability
- contractability
- emphasising incentives and institutions.

Moreover, the principal–agent framework for analysing public sector interactions is also highly consonant with democratic theory.

Bibliography

Alchian, A. A., Coase, R. H. (1977) *Economic Forces at Work*. Indianapolis, IN: Liberty Fund

Alchian, A., Demsetz, H. (1972) 'Production, Information Costs and Economic Organization,' *American Economic Review*, reprinted in Ouchi and Barney (1987)

Alcock, P., Glennerster, H., Oakley, A., Sinfield, A. (Eds) (2001) *Welfare and Wellbeing: Richard Titmuss's Contribution to Social Policy*. Bristol: The Policy Press

Alford, J., O'Neill, D. (1994) *The Contract State: Public Management and the Kennett Government*. Melbourne: Deakin University Press

Allison, G. T., Zelikow, Ph. (1999) *Essence of Decision: Explaining the Cuban Missile Crisis*. New York: Longman

Andersen, S. S. (1993) *The Struggle over North Sea Oil and Gas: Government Strategies in Denmark, Britain and Norway*. Oslo: Scandinavian University Press

Appleby, W. A. (1975) *Policy and Administration*. Tuscaloosa, AL: University of Alabama Press

Armstrong, K. A. (2000) *Regulation, Deregulation, Re-regulation*. London: Kogan Page

Arrow, K. J., Sen, A. K., Suzumura, K. (Eds) (2002) *Handbook of Social Choice and Welfare*, Vol. 1. Amsterdam: Elsevier

Ashburner, L., Fitzgerald, L., Pettigrew, A., Ferlie, E. (Ed.) (1996) *The New Public Management in Action*. Oxford: Oxford University Press

Baldwin, R., Cave, M. (1999) *Understanding Regulation: Theory, Strategy and Practice*. Oxford: Oxford University Press

Barber, B. R. (2004) *Strong Democracy: Participatory Politics for a New Age*. Berkeley, CA: University of California Press

Bardhan, P. (Ed.) (1989) *The Economic Theory of Agrarian Institutions*. Oxford: Clarendon Press

Barnard, Ch. I. (1972) *The Functions of the Executive*. Cambridge, MA: Harvard University Press

Barnard, Ch. I. (2003*) Organisation and Management: Selected Papers*. London: Routledge

Barr, N. (1993) *The Economics of the Welfare State*, Second Edition. Oxford: Oxford University Press

Bartholomew, J. (2004) *The Welfare State We're in: The Failure of the Welfare State*. London: Politico's Publishing

Barzel, Y. (1997) *Economic Analysis of Property Rights*, Second Edition. Cambridge: Cambridge University Press

Barzel, Y. (2002) *A Theory of the State: Economic Rights, Legal Rights, and the Scope of the State*. Cambridge: Cambridge University Press

Barzelay, M. (2001) *The New Public Management. Improving Research and Policy Dialogue.* Berkeley, CA: University of California Press

Baumol, W. J. (1997) *Microeconomics: Principles and Policy* (1988 update). New York: Thompson Learning

Baumol, W. J., Batey Blackman, S. A. (1991) *Perfect Markets and Easy Virtue.* Cambridge, MA: Blackwell

Beck, U. (2001) *La société du risque. Sur la voie d'une autre modernité.* Paris: Aubier

Becker, G. S. (1976) *The Economic Approach to Human Behavior.* Chicago: The University of Chicago Press

Becker, G. S., Becker, G. N. (1997) *The Economics of Life: From Baseball to Affirmative Action to Immigration – How Real-World Issues Affect Our Everyday Life.* New York: McGraw-Hill

Becker, G. S., Murphy, K. (2003) *Social Economics: Market Behavior in Social Environment.* Cambridge, MA: Harvard University Press

Becker, G. S., Febrero, R. I., Schwartz, P. (1995) *The Essence of Becker.* Stanford, CA: Hoover Institution Press

Ben Youssef, A., Ragni, L. Rallet, A. Torre, D. (2004) *Nouvelle économie, organisations et modes de coordination.* Paris: Editions L'Harmattan

Berg, S. V., Tschirhart, J. (1988) *Natural Monopoly Regulation.* New York: Cambridge University Press

Bilas, R. A. (1971) *Microeconomic Theory,* Second Edition. Tokyo: McGraw-Hill Kogakusha Ltd

Binmore, K. (1994) *Game Theory and the Social Contract, Vol. I: Playing Fair.* Cambridge, MA: The MIT Press

Binmore, K. (1998) *Game Theory and the Social Contract, Vol. II: Just Playing.* Cambridge, MA: The MIT Press

Blakemore, K. (2003) *Social Policy: An Introduction.* Maidenhead: Open University Press

Blaug, M. (1992) *The Methodology of Economics: Or How Economists Explain,* Second Edition. Cambridge: Cambridge University Press

Bonoli, G. (2000) *The Politics of Pension Reform: Institutions and Policy Change in Western Europe.* Cambridge: Cambridge University Press

Borins, S. (2001) 'Innovation, Success and Failure in Public Management Research: Some Methodological Reflections,' *Public Management Review* 3(1): 3–17

Boston, J. Martin, J., Pallot, J., Walsh, P. (1996) *Public Management: The New Zealand Model.* Auckland: Oxford University Press

Brams, S. J., Taylor, A. D. (1996) *Fair Division: From Cake-cutting to Dispute Resolution.* New York: Cambridge University Press

Bratton, J., Gold, J. (2003) *Human Resource Management: Theory and Practice.* Basingstoke: Palgrave Macmillan

Brennan, G., Buchanan, J. M. (2000) *The Reason of Rules: Constitutional Political Economy.* Indianapolis, IN: Liberty Fund

Brennan, G., Buchanan, J. M. (2001) *The Power to Tax: Analytical Foundations of a Fiscal Constitution.* Indianapolis, IN: Liberty Fund

Breton, A. (1996) *Competitive Governments: An Economic Theory of Politics and Public Finance.* Cambridge: Cambridge University Press

Broadbent, J., Guthrie, J. (1992) 'Changes in the Public Sector: a Review of Recent Alternative Accounting Research,' *Accounting, Auditing and Accountability Journal,* 5(2): 3–31

Brooks, R. and Razin, A. (Eds) *Social Security Reform.* Cambridge: Cambridge University Press

Brudney, J. L., O'Toole, L. J., Jr, Rainey, H. G. (Eds) (2000a) *Advancing Public Management. New Developments in Theory, Methods and Practice.* Washington, DC: Georgetown University Press

Brudney, J. L., O'Toole, L. J., Jr, Rainey, H. G. (2000b) 'Introduction: Public Management in an Era of Complexity and Challenge,' in J. L. Brudney, L. J. O'Toole, Jr, H. G. Rainey (Eds), *Advancing Public Management: New Developments in Theory, Methods, and Practice,* Washington, DC: Georgetown University Press, pp. 1–12

Brudney, J. L., O'Toole, L. J., Jr, Rainey, H. G. (2000c) 'Concluding Perspectives,' in J. L. Brudney, L. J. O'Toole, Jr, H. G. Rainey (Eds), *Advancing Public Management: New Developments in Theory, Methods, and Practice,* Washington, DC: Georgetown University Press, pp. 252–260

Buchanan, J. M., Musgrave, R. A. (1999) *Public Finance and Public Choice: Two Contrasting Visions of the State.* Cambridge, MA: The MIT Press

Buchanan, J. M., Tollison, R. D., Tullock, G. (1980) *Toward a Theory of the Rent-Seeking Society.* College Station: Texas A & M University Press

Buckley, P., Michie, J. (Eds) (1996) *Firms, Organisations and Contracts: A Reader in Industrial Organisation.* Oxford: Oxford University Press

Cabral, L. M. B. (2000) *Introduction to Industrial Organization.* Cambridge, MA: MIT Press

Caiden, N., Wildavsky, A. (1980) *Planning and Budgeting in Poor Countries.* Somerset, NJ: Transaction Publishers

Calabresi, G. (2000) *A Common Law for the Age of Statutes.* Clark, NJ: Lawbook Exchange

Calhoun, C. (Ed.) (1993) *Habermas and the Public Sphere.* Cambridge, MA: The MIT Press

Campbell, C., Wilson, G. K. (1995) *The End of Whitehall: Death of a Paradigm?* Oxford: Blackwell

Campbell, D. E. (1995) *Incentives: Motives and the Economics of Information.* New York: Cambridge University Press

Carlin, T. M., Guthrie, J. (2003) 'Accrual Output Based Budgeting Systems in Australia: The Rhetoric-Reality Gap,' *Public Management Review* 5(2): 145–162

Carlton, D. W., Perloff, J. M. (2004) *Modern Industrial Organisation.* New York: Addison-Wesley

Castles, F. G. (2004) *The Future of the Welfare State.* Oxford: Oxford University Press

Castles, S., Miller, M. J. (2003), *The Age of Migration: International Population Movements in the Modern World,* Third Edition. Basingstoke: Palgrave Macmillan

Choi, Y.-C. (1999) *The Dynamics of Public Service Contracting: The British Experience.* Bristol: The Policy Press

Christensen, T., Laegreid, P. (Eds) (2001) *New Public Management: The Transformation of Ideas and Practice.* Aldershot: Ashgate

Clifton, J., Comin, F., Diaz Fuentes, D. (Eds) (2003) *Privatisation in the European Union: Public Enterprises and Integration.* Boston, MA: Kluwer Academic Publishers

Coase, R. H. (1990) *Firm, the Market and the Law.* Chicago, IL: University of Chicago Press

Coase, R. H. (1995) *Essays on Economics and Economists.* Chicago, IL: University of Chicago Press

Cole, G. (2000) *Strategic Management: Theory and Practice.* London: Continuum

266 *Bibliography*

Coleman, J. L. (1988a) *Markets, Morals and the Law*. Cambridge: Cambridge University Press

Coleman, J. S. (1988b) 'Social Capital in the Creation of Human Capital,' *American Journal of Sociology* 94 (suppl): 95–120

Cooter, R., Ulen, T. (2003) *Law and Economics*. Reading, MA: Addison-Wesley

Craven, J. (1992) *Social Choice: A Framework for Collective Decisions and Individual Judgments*. Cambridge: Cambridge University Press

de Soto, H. (2000) *The Mystery of Capital: Why Capitalism Triumphs in the West and Fails Everywhere Else*. New York: Basic Books

Deakin, N. (2001) *In Search of Civil Society*. Basingstoke: Palgrave Macmillan

Denhardt, J., Denhardt, R. (2003) *The New Public Service: Serving, not Steering*. Armonk, NY: M. E. Sharpe

DiMaggio, P., Anheier, H. K. (1990) 'The Sociology of Nonprofit Organisations and Sectors,' *Annual Review of Sociology*, 16 (1), 137–159

Dine, J. (1997) *Company Law*. Basingstoke: Palgrave Macmillan

Dollery, B. E., Wallis, J. L. (1999) *Market Failure, Government Failure, Leadership and Public Policy*. Basingstoke: Macmillan

Dollery, B. E., Wallis, J. L. (2003) *The Political Economy of the Voluntary Sector: A Reappraisal of the Comparative Institutional Advantage of Voluntary Organisations*. Cheltenham: Edward Elgar

Drewry, G. (2005) 'Citizen's Charters – Service Quality Chameleons,' *Public Management Review* 7 (forthcoming September)

Dror, Y. (1971) *Design for Policy Sciences*. New York: Elsevier

Dror, Y. (1973) *Public Policymaking Reexamined*. Bedfordshire: Leonard Hill Books

Dunleavy, P. (1991) *Democracy, Bureaucracy and Public Choice: Economic Explanations in Political Science*. London: Harvester Wheatsheaf

Dunsire, A., Hood, C., Huby, M. (1989) *Cutback Management in Public Bureaucracies: Popular Theories and Observed Outcomes in Whitehall*. Cambridge: Cambridge University Press

Dutta, P. K. (2000) *Strategies and Games – Theory and Practice*. Cambridge, MA: The MIT Press

Dworkin, R. (1977) *Taking Rights Seriously*. London: Duckworth

Dworkin, R. (1998) *Law's Empire*. Oxford: Hart

Dworkin, R. (2000) *Sovereign Virtue: the Theory and Practice of Equality*. Cambridge, MA: Harvard University Press

Eatwell, J., Milgate, M., Newman, P. (1989a) *Allocation, Information and Markets*. London: Macmillan

Eatwell, J., Milgate, M., Newman, P. (1989b) *General Equilibrium*. London: Macmillan

Eatwell, J., Milgate, M., Newman, P. (1989c) *Social Economics*. London: Macmillan

Eatwell, J., Milgate, M., Newman, P. (1989d) *The Invisible Hand*. London: Macmillan

Eliassen, K. A., Sjovaag, M. (Eds) (1999) *European Telecommunications Liberalisation*. London: Routledge

Epstein, R. (1985) *Takings: Private Property and the Power of Eminent Domain*. Cambridge, MA: Harvard University Press

Esping-Andersen, G. (Ed.) (1996) *Welfare States in Transition: National Adaptations in Global Economies*. London: Sage Publications

Esping-Andersen, G. (Ed.) (2002) *Why We Need a New Welfare State*. Oxford: Oxford University Press

Etzioni, A. (1990) *The Moral Dimension: Toward a New Economics*. New York: Free Press

Etzioni, A. (1994) *The Spirit of the Community: The Reinvention of American Society.* New York: Touchstone

Etzioni, A. (2001) *Next: The Road to the Good Society.* New York: Basic Books

Exworthy, M., Halford, S. (Eds) (1999) *Professionals and the New Managerialism in the Public Sector.* Buckingham: Open University Press

Fama, E. F. (1976) *Foundations of Finance: Portfolio Decisions and Securities Prices.* New York: Basic Books

Fama, E. F., Miller, M. (1972) *The Theory of Finance.* New York: Holt, Rinehart and Winston

Ferlie, E., Ashburner, L., Fitzgerald, L., Pettigrew, A. (1996) *The New Public Management in Action.* Oxford: Oxford University Press

Finer, S. E. (1999) *The History of Government from the Earliest Times: Empires, Monarchies and the Modern State*, Vols 1–3. Oxford: Oxford University Press

Flynn, N. (2002) *Public Sector Management.* London: Financial Times Management

Flynn, R., Williams, G. (Eds) (1997) *Contracting for Health: Quasi-markets and the National Health Service.* Oxford: Oxford University Press

Forsythe, D. W. (2004) *Memos to the Governor: An Introduction to State Budgeting.* Washington, DC: Georgetown University Press

Frantz, R. S. (1997) *X-Efficiency: Theory, Evidence and Applications*, Second Edition. Boston, MA: Kluwer Academic Publishers

Frederickson, H. G., Johnston, J. M. (Eds) (1999) *Public Management Reform and Innovation. Research, Theory and Application.* Tuscaloosa, AL: The University of Alabama Press

Frederickson, H. G., Smith, K. B. (2003) *The Public Administration Theory Primer.* Boulder, CO: Westview Press

Friedman, D. D. (2001) *Law's Order: What Economics Has to Do with Law and Why It Matters.* Princeton, NJ: Princeton University Press

Friedman, M. (1953) *Essays in Positive Economics.* Chicago: University of Chicago Press

Friedman, M. (1969) *The Optimum Quantity of Money and Other Essays.* Chicago: Aldine Transaction

Fudenberg D., Tirole, J. (1991) *Game Theory.* Cambridge, MA: MIT Press

Fukuyama, F. (2004) *State Building: Governance and World Order in the Twenty-First Century.* London: Profile Books

Furubotn, E. G., Richter, R. (2000) *Institutions and Economic Theory: The Contribution of the New Institutional Economics.* Ann Arbor, MI: University of Michigan Press

Gauthier, D. (1987) *Morals by Agreement.* London: Clarendon Press

George, V., Taylor-Gooby, P. (Eds) (1996) *European Welfare Policy.* London: Macmillan Press

George, V., Wilding, P. (1985) *Ideology and Social Welfare.* London: Routledge & Kegan Paul

Gigerenzer, G., Selten, R. (Eds) (2002) *Bounded Rationality: The Adaptive Toolbox.* Cambridge, MA: The MIT Press

Gilbert, N. (2004) *Transformation of the Welfare State: The Silent Surrender of Public Responsibility.* Oxford: Oxford University Press

Gintis, H. (2000) *Game Theory Evolving – A Problem-Centered Introduction to Modeling Strategic Interaction.* Princeton, NJ: Princeton University Press

Glendinning, C., Powell, M., Rummery, K. (Eds) (2002) *Partnership's New Labour and The Governance of Welfare.* Bristol: The Policy Press

Golding, M., Edmundson, W. (Eds) (2004) *The Blackwell Guide to the Philosophy of Law and Legal Theory.* Oxford: Blackwell Publishers

Goodin, R. E., Headey, B., Muffels, R., Dirven, H.-J. (1999) *The Real Worlds of Welfare Capitalism.* Cambridge: Cambridge University Press

Goss, B. A. (Ed.) (1991) *Rational Expectations and Efficiency in Futures Markets.* London: Routledge

Gould, A. (1993) *Capitalist Welfare Systems.* New York: Longman

Gowing, M. K., Kraft, J. D., Campbell, J. (1998) *The New Organisational Reality: Downsizing, Restructuring and Revitalization.* Washington, DC: American Psychological Association

Graham, C. (1998) *Private Markets for Public Goods. Raising the Stakes in Economic Reform.* Washington, DC: The Brookings Institution

Green, M. T., Jones, L. R., Thompson, F. (2000) 'Local Heroes? Reinvention Labs in the Department of Defense,' in J. L. Brudney, L. J. O'Toole, Jr, H. G. Rainey (Eds), *Advancing Public Management: New Developments in Theory, Methods, and Practice,* Washington, DC: Georgetown University Press, pp. 153–172

Greene, J. (2003) *Cities and Privatization: Prospects for the New Century.* Englewood Cliffs, NJ: Prentice-Hall

Guthrie, J. (1998) 'Accrual Accounting in the Public Sector?' *Financial Accountability and Management,* 14(1): 1–19

Guthrie, J., Carlin, T. (1998) 'Review of Australian Experiences of Output Based Budgeting: A Critical Reflection,' *Conference on Output Based Accrual Budgets in the Public Sector,* Canberra, 30–31 March

Habermas, J. (1992) *The Structural Transformation of the Public Sphere: Inquiry into a Category of Bourgeois Society.* Cambridge, MA: The MIT Press

Hammond, T. H., Knott, J. H. (2000) 'Public Management, Administrative Leadership, and Policy Choice,' in J. L. Brudney, L. J. O'Toole, Jr, H. G. Rainey (Eds), *Advancing Public Management: New Developments in Theory, Methods, and Practice,* Washington, DC: Georgetown University Press, pp. 49–76

Handler, J. F. (2004) *Social Citizenship and Workfare in the United States and Western Europe: The Paradox of Inclusion.* Cambridge: Cambridge University Press

Harris, J. W. (1997) *Legal Philosophies.* London: Butterworths Law

Harsanyi, J. C. (1976) *Essays on Ethics, Social Behaviour and Scientific Explanation.* Dordrecht: D. Reidel

Harsanyi, J. C. (1982) *Papers in Game Theory.* Dordrecht: D. Reidel

Hayek, F. A. (1982) *Law, Legislation and Liberty. A New Statement of the Liberal Principles of Justice and Political Economy.* London: Routledge & Kegan Paul

Hayek, F. A. (1991) *The Counter-Revolution of Science: Studies of the Abuse of Reason.* Indianapolis, IN: Liberty Fund

Hayek, F. A. (1996) *Individualism and Economic Order.* Chicago, IL: University of Chicago Press

Hayek, F. A. (2001) *The Road to Serfdom.* London: Routledge

Henley, D. (1992) *Public Sector Accounting and Financial Control.* London: Thomson Learning

Hennessy, P. (2001) *Whitehall.* London: Pimlico

Hesse, J. J., Ellwein, T. (2004) *Das Regierungssystem der Bundesrepublik Deutschland,* 2 Bde. Berlin: Gruyter

Hill, L. B. (Ed.) (1992) *The State of Public Bureaucracy.* Armonk, NY: M. E. Sharpe

Hill, M., Hupe, P. (2002) *Implementing Public Policy.* London: Sage Publications

Hillier, B. (1997) *The Economics of Asymmetric Information.* Basingstoke: Macmillan

Hines, R. (1988) 'Financial Accounting in Communication Reality vs Construct Reality,' *Accounting, Organisations and Society,* 13(3): 251–263

Hirschman, A. O. (1982) *Shifting Involvements: Private Interests and Public Action.* Princeton, NJ: Princeton University Press

Hirst, P. (1994) *Associative Democracy: New Forms of Economic and Social Governance.* Amherst, MA: University of Massachusetts Press

Hobson, C. F. (2000) *The Great Chief Justice: John Marshall and the Rule of Law.* Kansas City: University Press of Kansas

Hodgson, G. M. (2004) *The Evolution of Institutional Economics.* London: Routledge

Hoekman, B. M., Mattoo, A., English P. (Eds) (2002) *Development, Trade, and the WTO: A Handbook* (World Bank Trade and Development Series). Herndon, VA: World Bank Publications

Hogwood, B. W., Gunn, L. A. (1984) *Policy Analysis for the Real World.* Oxford: Oxford University Press

Hohfeld, W. N. (2001) *Fundamental Legal Conceptions as Applied in Judicial Reasoning.* Aldershot: Ashgate

Holzmann, R., Stiglitz, J. (Eds) (2001) *New Ideas about Old Age Security: Toward Sustainable Pension Systems in the 21st Century.* Washington, DC: The World Bank

Hood, C. (1986) *Tools of Government.* Chatham, NJ: Chatham House

Hood, C. (1991) 'A Public Management for All Seasons,' *Public Administration,* 69(1): 3–19

Hood, C. (1995) 'Contemporary Public Management: A New Global Paradigm?' *Public Policy and Administration,* 10(2): 104–117

Hood, C. (1997) 'Which Contract State? Four Perspectives on Over-Outsourcing for Public Services,' *Australian Journal of Public Administration,* 56(3): 120–131

Hood, C. (2000) *The Art of the State: Culture, Rhetoric and Public Management.* Oxford: Clarendon Press

Hood, C., Rothstein, H., Baldwin, R. (2001) *The Government of Risk: Understanding Risk Regulation Regimes.* Oxford: Oxford University Press

Horwitz, S. (2001) *Microfoundations and Macroeconomics: An Austrian Perspective.* London: Routledge

Hughes, G., Lewis, G. (Eds) (1998) *Unsettling Welfare: The Reconstruction of Social Policy.* London: Routledge

Hyde, A. C. (Ed.) (1992) *Government Budgeting. Theory, Process, Politics.* Pacific Grove, CA: Brooks/Cole

Ingraham, P. W. (1995) *The Foundation of Merit: Public Service in American Democracy.* Baltimore, MD: Johns Hopkins University Press

Ingraham, P. W., Kneedler, A. E. (2000) 'Dissecting the Black Box: Toward a Model and Measures of Government Management Performance,' in J. L. Brudney, L. J. O'Toole, Jr, H. G. Rainey (Eds), *Advancing Public Management: New Developments in Theory, Methods, and Practice,* Washington, DC: Georgetown University Press, pp. 235–252

Ingraham, P. W., Joyce, P. G., Kneedler Donahue, A. (2003) *Government Performance. Why Management Matters.* Baltimore, MD: Johns Hopkins University Press

James, E., Rose-Ackerman, S. (2001) *The Nonprofit Enterprise in Market Economies.* London: Routledge

James, O., Rhodes, R. A. W. (Eds) (2003) *The Executive Agency Revolution in Whitehall: Public Interest versus Bureau-Shaping Perspectives.* Basingstoke: Palgrave Macmillan

Jensen, M., Meckling, W. (1976) 'Theory of the Firm: Managerial Behavior, Agency Costs and Ownership Structure,' *Journal of Financial Economics*, 3(3): 302–325

Johansen, L. (1965) *Public Economics*. Amsterdam: North-Holland Publishing

Johnson, R. N., Libecap, G. D. (1994) *The Federal Civil Service System and the Problem of Bureaucracy: The Economics and Politics of Institutional Change*. Chicago, IL: The University of Chicago Press

Joyce, P. (1999) *Strategic Management for the Public Services*. Buckingham: Open University Press

Kant, I. (1994) *Métaphysique des moeurs*. Paris: Flammarion

Kant, I. (1996) *The Metaphysics of Morals*, M. J. Gregor (Ed.). Cambridge: Cambridge University Press

Kantorowicz, E. H. (1998) *The King's Two Bodies: Study in Medieval Political Theology*. Princeton, NJ: Princeton University Press

Kaufman, H. (1976) *Are Government Organisations Immortal?* Washington, DC: The Brookings Institution

Kaufman, H. (1981) *The Administrative Behavior of Federal Bureau Chiefs*. Washington, DC: The Brookings Institution

Kaufman, H. (1989) *Red Tape: Its Origins, Uses and Abuses*. Washington, DC: The Brookings Institution

Kaufmann, F. X., Majone, G., Ostrom, V. (Eds) (1986) *Guidance, Control, and Evaluation in the Public Sector*. Berlin: Walter de Gruyter

Kelsen, H. (1997) *Introduction to the Problems of Legal Theory: A Translation of the First Edition of the Reine Rechtslehre or Pure Theory of Law*. S. L. Paulson, B. Litschewski Paulson (Trans.). Oxford: Clarendon Press

Kelsen, H. (1999) *General Theory of Law and State*. Clark, NJ: Lawbook Exchange

Kelsen, H. (2000) *What Is Justice: Justice, Law, and Politics in the Mirror of Science: Collected Essays*. Clark, NJ: Lawbook Exchange

Kelsey, J. (1995) *Economic Fundamentalism*. London: Pluto Press

Kernaghan, K., Marson, B., Borins, S. (2000) *The New Public Organisation*. Toronto: Institute of Public Administration of Canada

Kettl, D. F. (2000) *The Global Public Management Revolution: A Report on The Transformation of Governance*. Washington, DC: The Brookings Institution

Kettl, D. F. (2002) *The Transformation of Governance: Public Administration for Twenty-First Century America*. Baltimore, MD: The Johns Hopkins University Press

Kettl, D. F. (2003) *Team Bush: Leadership Lessons from the Bush White House*. New York: McGraw-Hill

Kettl, D. F., DiIulio, J. J. (Eds) (1995) *Inside the Reinvention Machine: Appraising Governmental Reform*. Washington, DC: The Brookings Institution

Khademian, A. M. (2000) 'Is Silly Putty Manageable? Looking for the Links Between Culture, Management, and Context,' in J. L. Brudney, L. J. O'Toole, Jr, H. G. Rainey (Eds), *Advancing Public Management: New Developments in Theory, Methods, and Practice*, Washington, DC: Georgetown University Press, pp. 19–32

Kiewiet, R., McCubbins, M. (1991) *The Logic of Delegation: Congressional Parties and the Appropriations Process*. Chicago: University of Chicago Press

Kingsley, G., Melkers, J. (2000) 'The Art of Partnering Across Sectors: the Influence of Centrality Strategies of State R & D Projects,' in J. L. Brudney, L. J. O'Toole, Jr, H. G. Rainey (Eds), *Advancing Public Management: New Developments in Theory, Methods, and Practice*, Washington, DC: Georgetown University Press, pp. 97–108

Kirzner, I. M. (2000) *The Driving Force of the Market: Essays in Austrian Economics*. (Foundations of the Market Economy S.) London: Routledge

Kleinman, M. (2002) *A European Welfare State? European Union Social Policy in Context.* Basingstoke: Palgrave Macmillan

Kooiman, J. (Ed.) (1993) *Modern Governance.* London: Sage

Kooiman, J. (2003) *Governing as Governance.* London: Sage

Kramer, M., Simmonds, N. E., Steiner, H. (1998) *A Debate Over Rights: Philosophical Enquiries.* Oxford: Oxford University Press

Kreps, D. M. (1990a) *A Course in Microeconomic Theory.* New York: Harvester Wheatsheaf

Kreps, D. M. (1990b) 'Corporate Culture and Economic Theory,' in J. A. Alt and K. A. Shepsle (Eds) *Perspectives on Positive Political Economy.* Cambridge: Cambridge University Press, pp. 90–143

Krueger, A. (1974) 'The Political Economy of the Rent-Seeking Society,' *American Economic Review,* 64(2): 291–303

Krugman, P. (2003) *The Great Unravelling: From Boom to Bust in Three Short Years.* London: Allen Lane

Kuran, T. (1990) 'Private and Public Preferences,' *Economics and Philosophy,* 6(1): 1–26

Kymlicka, W. (2004) *Contemporary Political Philosophy: An Introduction.* Oxford: Oxford University Press

Laffont, J.-J. (2001) *Incentives and Political Economy.* Oxford: Oxford University Press

Laffont, J.-J. (2003) *The Principal Agent Model: The Economic Theory of Incentives.* Cheltenham: Edward Elgar

Laffont, J.-J., Martimort, D. (2001) *The Theory of Incentives: The Principal–Agent Model.* Princeton, NJ: Princeton University Press

Laffont, J.-J., Tirole, J. (1993) *A Theory of Incentives in Procurement and Regulation.* Cambridge, MA: The MIT Press

Lambert, P. J., Lambert, P. (2002) The *Distribution and Redistribution of Income.* Manchester: Manchester University Press

Lane, J.-E. (2000) *The Public Sector: Concepts, Models and Approaches.* London: Sage Publications

Lavery, K. (1999) *Smart Contracting for Local Government Services: Processes and Experience.* Westport, CT: Greenwood Press

Lawton, A., Rose, A. (1991) *Organisation and Management in the Public Sector.* London: Pitman Publishing

Ledyard, J. (1995) 'Public Goods: A Survey of Experimental Research' in J. Kagel and A. Roth (Eds), *A Handbook of Experimental Economics,* Princeton, NJ: Princeton University Press, pp. 111–194

Lee, R. D., Johnson, R. W., Joyce, Ph. G. (2003) *Public Budgeting Systems.* Sudbury, MA: Jones and Bartlett

Leibenstein, H. (1966) 'Allocative vs X-Inefficiency,' *American Economic Review,* 56(2): 394–407

Leube, K. R., Moore, T. G. (Eds) (1986) *The Essence of Stigler.* Stanford, CA: Hoover Institution Press

Lewis, J. and Surender, R. (2004) *Welfare State Change.* Oxford: Oxford University Press

Libecap, G. (1989) *Contracting for Property Rights.* Cambridge: Cambridge University Press

Lindblom, C. E., Woathonse, E. J. (1994) *The Policy-Making Process.* Englewood Cliffs, NJ: Prentice-Hall

272   Bibliography

Llewellyn, N., Jones, G. (2003) 'Controversies and Conceptual Development: Examining Public Entrepreneurship,' *Public Management Review* 5(2): 245–266

Loughlin, M. (1992) *Public Law and Political Theory*. Oxford: Clarendon Press

Loughlin, M. (2003) *The Idea of Public Law*. Oxford: Oxford University Press

Lowi, Th. J. (1979) *The End of Liberalism: The Second Republic of the United States*. New York: Norton

Lynch, T., Lynch, C. (1997) 'The Road to Entrepreneurial Budgeting,' *Journal of Public Budgeting, Accounting and Financial Management*, 9(1): 161–180

Lynn, L. E. (2001) 'Globalization and Administrative Reform: What Is Happening in Theory?' *Public Management Review* 3(2): 191–208

Macho-Stadler, I., Perez-Castrillo, D. (1997) *An Introduction to the Economics of Information: Incentives and Contracts*. Oxford: Oxford University Press

Majone, G. (1996) *Regulating Europe*. New York: Routledge

Mandell, M. P., Steelman, T. A. (2003) 'Understanding What Can Be Accomplished Through Interorganisational Innovations: The Importance of Typologies, Context and Management Strategies,' *Public Management Review* 5(2): 197–224

Mandeville, B. (1990) *The Fable of the Bees: Or Private Vices, Public Benefits*. Washington, DC: Liberty Fund

Mansfield, E. (1997) *Applied Microeconomics*, Second Edition. New York: W. W. Norton

Mantzavinos, C. (2001) *Individuals, Institutions and Markets*. Cambridge: Cambridge University Press

March, J. G. (1989) *Decisions and Organizations*. Oxford: Blackwell

March, J. G., Olsen, J. P. (1980) *Ambiguity and Choice in Organizations*. Oxford: Oxford University Press

March, J. G., Olsen, J. P. (1996) *Democratic Governance*. New York: The Free Press

March, J. G., Simon, H. S. (1993) *Organizations*. Oxford: Blackwell

Marquand, D. (2004) *Decline of the Public: The Hollowing Out of Citizenship*. Cambridge: Polity Press

Martin, E. A. (Ed.) (2003) *A Dictionary of Law*. Oxford: Oxford University Press

Martin, S. (2002) 'The Modernization of UK Local Government: Markets, Managers, Monitors and Mixed Fortune,' *Public Management Review* 4(3): 291–308

März, E. (1991) *Joseph Schumpeter. Scholar, Teacher and Politician*. New Haven & London: Yale University Press

Massey, A. (1997) *Globalization and Marketization of Government Services: Comparing Contemporary Public Sector Developments*. Basingstoke: Palgrave Macmillan

Maynard-Moody, S., Leland, S. (2000) 'Stories from the Front Lines of Public Management: Street-Level Workers as Responsible Actors,' in J. L. Brudney, L. J. O'Toole, Jr, H. G. Rainey (Eds), *Advancing Public Management: New Developments in Theory, Methods, and Practice*, Washington, DC: Georgetown University Press, pp. 109–126

McCubbins, M. D., Noll, R. G., Weingast, B. R. (1987) 'Administrative Procedures as Instruments of Political Control,' *Journal of Law, Economics and Organization* 3: 243–7

McCubbins, M. D., Noll, R. G., Weingast, B. R. (1989) 'Structure and Process, Politics and Policy: Administrative Arrangements and the Political Control of Agencies,' *Virginia Law Review* 75: 430–82

McGregor, E. B. (2000) 'Making Sense of Change,' in J. L. Brudney, L. J. O'Toole, Jr, H. G. Rainey (Eds), *Advancing Public Management: New Developments in Theory, Methods, and Practice*, Washington, DC: Georgetown University Press, pp. 127–152

McLaughlin, K., Jeneï;, G. (2002) 'Comparative Perspectives on Modernizing Local Governance,' *Public Management Review* 4(3): 271–274

McLaughlin, K., Osborne, S. P., Ferlie, E. (Eds) (2001) *New Public Management: Current Trends and Future Prospects.* London: Routledge

McLeod, I. (1996) *Legal Method,* Second Edition. Basingstoke: Macmillan

McLeod, I. (2003) *Legal Theory.* Basingstoke: Palgrave Macmillan

McLoughlin, P., Rendell, C. (1992) *Law of Trusts.* London: The Macmillan Press

McMahon, A., Thomson, J., Williams, Ch. (2000) *Understanding the Australian Welfare State. Key Documents and Themes.* Croydon, Victoria: Tertiary Press

Medema, S. G., Mercuro, N. (1998) *Economics and the Law.* Princeton: Princeton University Press

Meier, K. J., Gill, J., Waller, G. (2000) 'Optimal Performance versus Risk Aversion: An Application of Substantively Weighted Analytical Techniques,' in J. L. Brudney, L. J. O'Toole, Jr, H. G. Rainey (Eds), *Advancing Public Management: New Developments in Theory, Methods, and Practice,* Washington, DC: Georgetown University Press, pp. 77–96

Meltsner, A. J., Bellavita, C. (1983) *The Policy Organisation.* Beverly Hills: Sage

Ménard, C. (1997) *L'économie des organisations.* Paris: La Découverte & Syros

Ménard, C. (Ed.) (2000) *Institutions, Contracts and Organizations: Perspectives from New Institutional Economics.* Cheltenham: Edward Elgar

Milgate, M. (2001) *Alliances, Outsourcing, and the Lean Organisation.* Westport, CT: Greenwood Press

Milgrom, P., Roberts, J. (1992) *Economics, Organisations and Management.* Englewood Cliffs, NJ: Prentice-Hall International

Miller, G. J., Hildreth, W. B., Rabin, J. (Eds) (2001) *Performance-Based Budgeting.* Boulder, CO: Westview Press

Miller, P. J. (Ed.) (1994) *Rational Expectations Revolution: Readings from the Front Line.* Cambridge, MA: The MIT Press

Miller, W. L. (1992) *The Business of May Next – James Madison and the Founding.* Charlottesville, VA: University Press of Virginia

Mintzberg, H., Ahlstrand, B., Lamparel, J., Lampel, J. (2001) *Strategy Safari: A Guided Tour Through the Wilds of Strategic Management.* London: Prentice-Hall

Moe, T. M. (1987) 'An Assessment of the Positive, Theory of Congressional Dominance,' *Legislative Studies Quarterly,* 12: 475–520

Modigliani, F. and Muralidhar, A. (2004) *Rethinking Pension Reform.* Cambridge: Cambridge University Press

Moore, M. H. (2003) *Creating Public Value: Strategic Management in Government.* Cambridge, MA: Harvard University Press

Morgan, B. (1999) 'Regulating the Regulators: Meta-regulation as a Strategy for Reinventing Government in Australia,' *Public Management Review,* 1(1): 49–65

Morgan, C., Murgatroyd, S. (1994) *Total Quality Management in the Public Sector: An International Perspective.* Buckingham: Open University Press

Mudambi, R., Ricketts, M. (Eds) (1997) *Organisation of the Firm: International Business Perspectives.* London: Routledge

Mueller, D. C. (2003) *Public Choice III.* Cambridge: Cambridge University Press

Musgrave, R. A. (2000) *Public Finance in a Democratic Society: The Foundations of Taxation and Expenditure.* Cheltenham: Edward Elgar

Musgrave, R. A., Musgrave, P. B. (1989) *Public Finance in Theory and Practice,* Fifth Edition. New York: McGraw-Hill

Myerson, R. B. (1997) *Game Theory: Analysis of Conflict.* Cambridge, MA: Harvard University Press

Nash, J. (2001) *The Essential John Nash.* H. W. Kuhn, S. Nasar (Eds). Princeton, NJ: Princeton University Press

Natemeyer, W. E. (Ed.) (1978) *Classics of Organisational Behavior.* Oak Park, IL: A. Moore

Niskanen, W. A. (2004) *Autocratic, Democratic and Optimal Government: Fiscal Choices and Economic Outcomes.* Cheltenham: Edward Elgar

Nozick, R. (2001) *Anarchy, State and Utopia.* Oxford: Blackwell

Nurmi, H. (1999) *Voting Paradoxes and How to Deal with Them.* New York: Springer-Verlag

Nyce, S. A. and Schieber, S. J. (2005) *The Economic Implications of Aging Societies* Cambridge: Cambridge University Press

O'Driscoll, G. P., Risso, M. (1985) *The Economics of Time and Ignorance.* Oxford: Blackwell

O'Faircheallaigh, C., Wanna, J., Weller, P. (1999) *Public Sector Management in Australia. New Challenges, New Directions,* Second Edition. South Yarra, Victoria: Macmillan

O'Looney, J. A. (1998) *Outsourcing State and Local Government Services: Decision-Making Strategies and Management Methods.* Westport, CT: Greenwood Press

O'Toole, L. J. Jr (2000) 'Different Public Managements? Implications of Structural Context in Hierarchies and Networks,' in J. L. Brudney, L. J. O'Toole, Jr, H. G. Rainey (Eds), *Advancing Public Management: New Developments in Theory, Methods, and Practice,* Washington, DC: Georgetown University Press, pp. 15–18

OECD (2001a) *Education at a Glance 2001.* Paris: OECD

OECD (2001b) *OECD Health Data 2001.* Paris: OECD

OECD (2003) *Social Expenditures Data.* Paris: OECD, available through http://www.sourceoecd.org

Okun, A. M. (1975) *Equality and Efficiency.* Washington, DC: Brookings Institution

Oleszek, W. J. (2001) *Congressional Procedures and the Policy Process,* Fifth Edition. Washington, DC: CQ Press

Oliver, E. L., Sanders, L. (2004) *E-Government Reconsidered: Renewal of Governance for the Knowledge Age.* Saskatchewan: University of Regina Canadian Plains Research Center

Olson, M. (2000) *Power and Prosperity: Outgrowing Communist and Capitalist Dictatorships.* New York: Basic Books

Olson, O., Guthrie, J., Humphrey, C. (1998) 'Global Warning! International Experiences with 'New' Public Financial Management (NPFM) Reforms: New World? Small World? Better World?,' in O. Olson, J. Guthrie, C. Humphrey (Eds), *Global Warning: Debating International Developments in New Public Financial Management,* Oslo: Cappelen, pp. 17–48

Olson, W. K. (2003) *The Rule of Lawyers: How the New Litigation Elite Threatens America's Rule of Law.* New York: St. Martin's Press

Ordeshook, P. C. (1986) *Game Theory and Political Theory.* Cambridge: Cambridge University Press

Osborne, D., Gaebler, T. (1992) *Reinventing Government: The Five Strategies for Reinventing Government.* New York: Plume

Osborne, D., Hutchinson, P. (2004) *The Price of Government: Getting the Results We Need in an Age of Permanent Fiscal Crisis.* New York: Basic Books

Osborne, D., Plastrik, P. (1997) *Banishing Bureaucracy: The Five Strategies for Reinventing Government*. New York: Addison-Wesley

Osborne, D., Plastrik, P. (2000) *The Reinventor's Fieldbook: Tools for Transforming Your Government*. San Francisco: Jossey-Bass

Ostrom, E., Dietz, Th., Dolsak, N. Stern, P. C., Stonich, S. Weber, E. U. (Eds) (2002) *The Drama of the Commons*. Washington, DC: National Academy Press

Ott, S. (2001) *The Nature of the Nonprofit Sector*. Boulder, CO: Westview Press

Ouchi, W. G., Barney, J. B. (Eds) (1987) *Organisational Economics: Toward a New Paradigm for Understanding and Studying Organisations*. San Francisco, CA: Jossey Bass

Padula, G. (2002) Madison v. Marshall: *Popular Sovereignty, Natural Law and the United States Constitution*. Boulder, CO: Rowman and Littlefield

Pallot, J. (1998a) 'New Public Management Reform in New Zealand: The Collective Strategy Phase,' *International Public Management Journal*, 1: 1–18

Pallot, J. (1998b) 'The New Zealand Revolution,' in O. Olson, J. Guthrie, C. Humphrey (Eds), *Global Warning: Debating International Developments in New Public Financial Management*, Oslo: Cappelen, pp. 156–184

Parker, L. D., Guthrie, J. (1993) 'The Australian Public Sector in the 1990s: New Accountability Regimes in Motion,' *Journal of International Accounting, Auditing and Taxation*, 2(1): 57–79

Partington, M. (2003) *An Introduction to the English Legal System*. Oxford: Oxford University Press

Pateman, C. (1970) *Participation and Democratic Theory*. Cambridge: Cambridge University Press

Pateman, C. (1985) *The Problem of Political Obligation: A Critical Analysis of Liberal Theory*. Cambridge: Polity Press

Peck, J. (2001) *Workfare States*. New York: Guilford Press

Percy-Smith, J. (Ed.) (2000) *Policy Responses to Social Exclusion: Towards Inclusion?* Maidenhead: Open University Press

Persson, T., Tabellini, G. (2002) *Political Economics: Explaining Economic Policy*. Cambridge, MA: MIT Press

Pierre, J., Peters. B. G. (2000) *Governance, Politics and the State*. Basingstoke: Macmillan

Pierson, P., (Ed.) (2001) *The New Politics of the Welfare State*. Oxford: Oxford University Press

Podilado, C., Hulme, D. (1999) 'Public Management Reform in Developing Countries: Issues and Outcomes,' *Public Management Review*, 1(1): 121–132

Polinksky, A. M. (2003) *An Introduction to Law and Economics*. New York: Aspen Publications

Pollitt, C. (2003) *The Essential Public Manager*. Philadelphia, PA: Open University Press

Pollitt, C., Bouckaert, G. (1999) *Public Management Reform: A Comparative Analysis*. Oxford: Oxford University Press

Posner, R. A. (1990) *The Problems of Jurisprudence*. Cambridge, MA: Harvard University Press

Posner, R. A. (1992) *Economic Analysis of Law*, Fourth Edition. Boston: Little, Brown and Company

Posner, R. A. (1999) *The Problematics of Moral and Legal Theory*. Cambridge, MA: Harvard University Press

Posner, R. A. (2001) *Frontiers of Legal Theory*. Cambridge, MA: Harvard University Press

Posner, R. A. (2003) *Law, Pragmatism, and Democracy*. Cambridge, MA: Harvard University Press

Potts, J. (2001) *The New Evolutionary Microeconomics: Complexity, Competence and Adaptive Behaviour*. Cheltenham: Edward Elgar

Pressman, J., Wildavsky, A. (1984) *Implementation*, Third Edition. Berkeley, CA: University of California Press

Price, C. (1993) *Time, Discounting and Value*. Oxford: Blackwell

Pugh, D. S. (Ed.) (1997) *Organisation Theory: Selected Readings*. London: Penguin

Pugh, D. S., Hickson, D. J. (Eds) (1997) *Writers on Organisations*. Thousand Oaks, CA: Sage

Putnam, R. D., Leonardi, R., Nanetti, R. Y. (1994) *Making Democracy Work*. Princeton, NJ: Princeton University Press

Putterman, L., Kriszner, R. S. (Eds) (2003) *The Economic Nature of The Firm*. Cambridge: Cambridge University Press

Quine, W. V. (1992) *Pursuit of Truth*. Cambridge, MA: Harvard University Press

Raadschelders, J. C. N. (1998) *Handbook of Administrative History*. Somerset, NJ: Transaction Publishers

Raiffa, H. (2002) *Negotiation Analysis: The Science and Art of Collaborative Decision Making*. Cambridge MA: Harvard University Press

Raphaelson, A. H. (Ed.) (1998) *Restructuring State and Local Services: Ideas, Proposals and Experiments*. Westport, CT: Greenwood Press

Rasmusen, E. (1994) *Games and Information. An Introduction to Game Theory*, Second Edition. Cambridge, MA: Blackwell

Rasmusen, E. (2001) *Games and Information: An Introduction to Game Theory*. Oxford: Blackwell

Rawls, J. (1995) *Political Liberalism*. New York: Columbia University Press

Rawls, J. (1999) *A Theory of Justice*. Oxford: Oxford University Press

Rawls, J. (2001) *Justice as Fairness: A Restatement*. Cambridge, MA: Harvard University Press

Regester, M., Larkin, J. (2002) *Risk Issues and Crisis Management. A Casebook of Best Practice*. London: Kogan Page

Richards, D., Norman, G., Pepall, L. (2004) *Industrial Organization: Contemporary Theory and Practice with Economic Applications*. New York: South Western College Publishing

Ricketts, M. (2002) *The Economics of Business Enterprise: An Introduction to Economic Organisation and the Theory of the Firm*. Cheltenham: Edward Elgar

Riker, W. H. (1988) *Liberalism Against Populism: A Confrontation Between the Theory of Democracy and the Theory of Social Choice*. Reissue Edition. Prospect Heights, IL: Waveland Press

Roberts, N. C. (2000) 'Organisational Configurations: Four Approaches to Public Sector Management,' J. L. Brudney, L. J. O'Toole, Jr, H. G. Rainey (Eds), *Advancing Public Management: New Developments in Theory, Methods, and Practice*, Washington, DC: Georgetown University Press, pp. 217–234

Romzek, B. S., Mohnston, J. M., 'Reforming State Social Services Through Contracting Linking Implementation and Organisational Culture,' in J. L. Brudney, L. J. O'Toole, Jr, H. G. Rainey (Eds), *Advancing Public Management: New Developments in Theory, Methods, and Practice*, Washington, DC: Georgetown University Press, pp. 173–196

Rose, R. (1981) *Understanding Big Government: The Programme Approach.* London: Sage

Rose, R. (1989) *Ordinary People in Public Policy: A Behavioural Analysis.* London: Sage

Rose-Ackerman, S. (1996) 'Altruism, Nonprofits, and Economic Theory,' *Journal of Economic Literature,* 34(2): 701–728

Rosen, H. S. (1988) *Public Finance,* Second Edition. Homewood, IL: Irwin

Rosen, H. S. (2001) *Public Finance,* Sixth Edition. New York: McGraw-Hill

Rothery, B., Robertson, I. (1995) *The Truth About Outsourcing.* Aldershot: Gower

Rousseau, J.-J. (1997) *The "Social Contract" and Other Later Political Writings: "Social Contract" and Other Later Political Writings,* Vol. 2. V. Gourevitch (Ed.). Cambridge Texts in the History of Political Thought. Cambridge: Cambridge University Press

Rubin, I. S. (1996) *The Politics of Public Budgeting: Getting and Spending, Borrowing and Balancing.* New York: Seven Bridges Press

Rutherford, M. (1996) *Institutions in Economics: The Old and the New Institutionalism.* Cambridge: Cambridge University Press

Sabatier, P. (1986) 'Top-Down and Bottom-Up Approaches to Implementation Research,' *Journal of Public Policy,* 6(1): 21–48

Sanger, B. M. (2003) *The Welfare Marketplace: Privatization and Welfare Reform* (a Center for Public Service Report). Washington, DC: The Brookings Institution

Schick, A. (2003) *The Federal Budget Process.* Hauppauge, NY: Nova Science Publishers

Schick, A., Lostracco, F. (2000) *The Federal Budget: Politics, Policy, Process.* Washington, DC: The Brookings Institution

Schumpeter, J. A. (2002) *The Theory of Economic Development.* Somerset, NJ: Transaction Publishers

Schumpeter, J. A., Clemence, R. V. (1989) *Essays: On Entrepreneurs, Innovations, Business Cycles and the Evolution of Capitalism.* Somerset, NJ: Transaction Publishers

Scott, S. (1975) *Governing California's Coast.* Berkeley, CA: Institute of Governmental Studies, University of California

Scott, W. R., Meyer, J. W. (1994) *Institutional Environments and Organisations. Structural Complexity and Individualism.* London: Sage Publications

Seidenstat, P. (Ed.) (1999) *Contracting out Government Services.* Westport, CT: Greenwood Press

Seymour, M., Moore, S. (2000) *Effective Crisis Management. Worldwide Principles and Practice.* London: Continuum

Shafritz, J. M. (1997) *Shafritz Classics of Public Administration.* London: Thomson Learning

Shafritz, J. M., Ott, J. S. (Eds) (1992) *Classics of Organisation Theory,* Third Edition. Pacific Grove, CA: Brooks/Cole Publishing Company

Shafritz, J. M., Russell, E. W. (2004) *Introducing Public Administration.* London: Longman

Sharpf, F. (2004) *Games Real Actors Play.* Boulder, CO: Westview Press

Sheffrin, S. M. (1996) *Rational Expectations.* Cambridge: Cambridge University Press

Shepsle, K. A., Bonchek, M. S. (1997) *Analyzing Politics: Rationality, Behavior, and Institutions.* New York: Norton

Sheridan, K. (Ed.) (1998) *Emerging Economic Systems in Asia: A Political and Economic Survey.* St Leonards, NSW: Allen & Unwin

Sherman, R. (1989) *The Regulation of Monopoly.* Cambridge: Cambridge University Press

Shichor, D., Gilbert, M. J. (2000) *Privatization in Criminal Justice: Past, Present, and Future.* Cincinnati, OH: Anderson

Shragge, E. (1997) *Workfare – Ideology for a New Under-Class*. Toronto, Garamond Press

Shy, O. (2001) *The Economics of Network Industries*. Cambridge: Cambridge University Press

Simmonds, N. E. (2002) *Central Issues in Jurisprudence: Justice, Law and Rights*. London: Sweet & Maxwell

Simon, H. A. (1997) *Models of Bounded Rationality and Other Topics in Economics: Empirically Grounded Economic Reason*. Cambridge, MA: The MIT Press

Skyrms, B. (1996) *Evolution of the Social Contract*. Cambridge: Cambridge University Press

Sky, O. (2001) *The Economics of Network Industries*. Cambridge: Cambridge University Press

Slovic, P. (2000) (Ed.) *The Perception of Risk*. London: Earthscan

Smith, M. J. (1999) *The Core Executive in Britain*. Basingstoke: Macmillan

Solow, R. M. (1998) *Work and Welfare*. Princeton, NJ: Princeton University Press

Solzhenitsyn, A. (2000) *One Day in the Life of Ivan Denisovich*. London: Penguin Books

Solzhenitsyn, A. (2002) *The Gulag Archipelago 1918–1956*. New York: Perennial

Spulber, D. F. (1989) *Regulation and Markets*. Cambridge, MA: The MIT Press

Stanley, M. (2000) *Politico's Guide to How to be a Civil Servant*. London: Politico's Publishing

Steane, P. (1999) 'Public Management Developments in Australia and New Zealand,' *Public Management Review*, 1(1): 133–142

Stigler, G. J. (Ed.) (1988) *Chicago Studies in Political Economy*. Chicago: University of Chicago Press

Stigler, G. J. (2000) *The Intellectual and the Marketplace*. Lincoln, NE: iUniverse

Stigler, G. J. (2003) *Memoirs of an Unregulated Economist*. Chicago: University of Chicago Press

Stiglitz, J. (2000) *Economics of the Public Sector*. New York: Norton

Stiglitz, J. (2003) *The Roaring Nineties: Seeds of Destruction*. London: Allen Lane

Stoner, J. R., Jr (1992) *Common Laws & Liberal Theory. Coke, Hobbes, and The Origins of American Constitutionalism*. Kansas City: University Press of Kansas

Suleiman, E. N. (2005) *Dismantling Democratic States*. Princeton, NJ: Princeton University Press

Sunstein, C. R. (2005) *Laws of Fear*. Cambridge: Cambridge University Press

Tangas, J. (2003) Changing Paradigms in Public Management: the Case of Victoria 1992–99. Unpublished PhD thesis. Melbourne: University of Melbourne

Tanzi, V., Schuknecht, L. (2000) *Public Spending in the 20th Century: A Global Perspective*. Cambridge: Cambridge University Press

Taylor, C. (1992) *Sources of the Self: Making of the Modern Identity*. Cambridge: Cambridge University Press

Taylor-Gooby, P. (Ed.) (2004) *New Risks, New Welfare*. Oxford: Oxford University Press

Ter-Minassian, T. (1997) *Fiscal Federalism in Theory and Practice*. Washington, DC: International Monetary Fund (IMF)

Thompson, F. J. (Ed.) (1979) *Classics of Public Personnel Policy*. Oak Park, IL: Moore Publishing

Thompson, J. R. (2000) 'Quasi Markets and Strategic Change in Public Organisations,' in J. L. Brudney, L. J. O'Toole, Jr, H. G. Rainey (Eds), *Advancing Public Management: New Developments in Theory, Methods, and Practice*, Washington, DC: Georgetown University Press, pp. 197–216

Thynne, I. (1994) 'The Incorporated Company as an Instrument of Government: A Quest for a Comparative Understanding,' *Governance*, 7(1): 59–80

Thynne, I., Wettenhall, R. (2004) 'Public Management and Organizational Authority' *International Review of Administrative Sciences*. 70: 609–621. London: Sage Publications

Tirole, J. (1988) *The Theory of Industrial Organisation*. Cambridge MA: The MIT Press

Tomkin, S. L. (1998) *Inside OMB: Politics and Process in the President's Budget Office*. Armonk, NY: M. E. Sharpe

Torres-Blay, O. (2004) *Economie d'entreprise: Organisation, stratégie et territoire à l'aube de la nouvelle économie*. Paris: Economica

Tsebelis, G. (2002) *Veto Players: How Political Institutions Work*. Princeton, NJ: Princeton University Press

Tullock, G. (1997) *Economics of Income Redistribution*. Boston, MA: Kluwer Academic Publishers

Vega-Redondo, F. (1996) *Evolution, Games, and Economic Behaviour*. New York: Oxford University Press

Vickers, J., Yarrow, G. (1989) *Privatization – An Economic Analysis*. Cambridge, MA: MIT Press

Viscusi, W. K, Vernon, J. M., Harrington, J. E. (1992) *Economics of Regulation and Antitrust*. Lexington, MA: D. C. Heath

von Neumann, J., Morgenstern, O. (2004) *Theory of Games and Economic Behavior*, 60th Anniversary Edition. Princeton, NJ: Princeton University Press

Vromen, J. (1995) *Economic Evolution: An Inquiry into the Foundations of New Institutional Economics*. London: Routledge

Waldo, D. (1984) *The Administrative State: A Study of the Political Theory of American Public Administration*. New York: Holmes & Meier Publishing

Wallis J., North, D.C. (1986) 'Measuring the Transaction Sector in the American Economy 1870–1970,' in S. L. Engerman, R. E. Gallman (Eds), *Long-Term Factors in American Economic Growth*. Chicago: University of Chicago Press

Walzer, M. (2004) *Spheres of Justice: A Defense of Pluralism and Equality*. New York: Basic Books

Weber, M. (1978) *Economy and Society I–II*. Berkeley, CA: University of California Press

Weber, M. (1994) *Political Writings*. P. Lassman (Ed.), R. Speirs (Trans.). Cambridge Texts in the History of Political Thought. Cambridge: Cambridge University Press

Weber, M. (2001) *Economie et société dans l'Antiquité*. Paris: Poche

Weber, M. (2003) *General Economic History*. New York: Dover

Wenin, L. (2003) *Economic Behaviour and Legal Institutions: An Introductory Text*. Singapore: World Scientific Publishing Group

Weisbrod, B. A. (1988) *The Nonprofit Economy*. Lexington, MA: D. C. Heath

Wettenhall, R. (1993) 'The Globalisation of Public Enterprises,' *International Review of Administrative Sciences*, 59(3): 387–408

White, J., Wildavsky, A. (1992) *The Deficit and the Public Interest: The Search for Responsible Budgeting in the 1980s*. Berkeley, CA: University of California Press

Wildavsky, A. (1986a) *Politics of the Budgetary Process*. New York: Little Brown

Wildavsky, A. (1986b) *Budgeting: A Comparative Theory of Budgetary Processes*, Revised Edition. Somerset, NJ: Transaction Publishers

Wildavsky, A. (1987) *Speaking Truth to Power: Art and Craft of Policy Analysis*. Somerset, NJ: Transaction Publishers

Wildavsky, A. (1988) *Searching for Safety*. Somerset, NJ: Transaction Publishers

Wildavsky, A. (1997)*But Is It True? A Citizen's Guide to Environmental Health and Safety Issues.* Cambridge, MA: Harvard University Press

Wildavsky, A. (2002) *The Revolt Against the Masses: And Other Essays on Politics and Public Policy.* Somerset, NJ: Transaction Publishers

Wildavsky, A., Caiden, N. (2003) *The New Politics of the Budgetary Process.* New York: Longman

Wildavsky, A., Swedlow, B. (Ed.), B. (2000) *Budgeting and Governing.* Somerset, NJ: Transaction Publishers

Williamson, O. E. (1986) *Economic Organisation: Firms, Markets and Policy Control.* Brighton: Harvester Wheatsheaf

Williamson, O. E. (1998) *The Economic Institutions of Capitalism.* New York: Free Press

Williamson, O. E. (1999) *The Mechanisms of Governance.* New York: Oxford University Press

Williamson, O. E., Masten, S. E. (Eds) (1999) *The Economics of Transaction Costs.* Cheltenham: Edward Elgar

Williamson, O. E., Winter, S. G., Coase, R. H. (1993) *The Nature of the Firm: Origins, Evolution and Development.* Oxford: Oxford University Press

Wilson, J. Q. (1991) *Bureaucracy: What Government Agencies Do and Why They Do It.* New York: Basic Books

Wise, M., Gibb, R. (1993) *Single Market to Social Europe.* Harlow, Essex: Longman Scientific & Technical

Wittfogel, K. A. (1981) *Oriental Despotism: A Comparative Study of Total Power.* New York: Random House

Wolf, C. (1989) *Markets or Governments.* Cambridge, MA: MIT Press

World Bank (1995) *Bureaucrats in Business: The Economics and Politics of Government Ownership.* New York: Oxford University Press

Index

Page numbers for figures have suffix **f**, those for tables have suffix **t**